Alaska Odyssey

Gospel of the Wilderness

Hal Thornton

Santa Barbara, California

Publisher's Cataloging-in-Publication
(Provided by Quality Books, Inc.)

Thornton, Hal, 1916–
    Alaska odyssey : gospel of the wilderness /
Hal Thornton. — 1st ed.
    p. cm.
    Includes biographical references.
    ISBN 0-9627114-4-6

    1. Thornton, Hal, 1916– 2. Christian biography.
3. Alaska—Biography. 4. Alaska—Description and travel.
I. Title.

BR1725.T495A3 2003   270.8'2'092
                                           QBI03–200625

Alaska Distributor
Wizard Works
P.O. Box 1125, Homer, AK 99603
907-235-8757 (ph./fax)
wizard@xyz.net

Thornton's Legacy Press
1255 Calle Cerrito Alto
Santa Barbara, CA 93101-4907

alaskaodyssey.com

Contents

Acknowledgments

My thanks to important and necessary friends:

Eli Luria for the cover art and inspiration. *Dr. Pete Diamond*, a scholar, for balancing my wilderness monologue. *Dr. Dale Lindsay Morgan*, a pastor, for balancing my religious perspectives. *Fred Allen*, a skilled photographer, for photo help. *Ann Miller* of Hope, Alaska, for the picture to illustrate my story of our pristine village. *Ruth Johannsen* for the back cover's special picture of a grand Mountain. *Janell Thornton Lewis* and her son *Riley* for shoving me into my computer. *Gene R. Kelley* and his wife *Maryellen*, for lots of good reasons. *Kathy Haley* of Moose River for Kenai Peninsula map. *Blas M. Garza*, a sax-playing veteran, for confirming Wildwood did exist. *Don George*, exponent of *The Island Within*, for inspiration. *Peggy and Jim Arness*, friends and Kenai survivors, for pictures and rekindling my embers. *Lisa Augustine* and *Jackie Benson Pels*, Kenai school girls turned authors.

Special thanks to *Jeanne Thornton*, the companion who witnessed and shared the most in the adventures in this book. I needed her support, approval, criticism, and her artistic talent that provided the inside-back-cover painting of our log cabin at Hope. Her greater achievement was raising our three daughters. (Joyce, Jeannette, and Janell.) More to the point, without these daughters we would have been deprived of our grandchildren. They were the motivation I needed for this autobiography.

Honorable mention to *Jo Evans*, my irrepressible niece. She has volunteered a few truths *About the Author*. She can hardly be objective because she owes me big time for taking her to Argentina, whereby she met her husband. She could have said more, much more, but may have felt restrained because she hopes for another trip, someday.

I also gratefully acknowledge below the many scholars who volunteered endorsements. Important people with impressive credentials responded; the sheer volume required impaneling a committee of judges.

Marion Anker	Muriel Ganapole	Paul Murray
Alison Bertsche	Philip Jerge	Larry Phillips
Jacquiline Anker	Gene Kelley	Leo Robidoux
Carol Brenner	Pat Golliher	Glenn Scheel
Millie Brombal	Roselinde Konrad	Bob Short
Susan Dahl	Maryellen Flynn Kelley	Dwaine Thwing
Jeannette Delimitros	Larry Lawrence	Sam Wake
Arlene Douglas	Bob McNary	Marian Winters

Technical support: *Arlene Douglas* for filling my computer gaps. *Anne Beckwith Johnson*, a fellow traveler, for manuscript insights. *Christine Nolt*, design editor and *Linda Gray*, text editor. *Robert Howard*, cover designer and *Tom Stanley*, art.

— Hal Thornton
2003

Foreword

A Biased Perspective

I am the middle daughter who actually got to be "born free." I was born in Anchorage at a military hospital while dad was in the Army. I've never quit feeling "free."

We get this one script to act out in this lifetime, and I got to be chosen by Hal and Jeanne. My dad had a lot of spirit, imagination, creativity, and ideas. He made things happen. We never knew how to fill in the line on the school papers that asked for *Father's Occupation?* He was a mechanic, a car dealer, a farmer, a construction worker in a hard hat, a builder, a horse trader, a gas station attendant, a commercial fisherman, a house mover, a subdivider, a contractor, an insurance agent, a chef, a rancher. He was a water ski boat operator on weekends, he was a movie critic, he was the president of the Lutheran Church congregation, he was Rotary president, and he was our dad. He chose his mate carefully and wisely and they made it last for a lifetime.

Our mom also wore many hats, and she typified Betty Crocker, the mythic mother, and we trusted implicitly in the veracity of the jingle that "*nothin' says lovin' like something from the oven.*"

My life in the home of happy Hal and joyful Jeanne was delightful, and there were surprises—trips to Caines Head in a small open dory boat, living conditions over a café in Kenai that would make any small studio look spacious. There was a

4th of July beach picnic where we ended up stranded in a Jeep between two rocks as the tides washed in around us; there were trips in a little tiny airplane with inclement weather conditions. All of these experiences, and many more, filled our spirits with adventure, and we have to keep looking now for refuel. Our mom and dad's achievements were monumental and could have filled up a Norman Rockwell coffee table book. There were lots of dragons, but somehow, through all the adventures, we girls always knew that Dad would fend them off. What fun!

— Joyce Thornton Jerge

Another Perspective

I have memories of Hope as a family place with lots of time spent at the "farm" up on the "bench" with my grandparents. I have wonderful memories of the beauty of the area—wild flowers of bright hues, tall grass, and veggie gardens. I remember the village dances and what fun they were from a shy child's viewpoint.

I remember the chicken raising and the neck wringing and the crazy leaping around they did minus their heads—and my cigar box with chicken feet saved.

With our move to Kenai I recall the disruption and pressures on my parents. Pressures caused by the financial strain of starting a business, running it, and raising two small girls simultaneously with providing moose meat for the table, making clothes, and building for the next business, one to have an apartment overhead that was unfinished when we moved in.

I cherished the fun of having the first bathtub in Kenai

and inviting friends to take a bath. I can never forget Mount Redoubt, that beautiful volcano framed in our front window. I remember Kenai having extremes in coloring. I remember it as black and shadowy at dusk with the sun setting against the trees and the light from the snowpack creating the effect of a negative.

We had a radio. What magic! I believed in The Lone Ranger. Dad and mom got us a piano. That was a rarity. School memories are of the rickety wooden structure with Mrs. Petersen teaching my first and second grade. She was able to hold a classroom's attention with few props and certainly no special interest teachers. She was a priceless pro.

There were activities that Dallas children would, as my father says, "give their eye teeth for." Dodging moose while walking to school, many beach experiences, catalog shopping and several weeks of eagerly waiting for the packages to arrive, house chores, and knowing everybody. My parents were involved with local politics, schools, thespians, and the Kenai Chapel. In many ways, small village life was full to the brim. Perhaps we've lost something with our gravitation to the big city.

— Alaska Jeannette (Thornton) Delimitros

The Third Daughter Speaking

I've enjoyed watching my father write *Alaska Odyssey: Gospel of the Wilderness*. Because I was born after Alaska, I never endured what had shaped my sisters and parents. Growing up in the States, I'd never bathed in a bucket, eaten moose meat, been in a jeep, or experienced the intense Alaska winters. I can see how each of my family members has been

9

affected by Alaska—my maverick sisters, my parents "can do" attitude, and the whole family's love of the warm California climate and beaches. The Alaska experience created a very close family that treasures each other and every day.

I grew up in Washington State and California and was the beneficiary of some of the skills that my parents and sisters developed in Alaska. My parents took me on many great vacations—many of them in a small plane piloted by my father—provided and cared for my horses and dogs, and they've maintained their pioneering outpost independence.

We've been very lucky; as my father often says, "We're all healthy and none of the kids or grandkids are in jail." We enjoyed a kind of freedom that my children will never know, and we survived and thrived.

And even though I've been fortunate enough to get a great "school education," I can't cook, sew, paint, or run a home as well as my mom, and I can't write, play bridge, or voice my opinion as well as my father. They received a lot of strength and a pioneering education.

— Janell Thornton Lewis

Part One: Preface to Alaska Odyssey

This octogenarian's experience is that your life gets better with aging. Why? Several good reasons come to mind: (1) Most of the suspense is behind you. (2) You've learned to live with aches and pains and they don't frighten you. (3) You no longer need pretend you're something you are not. (4) Your kids are grown and on their own, and it's no longer your business where they are and what they're doing. (5) And if the IRS puts you in jail, I think they have to take care of your medical.

Not least, a treasure trove of memories accumulates. Eight decades have piled up a smorgasbord of experiences I wish to enshrine with this book. I have aged into a museum piece. Not many folk have lived from World War I, through the Depression and World War II, to witness Y2K.

This autobiography is in two parts. The early chapters are about my career search and pioneering businesses. It boils down to a hard physical life rarely experienced in our affluent society. Later in my story, with economic freedom, I could allot time and money for social concerns and attitudes. If the reader wishes to be spared my philosophy, just skip Part Two.

The focus of the first part of this book is my business experiences in Alaska. I hope it will be valuable to persons searching endlessly for a career, for I have been there, done that. When Spencer Blickenstaff asked me to speak to his Santa Barbara Community College class on business, I protested that I lacked the credentials. He assured me I would be useful because my experiences could serve as a horrible example.

I asked the class, "Do you want to get rich?" They of course answered, "Yes!" My retort was, "Since you live in a free country, live in a great community, and can attend its super college, you are already richer than most of the world. Maybe all that is missing for you is money in the bank."

"Many of you will be short of capital. I can think of four legal ways to accumulate money: One way is thrift—save what you earn. A second way is to be smart—that's why you're in this class. A third way is to inherit or borrow—for that you need luck or charm, lacking all else, marry it."

In Alaska, lacking a trade or profession, a business of my own seemed my best option. I told the class that I'd tried half a dozen. Some succeeded, some failed. Try enough and the law of averages works for you. If more succeed than fail, you're ahead of the game, but don't try to sell that business plan to your banker.

Rather than stay in college, I chose to flee. Maybe I chose wrongly. Education is a valuable tool. There is life without it. One can get rich without it, have a good family without it. But whether working at a trade, practicing a profession, running a business, or writing a book, education makes it better and easier. So my story is an object lesson.

I believe in having a contingency plan. If all the evidence makes it clear that I am probably destined never to be rich, I can easily adjust my perspective. One way to do that is to lower my expectations. "So how did it work?" you ask. "I took a shortcut. I got rich the vicarious way. I guarantee this strategy. I write the formula in Chapter 13 "Enjoying the Bounties of the Benevolent Rich."

In training to be a bush pilot, I learned that if you are lost, call the tower and admit that you are lost. "What if there is no tower?" I asked. "Circle in place and think. If thinking doesn't help, search for an open field and pray for a soft soft landing." Then pick yourself up, hike out of the woods, and start over. This is a hard lesson in our career search.

My wife warns, "The sermonizing in your book is too opinionated." My defense is "Of course. I'm a grumpy old sourdough." I blame it on both nature and nurture. Nature: Human society bugs me. Nurture: My parents gave me bad genes.

Blaming the parents is such a soul-satisfying cover. I'm too slow for basketball and too light for football; I have bad vocal chords for singing and a weak memory for acting; my brain is wrong to be a physicist, and I'm too lazy for medical school. Not one of those deficiencies is my fault. It is my belief that our ancestors' shadows stay with us forever. Their genes permeate our persona. That is a burden we cannot shrug off. My story is proof you can succeed in spite of misguiding parents.

I contend that life is a journey in the wilderness. Most of us live with day-to-day frustrations and perplexities. Technology changes faster than we can read the operating manual; government scares us; overpopulation encroaches on our freedom; the bureaucrats are "bumblingcrats"; and religion—oh please, don't get me started. To be angry is to be normal, and to be sane is as tricky as Catch 22. For the beleaguered souls who wonder if there is ever an escape from the wilderness, be assured that you have company.

So does the scenario in this book have a happy ending? Definitely! I have a message of hope for those who, like me, start their career on the wrong foot: A bad start is painful. What counts most is a good finish. As Shakespeare wrote, All's well that ends . . ." Well?

So if it is a happy success story you need, know this one gets better as the chapters unfold. Trust me.

—H. T.

1

From Pulpit to Parka, Bible Belt to the Arctic

Could GOD be confused? The dean of the Pentecostal Bible college in Springfield, Missouri, summoned me to his office. "Thornton, why are you here?"

"I believe that God has called me to the ministry."

"Well, God has changed His mind and you should not return next term."

I mustered a weak defense. "My father is a minister. He assured me God wants me in the ministry. So I'd like a second opinion."

The dean was ready with a stinging retort. "Here's your second opinion: The ministry is already overflowing with failures. And if you want a third opinion, you don't have the charisma to be a leader, and you're out of step as a follower."

The voice inside told me the dean was right. So God had gotten His wires crossed. It was 1936, the Great Depression era (I never understood what made it "great.") My dad had opted to be an evangelist, giving up the security of a parsonage (I was born in a parsonage.) My mother had followed loyally, and there was no home for me to return to. It was not

the first and would not be the last of many times I would be homeless. The only useful skill I salvaged from high school was typing. I was expert at that, but it was not enough when a fourth of the workforce was unemployed. This lost kid was adrift in a leaky boat without a rudder.

Civilian Conservation Corps

For an interlude, I pretended there was a hiding place for me with my parents in the roving ministry, but all I was learning was U.S. geography—the hard way. There was only one light at the end of my tunnel—the Civilian Conservation Corps, or CCC. Once in a while, the government does something right. The CCC was the shining star in President Roosevelt's New Deal experiment. Economic need and age were the qualifiers for admission; charisma be damned.

The Army provided camps with room, board, clothing, and tough discipline. We worked for a technical branch of the government—Forestry, Park Service, or Conservation. We built roads, picnic areas, and nature trails and put out forest fires—all constructive projects. The CCC was a lifeline for thousands like me. It kept us off the street, taught us work skills, and gave us an anchor until the wind filled our sails. We were locked in until we could produce evidence of stable employment. Even Kirk Kirkorian, who would later become an enterprising billionaire, was once in our lifeboat.

The ship *North Star* (of Byrd's Antarctic fame) on-loaded two hundred of us CCC men at Seattle in late winter of 1939. We were volunteers, opting for the excitement of Alaska as a good trade-off for the comforts of stateside garrison life. The *North Star* was no "cruise ship." We bunked in the hold (I was a "leader," which rated me the comforts of steerage) and ate on deck. We had no showers, no laundry, no heat; we had wintry seas for the ten days up the inside passage and across the Gulf of Alaska en route to Seward.

CCC Salute at Franklin Roosevelt Memorial, Washington, D.C.

2

Hiding Out in the Shadow of a Giant: Mount McKinley

Upon docking at Seward, we transferred to train, and two days later we were dumped on a station platform in the middle of the Alaska Range.* Our tent camp, a mile from Park Headquarters, was left over from the previous year; likewise the ice in the water pipes. Bathing was out, body odor was in. For weeks we were to shiver and shake and dream of hot showers. In short order we set about sprucing up this "last frontier" for the benefit of a trickle of tourists. Trickle? We did not image—few, if any, dreamed—that this would some-day be a prime destination for a horde.

Ascending that mountain in the era before modern equipment and air support was risky and rare. Many were seduced, few suc-ceeded. Legend has it that the first humans to stand atop the North Peak were some Fairbanks sourdoughs, two probably, who took a dare by the saloon they inhabited. They relied

---

* In pretourist times, the Alaska Railroad's trains stopped overnight at Curry. Here, passengers either rented a room or stayed aboard while the crew took a required break. The hotel had insufficient number of rooms, and it was com-monplace for single travelers, even if strangers, to double up.

19

heavily on the adage that God takes care of fools and drunks. They had enough alcohol in their blood to fend off freezing, so they made it—how, is a mystery. In 1913, Archdeacon Stuck's party made it to the South Peak, that's the lower one. Grant Pearson, the park superintendent, is credited with the second successful assault—this climb to the higher peak in 1932. Until recent times, climbing Denali was as remote as making a million. In modern times, the two challenges have kept pace.

(I may be one of the oxygen-breathing cowards who can honestly say, "I will not be climbing that mountain. Low hummocks are more my style."—H.T.)

Nenana River

In 1939, entertainment in the future "Denali Park" was skimpy. Meeting the weekly passenger train, a healthy hike down from our camp, was the primary excitement and the only way to connect with civilization. Three buddies and I were at the platform when a man wearing a flight jacket stepped off the train, scanned the group of greeters, and spotted what he needed—our young foursome. Dressed in our CCC garb, my buddies and I looked right for his risky mission. This stranger was about to put some excitement into our routine, and if we performed we were to be rewarded with $5 each or he would give us an airplane flight over our camp and the park.

We were talking with a bush pilot who had cracked up somewhere in the taiga. The plane was on the opposite side of the Nenana River,[*] on its back in brush and muskeg. We only had to find it and bring out his passenger's luggage and two

---

[*] Rivers in the Alaska Interior have names ending in "na." It is the Alaska Native language for "river."

Plane forced down 12 miles from McKinley station.

parachutes. He drew a crude map in the dirt, promised to return in a week or two and waved good-bye as he reboarded the train to Fairbanks.

The CCC could function without us for a few days. This was adventure we needed. Crossing the river, however, was a challenge. The Nenana was swift, turbulent, and flooding with snow runoff. Such a problem did not deter us green-horns.

Risky possibilities were considered and discarded. Rumor had it that an old trapper of a bygone era had left a spruce plank rowboat near the river. Even if we were able to find it, it probably had rotted. No problem. We would wrap the boat in a waterproof tarp so it couldn't possibly leak. We weren't dummies. Thus we four kid cheechakos[*] equipped with two weatherworn oars, a tarp, and pack boards for the salvage, set off in search of an abandoned rowboat along a trackless river. Finding the river was easy. Our ears told us the way because it roared. Standing beside that torrent scared us. We guessed,

[*] "Cheechakos" were green newcomers to Alaska, becoming "sourdoughs" with time.

but didn't discuss, that a human could not survive thirty seconds in that icy water.

We located the boat. It provided only a feeble frame for our canvas tarp. It floated, but with only enough freeboard to allow for two passengers. To ferry the four of us across and return with luggage was going to require at least twelve crossings. We estimated 100 yards to reach the opposite bank, plus twice that in downstream drift. Twelve chances to drown. Sixty years later, lost baggage is a way of life. No air traveler will believe that someone else's lost baggage can be a cause for risking death!

Nenana River

We four took turns rowing across the deadly torrent. Call it blind luck or a contract with the devil, we all survived and collected our airplane ride into the park. This became my attempted drowning number one. Others would follow.

Kantishna Hike

One flirt with death did not satisfy me. The next opportunity to die came when my friend who worked the infirmary told me, "This trapper has been rescued near Wonder Lake and brought to our infirmary. He and his partner have set a trapline beyond the Kantishna River. He was trying to get across the river with all his clothes in a packsack. He was swept away by the current, lost his packsack, wound up on the opposite bank naked. Our crew at Wonder Lake spotted him just as he collapsed on a crest of a hill."

This story was intriguing. The guy was pitiful. Mosquitoes had nearly devoured him. He was a mass of bruises and lacerations. He begged us to try to get word to his partner that he was still alive and would get supplies back to him, somehow. If we could find his partner, he was sure we'd be treated to trapline running, gold panning, all that fun stuff. What a great way for us to get initiated to the true Alaska.

There was a second reason we should go for this opportunity. We had yet to see the mountain. McKinley's 20,300-foot lofty height wrapped it in clouds—clouds generated by its frigid surfaces. The mountain is not visible at the Park Headquarters. We had made the two-hour truck ride into the park to the nearest viewing point, and each time the mountain hid behind its cloud mantle. We would now camp on its doorstep.

Wonder Lake was the nearest road access to begin our hike. It is also the nearest approach to Mount McKinley. Alongside the lake, we found an old trapper's cabin. It was near midnight. We gave the clouds shrouding the mountain a final glance before unrolling our sleeping bags. Then I decided to brush my teeth—something no genuine wilderness man would ever do. I glanced toward the mountain just as the clouds parted, framing it like a picture in an art gallery. Above its peak was a full moon. I rushed into the cabin, grabbed my camera, which was loaded with infrared film, snapped one shot, and the clouds closed the curtain. Months later in Fairbanks, the photo shop that developed the picture offered to buy it. No way!

The next morning, we set out for the daylong hike to the Kantishna River. The weather was unusually warm and we stripped to our undershirts. The mosquitoes went for our bare skin. What a wonderful day to be trudging across the muskeg. The mountain was hidden in its cloud mantle and very much in charge of the weather. It was about to give us a lesson in meteorology. Any junior weatherman would know that the heated air in our valley would rise to clash with that immense icy slope. Very likely, a heavy rain should follow, maybe of cloudburst intensity, causing the Kantishna River to flood, which it did.

Arctic tundra is the hardest hiking imaginable, and it's even worse if your pack boards are overloaded. When you think your boot is on a solid clump, it slides into a hole, a knee-deep water bucket. We were north of the tree line; there was no firewood except for a few spindly birches along the riverbank. The shrubs we found were soaking wet. My buddy and I stumbled around on the tundra for two days, always drenched and often without reference points. We were shaking so bad we couldn't hold our compass steady. Our shoulders ached from overloaded pack boards, and we realized we must throw away the tasty grub we shouldn't have brought. Only the mosquitoes would eat well. We were tired, lost, and scared.

The desperate strategy we settled on was to find a high rise where our lifeless bodies would be easy to spot. By whom? What rescue party would look for us? We had not advised the camp where we were going. Greenhorns do stupid things.

Somehow we made it back to Wonder Lake, caught a ride on the road, and eventually checked in at our camp. Mission aborted. The trapper on the other side of the Kantishna would just have to agonize. End of heroics.

McKinley Wrap Up

My sojourn in McKinley Park was a liberating experience. Camp life in isolation had been good for my health; some persistent chronic problems simply disappeared. Six months without a church service or prayer meeting and I was not smitten by God. I was then 22 and happy with my work, exhilarated by the arctic environment, and enjoying camp life. For my first time, I felt I might have a future outside of heaven. If so, I doubted that it was back in the States.

It was a bleak fall day with winter tightening the noose when I waved good-bye to the train taking my buddies south. Our CCC group could return to the States, but I was staying. I returned to the deserted camp, buttoned up the office paperwork, and wrote myself a discharge that said I was a very capable company clerk.

When I said good-bye to Grant Pearson, the park superintendent, I shook a hand that had been to McKinley's north summit. It was as close as I would ever get to that pinnacle except in a pressurized plane. When the northbound train arrived, I felt I was boarding a friend. As we pulled out of the park station, my eyes clouded. I loved that park even though it nearly killed me twice. So I gave the station an affectionate good-bye wave, not guessing how important my next visit would be. The Alaska Range faded behind the train as we entered gently rolling valleys blanketed by fireweed, then the familiar tundra, trees stunted by permafrost, and endless panoramas. The best train ticket I ever bought delivered me to Fairbanks where I had been promised a job with the Army's "cold weather testing" project, with temporary offices in the Pioneer Hotel on First Street.

With my duffel bag over my shoulder, I strode across the Chena River bridge and stopped in front of the post office. I looked up and down Cushman Street and scanned Second Street. A friendly old-timer guessed my problem and directed me to Frances Doyle's boarding house. I would now have company with other misfits in this strange little town near the Arctic Circle. I found an instant family, a roof over my head, and best of all, I had a job. I mean a *real job!* At last, I could exhale. Life does have its sweet moments.

3

A New Life, New Wife: Pioneering at Fairbanks

Here I found myself in an unkempt little mining town of 3,000. Fairbanks prior to World War II was a hideout for runaways, like myself, seeking economic freedom. Since the only way in and out was by ship and two days by rail, it was beyond reach and ideal for escapees from the Depression, bad marriages, and scrapes with the law. I had joined a polyglot society of adventure seekers with a live-and-let-live attitude.

Years of failed job hunting had loaded me with anxiety. I timidly checked into the temporary offices of the Army Quartermaster. Surprise! I became the one-man personnel department of a new venture that must hire a sizable force to build Ladd Field. I was soon in love with my job, with Fairbanks, and with winter. With luck, I might even learn courting.

In Fairbanks, I found a community that welcomed me. I had my first real job, first independence, and euphoric joy in living. Something about the arctic was energizing. I was socializing with Presbyterians, Nazarenes, and Episcopalians— an ecumenical experience for a Pentecostal lad. Despite the male-female imbalance, I was even dating. At the retarded age of 23, I danced for the first time because the log house some guys and I rented had, of all things, a polished living room floor, the legacy of a prior tenant who taught dancing. We hastened to find a record player, and thereafter our bachelor pad was the dancinest spot in the private circuit. The strains of "Deep Purple," "Stardust," and "My Prayer" could be heard up and down our street.

This bachelor pad housed from four to eight guys in their prime of immaturity. The exact number depended on variables such as hunting season, sport fishing, or point driving[*] in the placer gold fields, a job that built muscles, tanned skin, and paid good money. My work was in an office, and I had to compete with muscle hunks from the placer fields for the privilege of a young woman's company.

By a stroke of luck, a new lad in town, Jack Currier, became one of our housemates. He was a young playboy with an entrée to a female covey of high school seniors and college froshies—all good-looking. That is an understatement. In my eyes, they were all rare beauties, look-alikes for Constance Bennett, Norma Shearer, Veronica Lake.

Jack would sometimes break through the front door with, "Roll back the carpet. The girls are right behind me." The social side of my youth began in that living room.

Across the street from our house at 9th and Cushman was the high school where the outer grounds were flooded for ice-skating and the gymnasium was opened to badminton. It was the only game at which I excelled, and it opened my eyes to Minnie M. She was in her early twenties, a good player with a cute figure and a winning smile with teeth that glistened. She

---

[*] Points were hollow drill steel rods, hammered into the permafrost, to conduct cold water for thawing the next year's sluicing area.

worked in a local mercantile store. Nearly every Sunday after our game, we would go down to the Model Café for refreshments and chitchat. Nothing more.

Being with Minnie must have made me a bit giddy. No, worse, it must have scrambled my brains. On a winter Sunday while facing one another across our hamburgers, she sought my opinion: "I'm thinking of running for queen of the Ice Carnival. What do you think?" Selection of the queen was based on popularity and charisma and on the ability to garner the most ticket sales that financed some of the fun. It was Fairbanks' biggest event.

Minnie was a natural. In a parka, she was a photographer's bonanza! It flattered me that she wanted my opinion. I must think carefully. But her charm had intoxicated my head.

"Don't do it," I implored. "Don't let yourself get hurt. Your stunning beauty won't be enough. Fairbanks is not going to let a native wear its crown."

Minnie wanted my encouragement, not my advice. I opened my big mouth and cut myself out of escorting the queen to the grand ball of the 1940 spectacle of the year.

The winner's prize, in addition to the notoriety and attention, was a round-trip ticket to

Minnie M. queen of the ice carnival, 1940

Washington, D.C. The prize trip was also the key to Minnie's future. She was smart enough to throw away the return ticket. She settled in St. Louis, married, and I hope she cashed in on her anonymity.

Young men in Fairbanks had a unique problem that outranked the cold weather, the lack of a car, the frozen sewers, or even the high price of a two-bit hamburger—how to find a date for Saturday night, a month hence. The ratio of lusty men to high school and college girls was about six to one.

Beating those odds required ingenuity, inner strength, heroic persuasion, bravado, and planning ahead! None of our group was sex crazed, as I recall, but we desperately longed for the stimulation of a soft, scented woman to sit beside in a movie or to hold in our arms at the Saturday night dance.

The dances were public affairs and had the support of the town's upper crust. Everyone showed up at the Eagle's Hall, with or without a date. For Fairbanks, it was a well-dressed crowd. Coats and ties were the norm, and in winter everyone arrived in parkas and galoshes over shoes for dancing. Each dance had a theme, with decorations draped from the rafters. There'd be a punchbowl spiked on the sly. Billy Root's orchestra provided music sweeter than Jimmy Dorsey's.

Exposing a date to the stag line that filled one-third of the floor was a disincentive to dating. The most a man could expect would be the first and last dance with his date. In between, the stags cut in. It was the accepted behavior that a community-spirited girl would share her arms with a different partner for nearly every dance. Thus the stags not only could dance but were saved the cost of a rented car and the meal or refreshments before or after the dance.

Even so, with all the hormone-driven bachelors at 901

Saturday night dance, Eagles Hall, Fairbanks, 1940.

Cushman Street, lining up a date was a mark of distinction. It proved one's machismo. To outhustle the pack was a real high—great for the ego.

For this, a phone was required. We had one that saw constant use. The local phone company consisted of a switchboard operator who knew the community like no one else. With her on your side, you had access to inside information, even to which store your lady prospect had been seen entering. So sometimes, the first step in obtaining a date was the tone of your voice when you first heard, "Number, please."

The girl whom you called must have weighed her opportunities with a gambler's instinct. Often, the girls would overbook, sorting out the best bets as the time neared, and in due time beg off with less desirable suitors. But most of the girls were real troupers and honest sorts, who would console the loser with a double date. That meant a mini-meeting before or after the real date. And it was not unusual to be told by your date that she must be returned to her apartment or cabin by a precise hour; you could only hope not to encounter your date-successor waiting at her door. The six-to-one factor was annoying to the men and a bonus to the women.

Cabin Fever. A unique manifestation of isolated living was a homing instinct that, for most of us, surfaced after two years. A hermit of the wilderness would be smitten with a laundry list of chores that needed stateside attention, and he or she would think of myriad reasons for a return to the "Lower 48." It happened to me in November, just as winter got real. My list included treatment for an imaginary sinus problem, having my teeth checked, getting new eyeglasses, looking up an old CCC buddy, seeing my parents, getting out of my parka and mukluks, and staring at "normal" people. There was one other chore on my list—while I'm in Seattle; no harm in being prepared.

These furloughs merited a party, and the guys in the house threw a big one. I got drunk—the first and last time of my life. I got an official OK to stowaway on the Army's *St. Mihiel*, a transport ship named for a WWI battle. It was unloading at Seward and, I thought, destined for Seattle. Instead, the captain thought San Francisco's Presidio. No harm, it is an attraction everyone needs to see. Loafing aboard ship and California sunshine took one of my concerns off the list. It cured my sinus trouble, which was probably caused by lack of sleep induced by our bachelor house.

How lucky! The CCC buddy I wanted to visit lived in San Francisco. He had been my mentor in the park and now invited me to join him in some mentoring with big-city night life: a front row table in plain view of a sinful strip show. Uh-oh. Women were undressing. And gyrating to the accompaniment of my favorite Rachmaninoff concerto. (So, up close and naked—that's what a live female looks like!) I wasn't ready for this. I told my buddy I really needed to be on my way to Seattle. *Point me toward the bus station.*

The boarding house I located on Seattle's Capitol Hill exposed me to a mix of girls and guys. Single working kids. They marveled at a contemporary who didn't need to work. New Year's Eve was my chance to see if I was out of my cocoon. I rented a tux, took a nervous date to the Washington Athletic Club—totally out of my element and hers. We both had an awkward evening, Two left feet on the dance floor, and I didn't know how to kiss her goodnight, and so much for crashing the upper crust.

Window-shopping in Seattle I spotted the most tentative challenge on my list. I entered a jewelry store:

"How much for that set of rings in the window?"

"$55.00. Would you like to examine them?"

"No, I don't know much about diamonds. Would you lay them away?"

"It depends on how long. When are you getting married?"

"I wish I knew."

"What is the ladies finger size?"

"I don't yet know who she is. I just want to be prepared."

"You're from Alaska, aren't you?"

I partied in Seattle until my money was gone, and I had to return north on the cheapest ticket. That would be second-class on Canadian Pacific's *Princess Cathleen* to Vancouver, *Princess Norah* on to Juneau, and Alaska Steamship's steerage to Seward. For the second time, I was in steerage, crossing the Gulf of Alaska in winter.

Back in our Fairbanks bachelor pad, totally recovered from cabin fever, girls were my continuous focus. Not surprising, then, that there came the time when my eyes focused on Jeanne Brenner, a promising prospect still in the bud. Her parents had brought her from Seward to enter the university. They were a solid "WASP" family of German descent, hardworking and honest Methodists out of the Midwest. Others in our household had already displayed serious interest in Jeanne, and it was a given that some had proposed to her. I asked the charming college freshman to go to a spring dance. She agreed.

For this landmark event, I rented a car and gave Jeanne her first corsage, made of flowers shipped from the States. Recently I had given some thought to my domestic future. However, much cogitation must lay the groundwork, and I was not yet decided the how, when, and who for the ring on layaway in Seattle. After the dance, instead of taking Jeanne directly home, I drove a roundabout way. The route via the farm loop road was a direction 180 degrees off course. Spring was in the air. Spring is also the time of year when permafrost boils are in the road. They are a plague. Jeanne maintained her distance on the front seat, and I had every honest intention for the evening to end in a most decent fashion. Her mother would be waiting up and I valued her trust.

Except we ran into this mud hole. The car was hopelessly stuck. It was midnight, and we would have to wait a reasonable time to rouse a farmer with a tractor. With hours of awkward waiting, there was plenty of time to reflect on what a dumb thing I had done. In the long twilight of Arctic summer, there was not even darkness to hide my pained expression. Jeanne was holding her distance.

In today's world of dating, it would appear silly to think that a boy and a girl on a date would not avail themselves of the obvious opportunity. But there we were, two virgins with a case of nerves, our car engulfed in mud. Conversation was awkward. The clock ticked slowly. I worried about keeping Jeanne out past her appointed check-in time and was embarrassed for getting my car stuck.

Perhaps the circumstance gave me the shove I needed. With no preliminaries and no rehearsal, I mumbled, "Jeanne, will you marry me?" Was it a question? Or an apology?

There in the mire of a sinkhole at midnight! What an all-wrong setting. Years later, my goof would be expressed perfectly in a popular song that laments, ". . . and then I go and spoil it all by saying something stupid like 'I love you.'" Of course I got the NO I deserved.

A month would be required to smooth it over and say it right: "Jeanne, seriously, please marry me . . . bear my children . . . let me die in your arms!" I received the answer I had hoped for: YES. No mention of a pre-nuptial.

Engagement

On the day we formalized our engagement, I made it plain to Jeanne that she had made the best choice. Memorial Day, 1941, I planned to impress this sweet young lady with a riverboat ride up the Chena. I owned a boat. I did not own an outboard motor, but that need could be solved by inviting an officer friend from Ladd Field. The boat was tied along the river below the Chena bridge. We hung the motor on the stern, climbed in, and shoved into a slow current.

Outboards can be ornery. I cranked and cranked but the motor only putted enough to hold us even in midstream. We

35

noticed a crowd gathering on both banks and the bridge. I was starting to sweat and cranked and cranked. Jeanne was irritated.

"Why the crowd?" she asked. "Get us out of here!" she pleaded.

Uh-oh! 11 a.m. Memorial Day, the sacred moment. A color guard marched onto the bridge, faced us, and fired. A bomber from Ladd Field flew over and dropped a wreath beside our boat. The lieutenant straightened to attention and saluted. Jeanne hid her face inside her coat. I continued my cranking. We were center stage for the pageantry.

Then I had this bright idea: *open the gas valve, you idiot.* The motor sprang to life, we glided under the bridge and as we did, kids above razzed us and pelted us with spent cartridges. Barely past the bridge, I ran the boat onto a sandbar. How memorable can Memorial Day be.

There's a lesson here: *Display your stupidity early so the wife can never say she didn't know.*

Wedding

Our wedding in the Presbyterian Church was not quite traditional. Jeanne was beautiful, as brides are meant to be. Her pink chiffon gown a sparkling contrast to our drab little town. Her radiance disguised her fears that she might be marrying a jerk. As she nervously walked down the aisle on the arm of her father, the pianist and soloist, good friends of ours, performed *Because God Made Thee Mine.* It brought tears to my eyes. Reverend Armstrong delivered the proper exhortations, we made some binding promises, and afterward a sit-down breakfast was served by the ladies in the church. We had scheduled the wedding for 6 a.m., so we could catch the eight o'clock train to Mount McKinley National Park. It was ridiculously early, but we had no choice—the Boy Scout troop would be on that train for their summer camp in the park and I was their adult monitor.

It was now apparent but also too late—Jeanne had just married a chronic scheduler. July 3, 1941, would tie her to a guy arranging for others while in search of himself.

Honeymoon in heaven! The McKinley Park hotel had been under construction when I was living in a tent in the nearby CCC camp two years earlier. Now my young bride and I were in their finest room and had the $12 a night to pay for it. I laid awake on my wedding night thinking. Was God making restitution for having me thrown out of Bible college? My life had turned around so fast. Should I thank God or Roosevelt or this pioneer territory?

Fairbanks, 7/3/41 6 a.m. Presbyterian Church

37

Then I shuddered as my thoughts returned to that weird encounter at the train station that led four of us to cross the Nenana in the rotted skiff. What if the Nenana had prevailed and fate closed the curtain on me. What of Jeanne? Given the imbalance of males to females in Alaska's interior, any girl possessing the attributes of a potential wife had only to sort through her numerous proposals. I assumed that the next in line as Jeanne's choice was a chap with a motorcycle. Not many swains in Fairbanks had wheels, and he had two. Undoubtedly a motorcycle would have changed Jeanne's whole lifestyle. She would have had harrowing rides on Alaska's gravel roads and skinned up arms and legs. Screams and squeals. Probably broken bones. Instead of being linked to a guy who wanted to save the world, her husband would savor it, hell-bent. So Jeanne had a narrow escape, too. Such crazy thoughts.

Had heaven chosen not to wait, I'm betting the other guy wouldn't be thinking about the river. He'd be too busy polishing his bike. It's still raining. I'm still awake. Jeanne's awake, too. I wonder what she's thinking—and I'm afraid to ask.

I did give the Scouts some thought. I was their adult monitor. We had shipped them into the park to a camp at mile 33 before the rains washed out a bridge behind them. They couldn't get to us, so this cloud had a rainbow. They had food and shelter and a phone. Their motto is "Be Prepared." Nothing I can do and it's my honeymoon.

To start married life, I rented a nearly new, cozy but tiny, log house. It even had indoor plumbing. How could everything be going so well! What a transition! Since leaving the Lower 48, I had gone from homeless to housed, from jobless to good pay, from lonely to married. I was in love with a lov-

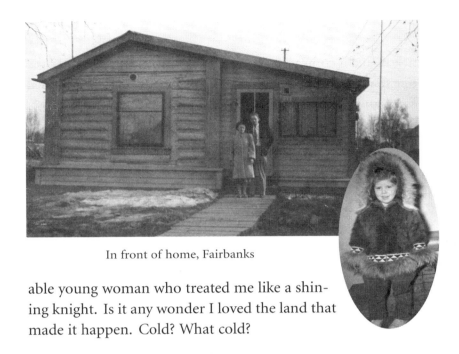

In front of home, Fairbanks

able young woman who treated me like a shining knight. Is it any wonder I loved the land that
made it happen. Cold? What cold?

Ladd Field

Ladd Field was, in its conception, stimulated by the Russ-
ian-Finnish war. Our military planners awoke to the realiza-
tion that warfare in an Arctic environment is a different ball
game. Hence the decision to install the "Cold Weather Test
Station" to be named Ladd Field. It's focus was on aviation,
and soon after completion, including a concrete runway, it
needed a supply function. I became its chief clerk.

The scope of cold weather adaptation was a veritable grab
bag. Special lubricants, special clothing, special transportation. This latter element entailed a means to rescue downed
plane crews, and this opened an unforgettable sortie.

A news story landed on my desk, telling of the rescue of a
stranded party in deep snow near Donner Pass. An inventor-
tinkerer named Tucker had developed a snow-traversing
machine that did the trick. We needed such equipment and

negotiated a contract for a similar concept patterned after the one that was so successful in the high Sierras. Tucker proposed a design larger than the news story machine, which was powered by a sixteen-horsepower motorcycle engine. He would build one with an eighty-horsepower aircraft engine. Five times the power should haul five times the payload? And five times faster? Whoa. We are definitely in unexplored territory.

I sent Mr. Tucker a contract for a single prototype for a price of $2,500. (Ten times that would have been realistic.) Delivery in sixty days. Inventors don't bother with practicality because six months would be too short. After much impatient waiting, I was dispatched to Los Angeles to expedite shipment. Incredible as it sounds sixty years later, I tried to save the Feds money by hitching a ride on a B-18 bomber destined for McClellan Field, then hitched a ride on a C-47 destined for Mines Field (stakeout for the future LAX).

On arrival, I was met, not by Mr. Tucker, but by Mr. Ward who owned a small manufacturing plant in Los Angeles. Tucker had gone to work for Ward because he had no capital to fulfill the contract. Ward learned of this and envisioned being the producer of the *Jeep of the arctic*. They did indeed have a machine, designed without a prototype, and it would be ready for testing in a week; I could witness the event.

In early December, our caravan set off from Los Angeles for the nearest snow, Mammoth Lakes. Hopes were high. The snow gizmo was on a trailer behind a Buick Roadmaster, followed by a retinue of interested parties, including the press. Mammoth Mountain did its best and we had more snow than was healthy. I was the sole attendee dressed for winter, which qualified me to sit on a fender and clear snow from the windshield.

We unloaded the thing into four feet of powder snow. The engine purred, the corkscrew-like flanges cut into the snow, everything functioning—except it didn't move. The observer sent by Continental Engine declared he knew how to make it work. When a person is drunk he knows a lot. He climbed onto the driver's seat, revved the engine to the max, let the clutch out, and we were blanketed by a blizzard. We heard steel whacking stone, and when the snow settled we stared down. The thing was sitting on bedrock. Mr. Tucker's dream turned nightmarish.

"I know it will work if the snow is right," he protested.

"We can't time a plane's forced landing to suit the snow." I replied. "And I can't sit around waiting for this cripple to be redesigned. I have a new bride back in Fairbanks and that's where I'm going."

The Mammoth area was deserted except for a sporting lodge that was buttoning up for the winter. They graciously opened their doors to our desolate party. The host told me there was a bus to Reno if I could get to the road. I hiked out. The road had been plowed.* There was no traffic, but in time, sure enough, the Reno bus. Most ski buffs reading this story will refuse to believe there was once a time, early December, ski season, powder snow, and the only traffic between L.A. and Reno was a lone bus.

---

* The next time I would see this road, it would be U.S.395, and the next time I would see the mountain it would be a popular ski resort, and we would own a condominium at 8,000 feet.

Getting Rich in Alaska

FIVE surefire ways of getting rich in Alaska, and how I tested each:

OIL: This is the easiest by far. You need only anticipate where the next strike will be and stake out a homestead. A near miss for me. I did this, but thirty years too soon.

FISHING: This can make you wealthy in a season. Two problems: you must pick the right era and right place. I did pick the right place, but forty years before the price was right. A-a-g-h!

GOLD MINING: Surefire hernia, sprained back, pneumonia, and attack by a bear. My brother-in-law showed me how very important the laws of economics. If costs go up and price comes down, shirt bound to be lost. Miner go broke? This one is for robust Swedes.

START A BUSINESS: Very challenging. You must exploit a service that's needed. I started my share. If the place or location or timing is wrong, just start over.

WIN THE NENANA ICE POOL! For over eighty years, this Alaska ritual has kept the locals guessing. It's their way of pooling their money so one, or a few, could make a trip "outside" in style. It's a fat purse, and I guarantee you will win if you put a $2 guess on every minute between April 19 and May 17.

Fairbanks had myriad smaller "breakup" pools for guessing only the minute. These were clocks drawn on cardboard on which the locals put their name and their $5 or $10 on the minute. The clock would be displayed in the window of the sponsor who, if he was honest, would take the money to Fairbanks' only bank and buy a cashier's check, which would be handed to the winner—when . . .

These pools were bets on the ice in the Chena River. When the tripod on the ice moved, it pulled a cord, which was attached to a switch on the bridge. This stopped the clock in the Model Café. An alert waitress notified the Northern Commercial Company,

42

which sounded a siren, and the town folks went into action: (1) Phone the Model Café. (2) Ask a waitress "What minute?" (3) Hurry to the sponsoring business to pick up the winner's check. (4) Hustle to the bank to cash check! Simple? No way!

Reading a stopped clock is not that cut and dried—not with money at stake. The poor waitress in the Model Café never dreamed she was igniting a dynamite fuse. As the holders of the cashier checks poured into the bank lobby, others who disagreed with how to read the clock were in hot pursuit, demanding that they were entitled to the check. I'm not making this up; I was the teller behind the counter.

When we lived in Fairbanks, we never heard the words *abortion* or *gay rights* or *gun control* or *sexual harassment*. We got our protesting from the annual ice breakup payoff. The following day, the newspaper would editorialize that next year it must be fixed. Soon everyone went back to work in the placer mine fields to wait for the same arguments the following year.

————————————

Ten Questions Most Frequently Asked by Stateside Dwellers

Q. How cold did it get up in Fairbanks?

A. Cold enough to make the power wires sing, the nail heads in your living room frost.

Q. How did you get around?

A. Since your car won't start, if you own one, walking works. Or call a cab.

Q. Did you ever live in an igloo?

A. Sure. We let our wood heater die out each night, so an igloo is what our cabin felt like each morning.

Q. Did you ever shoot a polar bear?

A. No, caribou tastes better. And 300 miles closer. And caribou don't maul you when they're mad.

Q. Ever freeze your body?

A. Sure. At 30-below, you freeze a cheek or an ear and don't feel pain, until later. I know.

Q. How did you dress to go out in the cold?

A. Wear everything you own. Footwear is the most demanding because feet sweat.

Q. What was the worst thing about the cold?

A. Glasses steam up, windows frost over solid, permafrost keeps shifting doors.

Q. I'll bet you couldn't wait for summer?

A. Hunting and fishing are macho stuff, but mosquitoes are worse than the cold.

Q. Did you feel threatened by the Eskimos?

A. Ours were called "Natives." No, they're peaceful and lovable folks.

Q. Why did you stay so long?

A. Camaraderie, freedom, aurora borealis, and the beautiful women.

Q. Are you sorry you left?

A. When I'm in Santa Barbara, No. If I'm anywhere else, Yes.

The Entrepreneur

For many of us, early Alaska was a do-it-yourself school. If a settler wanted a cabin, he became a carpenter. If he wanted running water, he sent to Sears for a manual on plumbing. If he wanted his vehicle to run, he learned mechanics. Self-education was a mean teacher, and we all made mistakes, lots of them, but we learned.

In Alaska of the 30s, it was endemic that newly arrived young bucks would spot voids in the local commerce, followed by the impulse to *give it a try*. I had no resistance to these temptations and succumbed readily. The place was a business beginner's dream. We didn't know the term *under-capitalized*. Never heard of a business plan. Cheechakos fresh from the States became opportunists overnight. Some made it, some didn't. I stumbled into numerous business ventures, tackling startups without the requisite smarts. My first of many such gambles was in the office equipment business (a loser because of wartime rationing). I became the jack-of-too-many trades and master of none. *My story is a beginner's textbook for free enterprise with a faulty bootstrap.*

For example: Rumor had it that Black Rapids Roadhouse was for sale. This possibility set my entrepreneurial glands in motion. Maybe it was the once-in-a-lifetime chance I had needed. What an opportunity! True, there were a few problems with the place. Its only dependable income was a small stipend for reporting weather. Its only traffic was when the road was open for a few months of Alaska's brief summer. And our three-year-old daughter would be needing playmates and eventually school. The only neighbor was a glacier across the river.

Black Rapids Glacier was not your run-of-the-mill chunk of ice. This one had spunk. It moved sometimes. All glaciers move, of course, but this one could move fast. In fact, it could rampage. And it made a racket. All of this gave it notoriety. If you want to hunker down beside a glacier, it may as well be one that knows how to break into the news.

The old log hostelry was near a pass through the Alaska Range, about a day's drive down the Richardson Trail to

Valdez. It was a leftover from the gold rush, when shelters were spaced a dog team's daily run apart. Roadhouses were vital links, lifesavers spotted about the interior, offering survival to the weary.

The Richardson trail consisted of only two tracks weaving across the lonely terrain. There was no roadbed, no drainage ditches, and no shoulders. To pass oncoming vehicles, usually trucks, meant squeezing onto the grass or brush alongside the roadway. The truck traffic was to and from Valdez. It was a much shorter route to the coast, and merchants used it to beat the train-shipping time via Seward by several days. The trucks were standard ton-and-a-half flatbeds, single rear axle. This before the days of 4-wheel drive. The drivers were paid by the trip, usually $40, for which reason they skipped sleep.

The Richardson Trail

This road had a unique handicap. Ninety miles from Fairbanks, near Big Delta, there was a ferry crossing of the Tanana River. The ferry was an economical marvel, a floating platform powered by the current, and required but a single attendant paid by the Alaska Road Commission (an arm of the U.S. Department of the Interior.) There came a time the ARC decided there should be some revenue from the road to ease the expense, so they levied a load tax against the truckers. The easiest way to collect it would be to nail their taxpayers at the ferry. It shut down at nighttime, and if one was driving the highway, it was critical to beat the closure time because motels were unheard of.

The truckers were a swashbuckling independent tribe and didn't cotton to being taxed. So they took the winch handle away from the custodian, drove on, and cranked the ferry into the current. That didn't need any skill. This defiance of the new rule required a marshal to come from Fairbanks. The truckers were lined up and waiting, took the marshal's gun away, and drove aboard.

Naturally, the marshal had to arrest a few. They came to trial, but where in Fairbanks could the government find a jury that didn't have friends among the truckers? So they were acquitted, and use of the Richardson was again toll-free.

———————

If we bought Black Rapids roadhouse, we wouldn't make much money, but we'd gather plenty of tall tales. Every trucker knew a near miss with death that would be grist for table chatter. We would be essential. We would be part of the folklore. We would even be a forerunner to the CB (the citizens' band radio) because the roadhouse was where the phone line from Fairbanks to Valdez had to relay by voice. We would be the "Hello, central" of the wilderness. We would also be isolated for the eight months the road was snowed in during the long winter. And what of our young daughter who would need school?

After lengthy deliberation (30 minutes, maybe an hour), Jeanne and I decided to drive down the trail and maybe buy that white elephant. Actually, it was my decision. Jeanne went along because divorce was anathema to her.

The owner of the Black Rapids Roadhouse was a widow—hard work had probably killed her husband—and she had a plausible reason to sell. Since we had no money, she would probably take a promissory note. As we drove up to the gravel parking area, I looked across the river to make sure the glacier was being a good neighbor and then headed for the door. It was locked! A scribbled sign told me that some lucky person had beat me to it. A missed opportunity, and by only a few days!

Wartime Dislocation

Wartime dislocation is a breeding ground for bad deci-

47

sions. Neither Jeanne nor I knew if we were coming or going. Jeanne had been evacuated to Kansas City by the military. I wangled a stateside transfer but no house included. In time, we fled Kansas City because we had not solved the housing problem, and we yearned for our cozy log home in Fairbanks. Despite major complications, we managed to return separately. I trespassed the Alcan Highway under construction (detailed in the next chapter); Jeanne and Jeannette, after much negotiation and anxiety, finally managed an Alaska Steamship sailing.

I made many restless moves to prepare Jeanne for my time in the service. Interim employment at Kansas City had been a hopeless headache, but in Fairbanks it was easy (more about that later). When the "greetings" finally arrived, Jeanne was displaced in Idaho with my parents, awaiting word for ship passage. Definitely a bad situation. The draft board listened to my story of a mother and baby stranded and granted me a month's delay. It was enough! In May, Jeanne and Jeannette arrived. I packed my bags, but days before my departure, the government decided that I was too old for military service. We could breathe again.

The John River Trading Company

A recent letter from Red, my old friend still in Fairbanks, teases me about a venture I would prefer to forget: The letter read: "This article came in our Sunday paper and I felt you would like to remember Hickel* and the great achievements of his time. As I recall, he also came to your rescue in Santa Bar-

---

* Walter Hickel went to Alaska in 1941, was active in business and oil development, became Secretary of the Interior for President Nixon in 1968, and then served two terms as governor of Alaska.

bara to help wash the oil off the sea birds after the big oil spill. Anyway, now you can drive to your trading post only to find no one there to trade with." /s/ Red Langley."

"Your trading post" referred to my next Alaskan gamble. Probably the stupidest. It had a name—the John River Trading Company. The article Red enclosed was an account of someone else's project touching the same location as mine. The reporter wrote of the construction of an ice road from Livengood to Bettles, then up the Koyukuk River, past the John River, eventually to reach Prudhoue Bay. The story carried a sideline of news that is a bit of an obituary for the folly into which Jeanne should have forbidden me to venture.

It happened quite understandably. Fred P. knocked at our door.

"Rumor has it that you want a roadhouse business. I have just the deal . . . we can be partners." (I could be the lucky chump.)

There was oil under the North Slope, as everyone in Fairbanks knew. Now, according to Fred, the Navy was going to make it accessible for warfare needs, and the first step was to build an emergency landing strip for planes unable to see their way across the Brooks Range.[*] The chosen site was by the Koyukuk River near the confluence of the John River. A few miles downstream was Bettles, a native village with a radio and a landing strip.

Fred's information on the strip location was top secret, as was the identity of the contractor, Lytle & Green. So we had the inside scoop. Always an advantage. Fred confided that they would be sending a tractor train overland as soon as the

---

[*] It needs explaining that once upon a time, airplanes had to fly by visual landmarks, aka VFR.

49

freeze-up permitted and we could get some of our building materials, maybe even nonperishable inventory, smuggled aboard.

It was certainly the opportunity of a lifetime. Fred and I, who knew nothing about each other, would form an entanglement, aka partnership. Fred would move to the location, and I would man the Fairbanks base. I was now a teller in the Fairbanks Bank and could be the liaison with civilization, purchase and forward supplies, etc., while receiving my $285 per month from the bank. Finally, we would have the roadhouse of my dreams and Jeanne's nightmares. From my viewpoint, it was the opportunity we were seeking.

A more difficult shoestring enterprise couldn't have been contrived. Fred was trying to construct something in frozen desolation. A large tent and a small one went North with the tractor train. Fred purchased an old building in Bettles, salvaged out the whipsawed boards and moved them by dog team up the frozen Koyukuk River. I dispatched supplies as radio requests came in, sending them by bush plane to Bettles for transshipment by dog team. The last consignment encountered spring thaw and required the dogs to pull through water flowing on top of the ice.

The wilderness exacts a toll. Fred's struggle with the isolation and the winter had been a lonely ordeal. So little wonder that he gave himself a well-earned fringe benefit in the form of a cook. She was a young and shapely native. Considering the absence of cosmetics and bathing facilities, she shouldn't have been a threat to Fred's marriage, but Fred had already stayed too long in the bush, away from his wife in Fairbanks.

By May, the contractors had a usable rough landing strip.

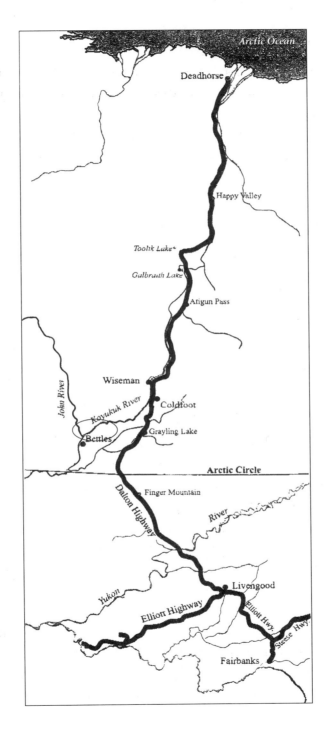

Arctic Ocean

Deadhorse

Happy Valley

Toolik Lake

Galbraith Lake

Atigun Pass

Wiseman

Coldfoot

John River

Koyukuk River

Grayling Lake

Bettles

Arctic Circle

Finger Mountain

Dalton Highway

River

Livengood

Yukon

Elliott Highway

Elliott Hwy.

Steese Hwy.

Fairbanks

"Everything for prospectors-miners-trappers"

JOHN RIVER TRADING CO.
GENERAL MERCHANDISE

Elbert H. Pitts
Harold Thornton
Co-owners

Mailing Address:
P. O. Box 1938
Fairbanks, Alaska

From now on our problems would be easy. The pieces were falling into place. I would accompany the load on the first plane to use the Navy's field. There was another reason for my trip. The draft board had now decided my age was just right. (I guess they figured an oldish recruit wouldn't do any real harm to the war.) I was to report for induction in a month.

Fred was gearing up for my visit. It would be the "grand opening"! Our tent-frame general store was primitive, and no words can do justice to its inadequacy. But it was only a beginning, someday to be enlarged and permanent. Of course. Even so, it was the best and only "shopping center" between Wiseman and Bettles, and the natives were quite excited by the promise of supplies and credit.

Our grand opening party started off quite orderly. Fifty or more natives had drifted in. There hadn't been an opening of a roadhouse on the Koyukuk for forty years, and this was a landmark event. The old and the young set up camp on the fringe of our clearing and gradually shuffled closer.

Fred had stocked our rough-hewn shelves with an assortment of staples and canned goods plus beer. The beer was against my wishes, but Fred insisted that the construction gang from Lytle & Green demanded it.

As the evening progressed, things got jolly. The sun in the north barely dipped to the horizon, making a blood-red ball in the sky that gave everything an eerie hue. An old-timer with a one-string fiddle emerged and began scratching out a discordant noise. His playing wasn't music, but it made the tribal toes twitch. Tapping became shuffling, which became swaying, which became stomping. A few hours of this and the crowd was sweaty, the air was smelly, the beer was flowing, the dancing intensified, the floor boards were convulsing, and the merchandise on the shelves was tumbling. By midnight, moccasin-clad feet were making a mixing bowl of our "store." It was a happening.

If I slept that night, it was fitfully. My memory has mercifully blotted it out. In the morning I surveyed the debris that represented Jeanne's and my life savings. Fred's Indian girl was stirring outside his sleeping tent. The river was threatening as it crowded its banks with spring runoff. The natives had moved out of sight. I felt helpless and displaced as I viewed the dismal scene and then scanned the sky for the bush plane that would take me back to Fairbanks.

The waiting seemed endless, but eventually I heard the far-off beat of a propeller, then a high-wing much abused plane came bumping down the rocky strip to our unloading

pallet. I helped the pilot off-load his cargo which I had ordered before leaving Fairbanks then climbed into the right seat beside the pilot. "Let's go!" I urged.

Ahead would be two interminable hours over trackless tundra dotted with ponds, then the Yukon River, and another hour to Fairbanks. Three hours of wilderness watching. A chance to think. Think about what I didn't want to think about. A pathetic tent store on the banks of the Koyukuk River? Thirteen weeks of recruit camp? Jeanne alone in Fairbanks? Fred's wife and kids?

I knew beyond doubt that I would never again see the John River Trading Company. At least Jeanne would be relieved. And Jeannette was too young to know she got lucky.

Next month I would be swearing in for a dead-end enlistment that paid $30 a month to start. Fortunately, I could not know that thirty years later the Alyeska pipeline near to our site would pay cat skinners and truck drivers $30 an hour. Their going near the North Slope would be tantamount to striking gold. Nor could I know that in a few years pressurized planes would soar past our emergency field and over the Brooks Range effortlessly and with instruments that could locate the Deadhorse field at Prudhoe Bay in a blinding ice fog.

4

World War II, Thousands of Miles From the Front

Tom Brokaw's book* praises my generation for its dedication to winning World War II. This epic in our country's history demanded the ultimate from both the military and the civilian workforce. I was in both. At the start, we could not guess how long it would last or be sure we would win. We could not guess the pain of the casualties, the separations, the shortages, or the housing problems we'd endure. Death—shortages—sweat—tears, all part of the cost.

Thirteen million[†] of us were in uniform and who can count the number in coveralls. Rosie the Riveter was a poster girl. Brokaw portrays us as noble achievers. It is well deserved by many. However, some of us, and this includes the professional brass, should be embarrassed for sharing Brokaw's plaudits, unless dislocations, separation from loved ones, miserable housing, and frustration qualifies us.

War is a horrendous waste of lives and material. Because

---

* *The Greatest Generation.*
† As of Veterans Day, 2002, the government estimates that WWII veterans are dying at the rate of 1,000 a day.

of its very nature, blunders are inevitable. The military is a feudal system to enforce a discipline that sometimes suffocates logic and wisdom. Hurry up and wait. Slow down. Order twice what is needed because half won't arrive. Try to outguess the enemy, and polish your muddy boots. Do as you're told even if you know it is stupid.

As a civilian with the Air Force at Ladd Field and later a tech sergeant at Fort Richardson, I was witness to much too much SNAFU—situation normal all fouled up.

Ladd Field, Fairbanks, 1939

My starting job was doing the construction payrolls. When the building was finished (actually, it never is), I moved to civilian chief of the Air Corps Supply. In November of 1941, the officer in charge put me on orders to Sacramento Air Depot where I was to learn how to cut the red tape. Then I was to continue to Los Angeles to expedite delivery of the snow tractor we had on order (described in Chapter 3). I wanted to save the government money, so opted to hitch a round-trip ride on a B-18 bomber that was bound for McClellan Field for installation of cockpit heaters. That might make sense, except as I was told by the officers who flew them, this slow plane was good only for submarine patrol in the Caribbean. So why was it sent to Alaska?

Weeks dragged by. My mission was ended and I wanted to get back to work. But the old bomber just dozed under its wing covers. Then came December 7th. Suddenly, we were at war and I was sweating. My boss at Ladd Field telegraphed, "What's delaying you?"

I inquired of the officers who flew us to Sacramento,

"Why don't we dash home?" Their answer was the same as I had heard before we were facing a war: "The heaters aren't here yet."

Then one day on the streets of Sacramento, I ran into the plane's crew chief. "Where do you stay? I never see you at the quarters."

He told me he had rented an apartment and brought his wife down. The light dawned. Even with the war, my B-18 flight crew had no intention of returning until the snow melted. Other planes were now being shot down, and this crew was vacationing in the warm sun. I hitched a ride on the first plane north.

Lovesick and Lonely

I was a newlywed husband, now separated from my young bride for seven long weeks without the voluminous mail that had piled up somewhere. Jeanne had enriched my life in all the ways a young woman has skills for. When I came home from work, she greeted me dressed for a date. Makeup, seductive dress, high heels, and a greeting like I was the most important thing in her life. It gave me good reason to hustle out of my parka, galoshes, and fur hat and de-steam my specs. I could smell a hot dinner on the cookstove mingled with the scent of perfume. The table would be set with our wedding silver.

Outside, the wires are singing and the moon is glistening on the snow. Inside, Jack Frost has coated the nail heads and blanked the windows, and the permafrost has heaved the kitchen floor; the cellar drum furnace can barely heat the room and we have our love to keep us warm. I'm soaking up the aura of a special evening.

What a surprise. This new wife blossomed in the mold of "Evangeline" as immortalized by the Poet Longfellow:

57

"She . . . would bring to her husband's house delight
and abundance, filling it with love and . . .
on whose spacious shelves were . . .
Linen and woolen stuffs, by [her] hand woven."

I had married a genuine homemaker. She could cook, knew
how to sew, and would recite poetry and sing to me. I told
myself, *This is too good to be true: a guaranteed date if I want,*
plus romance in the bedroom afterward. Can I really be this
lucky?

———————

The DC-3 I had chanced to catch arrived back over Fairbanks behind another plane that stirred up the atmosphere by
landing and socked the field in. This is an Arctic phenomenon that occurs when superchilled air is molested. We flew
back to Big Delta to wait. It was my birthday, and I was ninety
miles separated from a welcoming kiss from my new wife. I
had a selfish right to be mad over the delay in Sacramento.

In remembering back, it is hard to believe the anxiety
during the winter following Pearl Harbor. Outguessing the
Japanese intent was a stab in the dark. The most likely threat
to Fairbanks was believed to be an incendiary attack. Most of
us stashed footlockers out and away from our dwellings.
These contained emergency blankets, clothing, and supplies.
Ours was covered with a canvas and buried under snow.

The thought of being dislodged by fire gave good reason
for blackouts. Fairbanks soon had black oilcloth shades seal-
ing all of its windows. All street lights were out. Vehicles were
required to drive without lights. (Military vehicles came
equipped with blackout lights. These were miniature slits that
emitted only a warning for oncoming traffic.) Volunteer air-
raid wardens patrolled the streets watching for glimmers of
light escaping past the curtains. The feeling was eerie.

58

Spring of 1942 was a time of constant bad news. Japan's conquests seemed endless. Even the most optimistic forecasts were for a long war. Our government was evacuating dependents of military personnel and key civilians. I was considered "key." Jeanne's orders were for air to Juneau, ship to Seattle, train to Kansas City. When we said good-bye at the Fairbanks airfield, we choked because of the possibility we would never meet again.

Ladd Field was now a transfer point for airplanes being delivered to Russia. Russian crews were housed on the field, and I was moved into quarters adjacent to them. They regularly awakened me early mornings with a roll call formation outside my window. For them, our Arctic was like being back home, and this was a choice assignment because to them Fairbanks was a shopping mecca. My small town was a transfer point for more than airplanes. They reveled in the availability of consumer goodies.

I learned that a squadron of B-26s, intended for Aleutian duty or transfer to Russia had heavy losses from refueling at the gravel fields in Canada. *Why were B-26s in route?* Who in the Pentagon had chosen to send north these *bumblebees* with range too short for the Islands or Siberia and props too low for gravel fields? Surely they would have run out of fuel and ditched in the Aleutians or cracked up on Siberia's improvised fields. It was convenient that their wreckage was in Canada. Now, if they had any salvage value, it was more accessible. In addition to the loss of planes, it troubled me because workers in the Martin plant who assembled those planes believed each bomber was their contribution to the war effort. I hoped they might never know.

Jeanne's evacuation to Kansas City turned our lives upside

down. In time, I managed to get us together, but to do so I gave up my draft deferment. In Kansas City with an A-1 draft card, I was virtually unemployable. It was just a matter of time and my call up "Greetings" would arrive. And we were living with Jeanne's parents. In far-off Fairbanks we had a cozy log house. We could be with Alaskan friends. Tough decision time. We opted to go back regardless of transportation obstacles.

Bright idea! In Fairbanks, I had been a good customer for George Nehrbus's U-Drive. Many of us young bucks rented his cars if we wanted to impress a date. Oh sure, dates were willing to walk, but a car! That made it special. I wrote George, asking if he had a car in the States he wanted brought up the Alcan. I added, "Incidentally, my friend Red Langley is in Tacoma and would also like to drive a car back." Immediately came a letter with a $1,000 check and a wartime ration certificate to legalize the purchase. Nehrbus was renting cars to Kansas City Bridge, the general contractor for Alcan construction. Thus the entitlement.

The Alcan Highway

"Buy a '40 or '41 Ford sedan. This certificate will get you through the MP check stations on the Alcan. I'm also sending same to your friend Langley." The choice of "Ford" was an easy guess. That flat head V-8 would start at lower temperatures than any other make. '41s were the last of civilian production. I located a dandy with money to spare for the trip. Bingo! We had a solution. Maybe.

The Military Police check stations were taken care of. Now what about gas? By phone, Red and I concluded that if we loaded our back seats with "case gasoline"[*] at Edmonton, we could cover the 1,400 miles from Dawson Creek to Fairbanks. We scheduled to meet in Northern Idaho. Still lots of missing pieces in our puzzle and nothing is certain in war time, but we were on our way.

Planning is usually easier than execution. At the Canadian border we asked for ration coupons to get us to Dawson Creek. The border patrol told us, "You get 12 gallons, imperial" ("imperial?" Why can't the British be more like us?). Not half enough. We did a U-turn to top off our tanks, took our stingy Canadian ration tickets, and 700 miles later coasted into Edmonton on empty. This city on the fringe of the arctic never heard of case gas.

"Let's go to Kansas City Bridge. They must have a regional office here."

They did. We told them our plight. The man in charge opened a drawer full of Canadian ration coupons and told us to help ourselves. We were OK for the 500 miles to Dawson Creek, after which there would be no gas stations. Then what? That left a 1,500-mile gap for running on *empty*.

Edmonton to Dawson Creek was almost impassable. Spring thaw had turned the dirt road into a ribbon of mud. Night driving when temperatures dropped and froze the mud was our best option. At Grande Prairie, we were desperate for a night's sleep so made it a day's sleep, on the car seat. We nervously crossed the Athabasca River on the ice, inched our way over an under-construction Peace River bridge, slipped and lurched into Dawson Creek. Eventually, we stared at milepost

---

[*] In the Arctic, gasoline (also kerosene and pressure appliance fuel "blazo") was available in five-gallon square cans and packed two to a wooden box. The ideal way for transporting by bush plane.

1 of the Alcan Highway and saluted, but with grave concerns.

With topped tanks we forged ahead into no-man's land. The MP check stations were about fifty miles apart and all had gas pumps for the construction equipment. Our Kansas City Bridge certificates were a godsend, and fortunately, the MPs were a disgruntled bunch. They complained that the Army had promised them a short tour and quick rotation. The Army reneged. Instead, they got mosquitoes, freezing, and no entertainment.

"We need gas. Can you help us?"

"Friggin Army! There are the pumps. Take what you need . . ."

The temperature was favoring us. As we progressed North, the daytime thermometer dropped to freezing, then zero, then below zero. The lower the temperature, the better the traction. We were now making good time on graded ice and packed snow. Detours onto the tote road were common and skirting bridge construction frequent. The crews were friendly and the only traffic was their vehicles. Bunks and meals were easy to find in construction camps.

Fort Nelson and Watson Lake were small settlements that gave us a break in the isolation. Everything was going well until Red's Ford quit and I had to tow him 180 miles into Whitehorse. This pioneer settlement was far from the worst place to be stuck, and it had a friendly mechanic.

Kluane Lake to Northcross to Tanacross to Big Delta were welcome pit stops and great scenery. To our left was the snow-covered Alaska Range, a dramatic vista. And on our right, the Tanana River, which we had explored on fishing trips. Red and I were on the home stretch and could now breathe easier.

The biggest surprise, near Big Delta we could cross the Tanana River on a bridge under construction. Wow! No more ferry! It was the longest bridge span we had crept across since Peace River. 500-feet long, cantilever design. This bridge deserves a salute. Construction had been going on here through the winter even though Big Delta's temperatures are off the charts if wind chill is factored. Arctic conditions have unimaginable complications, and bridge building brings out the worst. The water and aggregate for concrete must be heated and kept heated until set, the steel is ice coated and slippery, machinery is balky and breaks, and materials get lost under the snow. Workers must avoid skin contact with all metal, so how do frozen fingers in a heavy mitt pick a nut or rivet out of a bucket? At twenty below and colder, a workman can deliver only a small fraction of normal productivity.

Ralph Soberg was running the Big Delta job. It takes a rugged Norwegian. Who else would risk his life wrestling steel girders into place, high above a river of icebergs, sucking thirty-below air into his lungs? Ralph had experienced a dozen episodes that should have killed him, but didn't, and he lived to pen his story,[*] which is hardship adventure to the max.

I first crossed a Ralph Soberg bridge under construction in Mount McKinley Park, later on the Tok Cutoff, next in 1947 at Moose River on the Kenai Peninsula, and next the Kenai River when the Sterling Highway released Homer from its isolation. I wish Soberg could know how often my travels needed his bridges while under construction, and many times since.

---

[*] *Bridging Alaska* by Ralph Soberg, 1991, Hardscratch Press, Walnut Creek, CA.

Eight days and 3,000 miles from the U.S. border, we drove into Fairbanks and could deliver to George Nehrbus his two Fords. Those pre-war cars were tough. They had survived a beating and were in good running order without a ding or a dent. They even had gas in the tanks. Red and I were tired, dirty, and happy. George was as relieved as we were and broke open a bottle of champagne.

For Alaska, the Alcan was the spoils of war. For Canada, it opened a wilderness. For Red and me, it returned us to the land where we belonged. Jeanne and Jeannette would soon return by ship, I hoped.

Canol

CANOL! The name for an unbelievable wartime waste few people heard of. The purpose was to tap a partially developed oil field at Norman Wells on the Mackenzie River, pump the crude to a proposed refinery at Whitehorse, then pipe the product to Fairbanks. Our country had been at war five months, workers were in short supply everywhere. Most products, including steel and machinery, were being tightly controlled, and guess what?

The War Department set in motion a crazy scheme that sent 25,000 men, 1,600 miles of steel pipe, and untold money, to an inaccessible frozen swamp 1,500 miles north of the end of civilization. Hey, guys, the war's in the other direction!

Impossible madness! To exploit Norman Wells meant defying torturous cold and spring breakups. It required constructing a thousand miles of access road over uncharted Canadian mountains and canyons, an endless supply of barges and trucks and bulldozers, and camp equipment, tools, and supplies. The refinery was built at Whitehorse; it pumped product the 625 miles to Fairbanks through a small four-inch pipe laid on the surface along the Alcan roadway. Two booster stations pushed the fuel at 1,600 psi to our tanks at Fairbanks. Standard Oil had a contract to manage it, and I was hired to run the supply at the Fairbanks tank farm.

When it was too late, a person of rare intelligence in Washington demanded an accounting of cost for the delivered fuel. As I recall, it was $45 a barrel. Same could be bought at the Fairbanks Standard Oil bulk plant for $5 a barrel. It was about then that Congress woke up and a Republican senator from Oklahoma (an oil state) assailed the War Department for a "bullheaded and arbitrary attitude" in going ahead with the project against the advice of "petroleum experts." Amazing what happens when there's no budget and limitless money. I wish I could say I made this up, that all the shortages and rationing were for winning the war, that bonds the little people were buying were necessary to finance the war, but how to explain Canol. This extravaganza was quietly shut down and most of its assets given to Canada, the rest sold for peanuts.

It didn't need genius to see my tenure was short. The good news: Jeanne was now situated in our log home where she could wait out my time in the service. I took a job in the Fairbanks Bank (one more line on my resume) while waiting for my draft orders. More good news: I was sent to Fort Richardson, near Anchorage.

Recruit Camp

Recruit camp was debasing. My drill sergeant was a kid who couldn't have made tenderfoot scout. But he had three stripes. I was an adult, married with a child, had performed

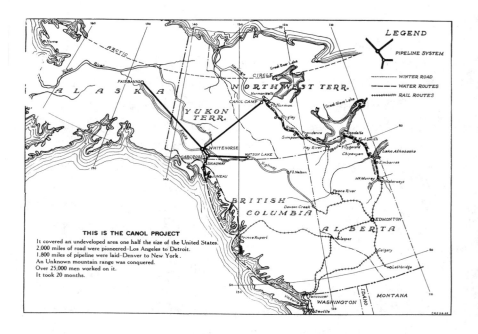

THIS IS THE CANOL PROJECT

It covered an undeveloped area one half the size of the United States.
2,000 miles of road were pioneered–Los Angeles to Detroit.
1,800 miles of pipeline were laid–Denver to New York .
An Unknown mountain range was conquered.
Over 25,000 men worked on it.
It took 20 months.

in numerous responsible positions and now I'm a dogface. The war is thousands of miles away, and what my cadre is enduring on bivouac and marches has no relevance. Eisenhower himself, if treated like a recruit, would have difficulty passing inspection.

The education we got in recruit training was a bit earthy. On bivouac, our C-ration contained cigarettes. To check out with a pass to town, we walked by a handout of condoms. To collect our pay, we dropped our pants for "short arm inspection."

If you see a squad of GIs training, you need only one guess as to what they're thinking about. It is not how to win the war; it's not how to be a better soldier, not how to shoot straighter. They are thinking about women. South Pacific's "There Is Nothing Like a Dame" tells it best. Our platoon sang as it shouted cadence. Always songs about girls.

"Oh, what do you know she smiled at me in my
dreams last night,

my dreams are getting better all the time."

The military is notorious for scrambling personnel geo-
graphically. It is the norm that easterners are sent west and
southerners are sent north. Trains, we called them "troop
trains," were crowded with servicemen moving cross-country.
Alaska was the exception. (I must credit the Army with the
good sense to assign us in our own territory.)

Military wives in large numbers tried to be near their men
if possible. Jeanne buttoned up our Fairbanks home and
arrived in Anchorage, a small town of 3,500 population that
was now required to absorb the out-fall from a bustling military base. Jeanne immediately discovered why *war is hell*—
that hell is not confined to the battlefield. She knew we could
not survive on my private's pay. She would have to go to
work. She would first need a caretaker for our infant. What
she found was the babysitter from hell. This witch was not
above exploiting a desperate housing shortage. She offered
Jeanne a couch in her living room for today's equivalent of
$500 a month. Of course, she would not feed Jeannette a
breakfast. Jeanne quickly found a job at Elmendorf Field, and
each morning as she left her little girl to go to work, I'm sure
a lot of tears ran down her cheeks.

In time, Jeanne located Seward friends, also with hus-
bands in the service. Ama and Billie came to the rescue with
loving child care and housing solutions. And in time, on
weekends, Jeanne, with Jeannette, could catch a bus to the
DC-3 recruit area and we could sneak through the woods to
a movie theater at a military hospital. Sometimes we had

what Jeannette called a "picnic," which might be no more than a roll of Lifesavers and time together in the woods. (I must interject a tribute to this toddler. Jeannette seemed to instinctively know her parents were under great stress and she should not add to it. Her behavior delighted us. Never a whimper. Her crib was a dresser drawer or a crate and never a complaint, not once. I whispered to Jeanne, "If girls are this easy, we should have another.") The short visits by my little family were a brief reprieve from recruit life. Wartime separation is hell. Being a camp follower lets wives share the hell. I am proud to include here a picture of Jeanne doing her part. Her effort was duplicated all over the U.S. a million times.

My Aleutian Fantasy

The drill sarge popped into our Quonset hut and shouted for Private Thornton to report to the camp commander.

"Thornton, I get scuttlebutt from the barracks that you know more than our top planners about how to win the war in the Aleutians. Why don't you share it with me, and it had better be good!"

"Yes SIR! Well, you see those barren rocks at the end of the chain, Kiska and Attu, are closer to Tokyo than to our base here at Elmendorf Field. That means their supply line is shorter than ours. So instead of trying to bomb them, we should drop back."

"Private, did it enter your head that next they'll move on Amchitka and Adak?"

"Yes SIR. And that's the good part. We keep luring them closer and their supply lines get longer. We relocate the Aleut natives same as we did the Japanese on the West Coast, and we let the enemy have Unalaska Island. Let 'em stagger around in the wind and fog at Dutch Harbor. Let 'em starve and freeze their butts. They're 3,000 miles from their supply base and will lose lots of planes and ships due to the miserable weather.

Better them than us.[*] Now, they're a short run from our ships at Kodiak and only 800 miles from our bombers at Elmendorf. We can make an occasional sortie just to keep them nervous. They'll build docks, warehouses, and camps that we'll own as booty when they lose the war."

"Thornton, your strategy is ingenious. How come you're only a private?"

"Good question, SIR. I think the sarge doesn't like me. He reads me off if I get out of step in close-order drill; tells me I don't shout cadence loud enough. He thinks I have a bad attitude. SIR."

When my miserable thirteen weeks of recruit camp came to an end, I didn't expect "graduation" hoopla. We had achieved zilch. Why advertise? But there was a ceremony. Col. Marvin "Muktuk" Marston had founded the Eskimo Scouts, and he gave an address. Most of our class were Aleuts from the Islands, and to them, Marston was God's helper. I remember one inspirational tip from his speech. He told these grinning happy native kids, "If you're assigned to drive the honey wagon, be the best honey wagon driver in the Army." It must have been good advice because we won the war.

I guess my footlocker passed inspection because I was given a rifleman's medal (M-16) and sent to HQ, Alaska Command. My office skills had saved me in the CCC, and now it had repeated. It was a lucky assignment, and I could resume being a human with an identity.

I was soon senior non-com in the personnel office quickly worked up to five stripes. Since new officers rotated through

* Brian Garfield's book *The Thousand Mile War* (Bantam edition 1982) estimates the Aleutian campaign cost us 10,000 lives, scores of ships, hundreds of airplanes.

frequently, assigned and reassigned, I ran the office and prepared the reports an officer would sign. They checked on our morale, got briefed on the state of affairs, OK'd what was put in front of them, and shoved off to the officer's club to win the war. I was the colonel's "Radar" (*M.A.S.H.* may be an exaggeration, but it depicts much truth). I sure didn't complain because garrison life was safe. PX and commissary purchases were a subsidized benefit and entertainments were virtually free. My job plus the stripes on my sleeve reaped a bit of respect and from my pay we were able to squirrel away some savings. The best was base housing, including furniture and utilities for rent less than Jeanne paid to sleep on the baby-sitter's couch when she arrived in Anchorage. We were able to bring our second baby home to the best shelter we had experienced in our married life.

Private Thornton—Recruit Camp, Fort Richardson, Alaska, WWII

My work put me in position to note that over 100,000 Army troops, plus Navy and Coast Guard, were stationed in Alaska. In my judgment, if regulations permit a non-com to have judgment, most of our troops were doing housekeeping chores, unrelated to winning a war. Manpower that was needed elsewhere was being wasted in Alaska. In warfare, it's generally the infantry that does the fighting, the dirty work, and Alaska had one regiment of infantry to do the fighting. It was a black contingent scattered along the Aleutian chain. Their duty—longshore work. Millions of us should not want to hear, "What did you do in the war, Daddy?"

In recruit camp, I had a buddy who borrowed our money. Not part of my $30 but from Jeanne's pay. She was doing her part for the war, same as Rosie the Riveter. Alex said he'd pay me back someday. Together we were assigned to the HQ. Alex's duty was composing the accolades that justified medals. He made up good stuff. One day he told me he was going to get me a decoration. I objected, "You could be busted back to private."

I was winding up my enlistment, and the colonel arranged a party for our detachment. He surprised me with an Army Commendation Medal. The citation read, "For meritorious service . . . Sergeant Thornton, Chief Clerk, demonstrated outstanding initiative and ability in completing a difficult

assignment. /s/ by direction of the Secretary of War." Yee gods! What a crock! Had I earned the Medal of Honor[*] I would have reason for pride. Alex's payback could be worn beside my Rifleman medal and the "ruptured duck" medal we all got with our honorable discharge. I would someday be a decorated veteran.

There isn't a GI living whose memory doesn't hide his wartime list

---

[*] The Medal of Honor is awarded for *special valor*. There have been 3,459 recipients since the Civil War, 141 still living. There is only one way to get it: the hard way.

of stupid orders and actions or waste. But we won. We won the war in spite of waste and bureaucracy. We won because of industrial muscle, abundance of natural resources, and willingness to spend whatever it takes. We won because millions of women pitched in, including Jeanne and her mother. Of most importance, *we won because we had enough brave troops . . . and Eisenhower in command.*

Eisenhower

From the perspective of a five-stripe sergeant in World War II, I believe it was our country's good fortune that at a crucial time in history Dwight Eisenhower (1890–1969) was available for Supreme Commander of the integrated European Defense Forces. He knew how to command; he had the backbone to control the jealousy of competing brass and national loyalties; he had the wisdom to see the big picture. I believe General Eisenhower infused most of us GIs with pride. Ike had the right stuff.

Millions of us veterans never dodged a bullet. But if Tom Brokaw says we are the "Greatest Generation," who am I to argue?

Demobilization

The war was over and it was time to go home. Demobilization was the order and the troops could shout HURRAY! Except this sergeant had sold his home in Fairbanks and foresaw no job. The colonel who ruled over my destiny had an answer:

"We can send you to officer's candidate school. Or we can

Bill Mauldin, the famous cartoonist for *Stars and Stripes*, stripped the glamour from warfare. I wish he could have put his pen to Alaska. Mauldin's cartoons were an enlisted man's tonic. He was self-educated, never graduated from high school, but won two Pulitzer prizes.

His cartoons told the story about the hardships of the war in Italy better than any news release. They embraced the plight of the average "dogface" and won Mauldin the love of millions who were serving in the crucible of misery. General Patton tried to muzzle Mauldin because Willie and Joe, his two famous privates, were contemptuous of the officer corp. One of his prize cartoons has an officer, newly arrived on the fighting front, admiring the French Alps with a caption, "Is there a view for the enlisted men?"

General Eisenhower got his chuckles from Mauldin's humor and shielded him from General Patton, even ordering that the cartoonist have his own Jeep so he could go anywhere he wanted. Where Mauldin wanted to go was the battle front. He was wounded and awarded a purple heart.

This picture of Sgt. Thornton in uniform, reading Bill Mauldin's Up Front while seated n the comforts of his Fort Richardson apartment, echoes the injustices Mauldin portrayed. I am the picture proof that military service is not a level playing field. War sacrifice is not one size fits all.

Bill Mauldin died as this story was readying for press. It saddens me that he will never know that his cartoon Jeep was the model used by Eli Luria for the cover of this book.

send you on temporary duty to our Fort Lawton assignment office."

TDY was usually a soft berth, well used and abused by most military who had a smidgeon of control of their personal destiny. I knew I couldn't be discharged while away from my post on TDY. I also knew they'd have to send me back to Fort Richardson for mustering out—after winter was over, I hoped. Request granted.

My military travel orders sent me to Seattle ahead of the family, which allowed time to search for a dwelling. Within a few weeks, Jeanne closed our Fort Richardson apartment, and with Jeannette and Joyce, then three months old, climbed aboard a commercial DC-4* at Elmendorf Field for a long and rough flight out of the Alaska winter.

Wartime dislocations were still prevalent and housing scarce. I was lucky to rent a shelter from Renton Highlands public housing.† The furniture was sparse; heat and cooking was with coal stoves, so we lived in soot. No matter, we had experienced much worse; plus, we were together.

To further brighten the Seattle sojourn, we had decent wheels. I met my little family with a new Chevrolet (one of the first off the line after postwar production resumed), wheedled for a price-controlled $1,300. Many such purchases entailed buying the salesman's necktie. My uniform got me past this ambush and saved me several hundred dollars.

Seattle's winter was like springtime to Jeanne and me. We

---

* The DC-4 was a four-engine successor to the DC-3, not pressurized. Until the advent of pressurization and jet engines, planes were not able to fly above weather turbulence.
† This was divine justice of a sort because many years later I managed the "public housing" in Santa Barbara; thus I could claim experience on both sides of the subsidy.

hustled the purchase of things we might need in a business at Hope (detailed in the following chapter), and I bought a surplus Navy jeep. I went through the motions of being useful to the Army while awaiting a spring sailing of the ship I knew to be the Army's coziest transport. (In my assignment work at Fort Richardson, I discerned that the GIs from stateside who arrived via the S.S. *Thistle,* a converted hospital ship, were happy soldiers.)

Our new daughter's first Easter was celebrated aboard ship with an Easter basket provided by the ship's crew. We cruised in style, debarked at the port of Whittier, then on by train to Fort Richardson for my "processing." Our Army experience had a gloomy start but a rosy finish.

Not so for 300,000 who would not be coming home. War is so grossly unjust. Ten million allies and 11 million axis soldiers would never come home. All this because Germany and Japan, and Italy, too, were captives of paranoid regimes. All because they had massive military machines and madmen itching to use them. And the Russians? Stalin accounted for unbelievable losses among his own people. Dictators with military might are loose cannons on the deck. Add all the casualties inflicted by World War II and the estimate is 50 million—but who can know?

At the Nuremberg Tribunal, the Chief U. S. Prosecutor, Supreme Court Justice Robert L. Jackson, spoke this summation:

> We must make clear to the Germans that the wrong
> for which their fallen leaders are on trial is not that thy
> lost the war, but that they started it. And we must not
> allow ourselves to be drawn into a trial of the causes
> of the war, for our position is that no grievances or

policies will justify resort to aggressive war. It is utterly renounced and condemned as an instrument of policy.

The war may be over, but the heartbreak lives on. There is no way to quantify the collective pain. What a terrible price nationalism extracts. It is a mockery to pretend anyone wins a war.

Japan's surrender was radio-broadcast by its "divine ruler" (Hirohito) to his devastated people on August 15, 1945. The peace treaty was signed on the main deck of the battleship *Missouri*. For the closing act of World War II, General Douglas MacArthur gave this stirring benediction:

> It is my earnest hope—indeed the hope of all mankind—that from this solemn occasion a better world shall emerge out of the blood and carnage of the past, a world founded upon faith and understanding, a world dedicated to the dignity of man and the fulfillment of his most cherished wish for freedom, tolerance and justice . . . Let us pray that peace be now restored to the world, and that God will preserve it always. These proceedings are closed.

After discharge, we had to start life anew. Jeanne and our two kids flew to Hope on a small bush plane that landed on the tide flat. I followed after the red tape unwound. The wartime disruption in our life was boiler-plated in the discharge I held:

"Awarded as a testimonial of Honest and Faithful Service to this country." That was the Army's parting salute to Tech. Sgt. Thornton.

5

Living on Moose, Salmon, and Love: Hope, Alaska

Hope, a sleepy little settlement on the opposite side of Turnagin Arm, seemed a logical choice. This village beckoned us for several reasons. Jeanne and her parents had moved to Hope* from Kansas City in 1936 to join brothers Ed and Forest. A third brother, Richard, soon followed, and for a while, the entire Brenner family was united in a mining venture. Ed went to Fairbanks to enter the university, and soon after, the parents and Jeanne followed. That's how the young daughter met her husband. After the war, the parents and Ed returned to Hope to mine again. Ed now had the gold fever bad. If mining didn't work, they could cocoon along with a few ancients who refused to believe the mining era had ended.

Hope's alluvial soil is rich and its scenery is priceless. The way it nestles against the mountains along the south shore of Turnagin Arm is art gallery material. It also had an isolation that matched the gold miner mentality. Society's dropouts loved it. The Seward marshal used to boast that he'd never made a trip to Hope to solve a crime. Of course, the game

* See the back inside cover for Ann Miller's photograph of Hope.

79

warden didn't share that complacency, but for Hope people, shooting illegal moose was good clean sport. They did it to put meat on the table, and sometimes it was the only fun in town. So Jeanne and I found ourselves in Utopia, except there was no way to make a living. That could be offset by the advantages of family—cousins for our two young daughters and a sister-in-law for Jeanne. Yes, Hope was perfect.

Hope had a fanciful history. And what a tide! Its claim to fame is Turnagin Arm's forty-foot tide change, second highest on earth, next to the Bay of Fundy. A tide such as Hope's is bragging material. It can be lethal if you're in it with a small boat, if a person tried to swim in it—nobody does—it would be a mud bath from which there is no return. No daredevil would surf in it. To approach Hope by water was akin to suicide. That tide would run out faster than a boatman could row for shore and the boat would settle into bottomless mud. Its bore was like the "tube" on Hawaii's north shore. When you can hear a tide before you see it, that's a force to be reckoned with. And of course, there's no way to make a living

from a tide that comes in with a bore that roars.

Hope had its origin in the leftovers from a gold camp named Sunrise, which was half a day's hike away, the spillover from the Klondike rush. Around Hope, there was just enough gold dust to keep the miners digging, or more accurately, "sluicing," because it was mainly placer. There was never enough to send anyone home rich, and many wanted to stay because it was an appealing little sanctuary. Once planted, folks got comfortable even if they starved, and that was something the locals wouldn't allow to happen.

We purchased a little cottage on the Forest Service bench about a mile from the village. By midsummer, we moved it down to the settlement and planted it along Hope's only access road. I added a sleeping room, a floor furnace, and a sink with a bucket. The land we purchased included an old quaint log cabin, a shed or two, some berry bushes, and that standard wilderness essential—an outhouse.

Of course, Hope had no employment. An insignificant detail, but nagging. The Alaska option of that era, for two people in need of an income and no identifiable skill, was to start a business. The one and only business in Hope was Doc Nearhouse's store. Doc was a landmark and dispensed everything tangible. Having no specialty and wishing no competition, we opted to supply Hope's missing services. Novices do that better than something requiring special smarts.

We became the wilderness catchall. We offered Jeep taxi for old miners trying to find their lost claims, cabins for transients, radio messages, fresh eggs, fryers, and berries.

Too much work, too little money! Jeanne and her mother raised chickens to sell in Seward. They canned a mountain of moose and salmon. When the salmon supply outran the jars, we sold the surplus in Seward (at the risk of going to jail). We took in boarders. We did subsistence gardening. We bounced the Jeep from the valley to the mountaintop on mining treks. Jeanne performed admirably, caring for our two youngsters and a husband. There were no modern conveniences, no stores, and no medics.

Hope lifestyle permitted a bit of socializing. There was the Saturday night dance. We went on picnics, snagged salmon in the river, and dodged the game warden. Once in awhile, Jeanne's dad hooked his team to a sleigh and gave the villagers a trot through the woods. These were his proudest moments. Hope's religious action was a mission church (Methodist), but the home folks didn't need salvation. It was a well-behaved little community and didn't admit to sin. Shooting an illegal moose, always for food, was considered a virtue. Most of the travel to and from Hope was to Seward, a seventy-five-mile gravel road through photogenic wilds. A bush plane could make it from Anchorage in thirty minutes if it wished to risk landing on the tide flat in front of the village, but few chose that option.

The Postmistress

Once upon a time, postmasterships were regarded as a patronage handout. Before civil service, an ambitious person needing a job could pick up a hammer, some tacks, and nail a bunch of political posters to the phone poles, knock on some doors, and if his candidate was elected, he might get an appointment with economic security while he managed the mails until the next election.

However, for small rural post offices, especially in the early days in Alaska, the job went to whoever had a centrally located shelter. The remuneration was insignificant. It was just a job somebody had to do. The Hope position came vacant. Jeanne was appointed.

The pay was about $125 per month, which went quite well with a lifestyle that had no shopping temptations. Odds and ends would make up the rest of the money we needed, and the easy post office schedule left lots of open time.

Serving Hope's sparse population (about 75 souls) could be done with a Wednesday afternoon opening when the villagers could buy their money orders to Sears Roebuck. After close up, we sacked the mail and left it by the door. Early the next morning, the trucker from Seward, making his weekly run, would pick it up, and our job was over until Saturday night at the dance.

There was nothing organized in Hope, but Saturday night, the handful of active inhabitants would gather for a dance or maybe a potluck at the rustic little community building. There would be a violin and harmonica, occasionally an accordion, and our glands would start to activate a bit. The kids would sleep along the wall. Sometime during the tail end of the activity, a villager would alert Jeanne or me that the mail truck

Anna Sweden and Jeanne

had returned from Seward.

Mail was always top priority, and we would start sorting immediately. It might take half an hour, and by then, variously delegated leaders were trekking over from the dance to our little rustic post office to pick up the mail for those remaining at the party. By midnight, our duty was over, except for some recluses too infirm to make the dance who would mosey over on Sunday morning for their mail. That would wrap it up until Wednesday.

In addition to our $125, we acquired a wealth of information. We knew who was sick, who was missing, who was mad, who could afford packages from Sears, and of course, we had the magazines and postcards to browse.

There's a good feeling about being indispensable, and Jeanne was just that and more to several of the ancients. Any weather-beaten old survivor of the mining era living out his days in a squatty cabin welcomed the lift of a feminine aura. With Jeanne behind the window, Sunday morning at our post office could rekindle the dying embers of a flame from yesteryear. The touch of her hand might revive his pulse. Mail took on added meaning when handed out by a pretty young lady. The old coots came in person, able or not, just for the sight of a full skirt and a frilly blouse, a soft voice and a warm smile.

Our crowded world has taken the human touch out of most transactions. Most, but not all. There's still the little post office on Santa Barbara's West Side. Anna rules it. Norman Rockwell would have immortalized her. She's formidable but she's gorgeous. When she retires, as soon she must, I'll feel abandoned, because I need Anna like old-timers in Hope needed Jeanne. Later in Kenai, Joyce Rheingans filled a similar need. She was another postmistress with charm and beauty.

I have been served by three gorgeous postmistresses . . .
I'm a lucky man.

Alaska Nellie

At mile 23, Jeanne and I turned off
the Seward road toward Nellie's cabin
by Kenai Lake. We had a special reason
to meet Nellie Lawing. Jeanne's brother
Forest had helped her write the story of
her life in the North.

Our visit was well rewarded. Nellie
took us across the railroad tracks to her
"museum" where an amazing display of
mounted trophy heads lined the walls. While listening to
Nellie's guided tour, we heard a loud pop.

Joyce Rheingans, Kenai

"Excuse me while I check my trapline." She returned,
explaining that a weasel had intruded into her sacred display
case. Nellie was in love with scads of pets, especially her rabbits.

Nellie's claim to fame stems from wild adventures in
Alaska before civilization. She went North as a young woman
in 1915 and found work cooking in the construction camps
run by the contractors building the railroad. When the railroad was completed, she was hooked on the country and settled into her cabin by Kenai Lake—for life. She married a
man named Lawing, and the railroad made Lawing a whistle-
stop. When you drive the road, you'll see the Lawing sign.
Nothing remains except Nellie's cabin.

The museum is no more. Nellie's guest book contained
15,000 names. Notables including a U.S. president, a secretary of the interior, a U.S. postmaster general, artists, writers,

and big game hunters. I understand the exhibits were given to the state, and I have no knowledge of where they repose. If they're lost, it's a sad loss. They're history, and so is Nellie.

Jeanne has just finished rereading *Alaska Nellie.* Many of the pages are marred by pencil scribbling. Jeanne cherishes vandalism by her toddler because it's "cute." So whoever comes into possession of this house, don't let this book wind up in the discards because it's valuable art and a unique memento.

Meat on the Table

In the interior, caribou was the sourdough's menu. On the Kenai Peninsula, it was salmon in the summer and moose in the winter. These staples were the bounty of the land, the reward for living in isolation. Early residents regarded free meat as their entitlement. The Fish and Wildlife Service (FWS) didn't always agree.

FWS wardens patrolled the Kenai with a Widgeon plane and by four-wheel drive vehicles. They were a dedicated lot. Most of them would arrest their own mother. A murderer would have a better chance of getting off than someone caught hiding wild game shot illegally. FWS in Kenai meant Dave Spencer and Jimmy Petersen. They were incorruptible, and they were friends. When Jimmy disappeared in Skilak Lake, the pain was like losing family.

The sport, if that's the right term, was more than stalking the prey. It was outfoxing the game wardens. Their mission was to enforce "the law." The hunter's mission was to put food on the table without getting caught. These motivations were not compatible. The FWS had one important clue—blood on the snow was a red flag.

Author With Moose

"The law" was just plain unreasonable. It specified that (1) only bulls could be taken, (2) one mile from the road, and (3) in open season. A wizard in Washington decided when we could hunt, but Mother Nature decided when to send a freeze so the meat would keep. There was no electricity in the bush; hence there were no refrigerators. "Bulls only" makes sense, but a cow makes better eating. And "one mile" is unthinkable. What half-sane native is going to lug 700 pounds of moose a mile through brush and swamp? Not when the moose is ignoring the rules and is willing to pack its own carcass to within gunshot distance of the road.

Another quirk of the law said the animal must not be spotted from the air. Often wondered why my neighbor, Jim Hartley, was airborne so early and so often in the fall. I guessed he just liked to see the sunrise from 1,000 feet above the woods.

The settlers on the peninsula observed a code. They shared. If a neighbor got lucky, we could count on eating. And when a pan of liver or roast showed up, we did not ask if it was "legal." We were hungry and gave thanks. Jeanne's father was a butcher by trade—therefore, a good companion on a hunt. He joked that he didn't know if legal game was edible.

In Fairbanks, it was typical to start the winter with three frozen caribou hanging in a shed; on the Kenai, one moose was sufficient unless the family was large. The best moose (cow or bull) is a three-year-old shot before the rutting excitement. Best target is a lung shot, which brings the moose down before it can heat up or run far.

Salmon are another of God's miracles. Best species is a king (aka chinook if you're West Coast); equally good but smaller is a silver (cohoe)—both favorites for barbecuing. Reds (sockeye) are for canning because of their oil content. Humpys (humpback) are pink salmon, and chums (dog) are okay if you're hungry.

Once the salmon nears its spawning ground, they stop feeding. They can survive a thousand miles up the Yukon River, and along their route native settlements put fish wheels in the river, dry their catch over rope lines, and have a winter's supply of dog food. Salmon are a priceless resource. Kenai and Hope were blessed with them.

Paul Murray and King Salmon

Newly arrived at Hope, I quickly

88

learned a gill net was needed. Bob Mathison made occasional runs to Anchorage with his power barge (the Yentna), and I went along. Bob tied up at the cannery on Ship Creek where I bought a used king net (called a "web" by the trade). Wearing hip boots for sloshing in the tidal mud, I put the net along Resurrection Creek, and we were jubilant with our harvest of beautiful kings, the largest probably fifty pounds. Lacking refrigeration, Jeanne hurriedly canned as many as possible in "Kerr" jars, the cartons stacked high in a corner. The larder was swamped. What to do with the surplus? Sell it in Seward? Commercial fishing in the Hope area was not legal, but sometimes you do what you gotta do.

Moose all winter and salmon all summer was our balanced diet. Free meat but a lot of work. And our game warden score? Arrests: 0. Near misses: plenty. We poachers could swear with pride President Nixon's famous denial: "I am not a crook."

From Hope to Seward was a lonely drive. A person on foot was certain to be offered a ride. The road was narrow and twisting. Snow was plowed by a road maintenance rotary "snow-go," which cut a vertical bank, like slicing a cake. It made foraging difficult for the moose who owned the road. They might trot ahead of your vehicle or might stop, block your way, and stare you down, as if to say, "You climb over to the deep snow, I'm tired."

There were a few scattered shelters along the road, rarely occupied, and our vehicle might be the only traffic of the day. Moose Pass, the only settlement after 45 miles, was a haven because two couples from Jeanne's Seward school days lived there. Laubschers or Saxtons were obligated by pioneer tradition to offer us shelter. It meant they must defrost us, then feed us, help us with any repairs our Jeep needed, and offer a bed in a corner of their dwelling. Even if we asked to borrow money or needed help packing a moose out, they were stuck with us. ("Oh Lord, here come Thorntons, just when I wanted a quiet night alone. . .") Of course, we would do the same for them, except luckily we weren't on their travel route.

Continuing from Moose Pass, another thirty miles of narrow twisting road, requiring slalom skills to dodge chuckholes so thick they can't be dodged, brought us to more modest temperatures with the deep snow gradually changing to ice, sleet, and rain. We reach the head of Resurrection Bay, a marvelous waterfront for the relatively young town of Seward. In this shopping mecca of 1,500 hardy individualists, we provisioned for the month to follow back in Hope or Kenai. This chore took most of the day and thus required overnighting in Seward. Our haven here was Sumes', still drawing on Jeanne's school days connections.

Friendships in the bush were a priceless currency. When I was drafted, and Jeanne, with our infant daughter, moved to Anchorage and a housing crisis, the Laubschers and Sumes came to the rescue. Isolation and pioneering gives friendship a different meaning. When someone tells you, "I love Alaska," it is most likely they mean they love the people in Alaska.

Marathoning

"No!" I reasoned with Janell. "You surely don't mean the 26 miler? Please, tell me that your plan is to go a few miles and then catch a cab back?" It was the plea of a parent on thin ice. As an adult, this daughter didn't need my permission. Past experience had proven that. I lamely conclude with, "I know you're too smart to finish on a stretcher."

90

Janell's answer was impatient. "Yes—and you did a crazier thing when you were in Alaska."

She's got me. She recollects some family history that predates her birth—like my own marathon. It was more a shuffle than a run. And it served no useful purpose other than to prove to myself that I could hike thirty miles nonstop—without competition.

At family get-togethers, I had recited it, partly in jest and partly a boast, and too often. The setting was January in Alaska in 1948. In our surplus military jeep, with Jeannette, our five-year old daughter, we were returning from my second trip to Kenai to our tiny cottage in the village of Hope.

The trip's purpose was to brainwash Jeanne into agreeing to a move to Kenai. Winter was not the thinking man's choice for off-road exploring, and winter travel was especially wrong for the safety of my family. In an era before seat belts, we skidded, churned, and bounced in an open-air, unheated jeep. From the end of the road at Hinton's Lodge, we crawled across an uncharted wilderness. (Modern four-wheel drive aficionados would kill for such an opportunity.) By pioneering criteria, the hardships were within tolerable levels, the trip even marginally successful, except . . .

Except on return: still thirty miles short of Hope and home, a snowslide blocked our road. A full moon looked down on our predicament—and perhaps accounted for my next lunacy. I decided Jeanne should drive the jeep back to Moose Pass, perhaps fifteen miles, where either the Saxtons or Laubachers, would shelter them until the road was opened. I would hike the thirty miles home to Hope. As I recall, I used our post office responsibilities to justify this impulsive madness.

With adequate clothing (parka, mitts, and shoepacs), but

no emergency provisions, and snowshoes tucked under my arm, I waved good-bye to Jeanne and Jeannette. As they drove out of sight, my bridge was burned. There was no turning back.

I picked my way across the slide—its mass was about 100 yards wide—and past that obstacle, I discovered that the roadway had been recently plowed by the equipment from the Hope end. Lucky day—I wouldn't need the snowshoes, so I jabbed them into the vertical snow bank where they would be visible to Jeanne when she eventually drove through.

The mission was simple enough. Just keep the toes pointed toward Turnagin Arm and put one foot ahead of the other for thirty long miles.

The plowed roadway was covered by an inch of new snow. Deep shoe-tread marks, at least 60,000 of them, would attest to this night's achievement. The air was calm, the temperature in the zero range, so there would be little danger of frosted lungs, and perspiration would be tolerable. There would be no passing vehicles and, unfortunately, no dwellings before Hope. Not one inhabitant, except! Fear gripped me. Moose! I had overlooked the likelihood of moose in the roadway. What a dumb oversight!

Moose are attracted to a graded roadway because it makes for easier foraging. They survive readily on branches that are reachable from the road. If I encountered moose blocking my route, I had no means of scaring them back into the deep snow. I knew from experience that only a noisy Jeep backfiring would hustle them off the road.

Occasionally, I could spot them out in the trees. I presumed they had been routed a safe distance by the rotary snowplow that throws the white stuff high and far in an arching plume. It cuts a vertical bank that acts like a fence after the moose return to the roadbed. Weariness was now a side issue. How far could I hope to get before there'd be a big hulk blocking my way? What would I do? I could not leave the roadway to skirt them because my snowshoes were now far behind. I had to keep going.

Step after step and mile after mile, my eyes fearfully searched the moonlit roadway. Physical endurance was no longer the challenge. Anxiety was a drain on my energy; moose were the enemy. One ugly moose blocking my way could convert this folly into a black comedy. I knew the scenario from Fairbanks days; the danger of subzero drowsiness, especially applicable after excess drinking. According to barroom wisdom, if a drunk submits to the sleep urge while staggering homeward, the nap can be fatal. The guys in the Pioneer Bar agreed that it was a fairly painless way to tell this earth good-bye. Was Jeanne ready for young widowhood?

Nine hours of plodding, and I was out of the mountains and along Turnagin Arm. Only a few miles remained. Moose fear was joined by exhaustion. In marathon parlance, I hit the wall. I was no longer able to use my head and my legs at the same time. I would sit down to rest, which allowed blood to return to my brain, which would then tell me to move or freeze. The distances between sit-downs grew shorter, my brain glazed over.

It was a night to remember. Or better to forget. But tomorrow came, and I was back in our house. If I could limp next door I would open the post office on schedule. Probably nobody would come. And before nightfall, Jeanne and Jeannette would drive into Hope and make me look stupid. I was thirty, going on fifty, or nineteen?

It became apparent that a livelihood in Hope was as tough as I'd been warned. Hope would sit out the postwar boom. My career planning had a serious flaw. I had started something I would not finish. Lying alongside Hope's sole road was my ugly black fuel tank for the gas station that might someday replace the 55-gallon drums behind everyone's cabin. I had excavated a basement hole that resembled a gravel pit. Beside the hole was a pile of rough framing lumber from Turpin's mill. I had carefully stickered it to dry. It was intended for the roadhouse Jeanne and I thought we needed. Maybe Mathison's barge could move that lumber and the tank to Kenai. It was worth exploring. We could transplant our Hope folly to the opposite side of the peninsula where on this trip I had written a check for a fish site on Cook Inlet. Might be a good idea, or maybe not. I needed to learn how stake netting is done, assuming I could find my site. To do that required a dory, and Bob DeFrance of Hope had just built one. Yes, I had a lot of loose ends to tie, not least of which was to borrow the money needed. Edwin and Elizabeth Brenner (Jeanne's parents) were quick to volunteer a lot of free labor, and they were willing to loan us $1,500. If that was not enough capital to launch a business venture from the dirt up, Jeanne would have to continue selling illegal fish to the Methodist TB Sanitarium in Seward. (Those patients were lucky to be eating choice king salmon) Since our cost was only the labor to net, clean, and transport, we were able to sell at a fraction of the market price-25 cents a pound-and make a tidy profit. Volume was our problem.

There's always a problem. Jeanne had two little children to care for, and lugging a thirty- to fifty-pound king salmon a hundred yards or more, from the net mired in the muddy

94

tidal estuary to the Jeep, was for man-sized muscle and hip boots. Instead, Jeanne turned her energy to selling eggs, fryers, and garden produce.

My head was still in the depression and my business plan was worse than primitive. I can share a lesson from this: If we can't afford an MBA consultant, we must be undercapitalized.

GILL-NETTING IS MUSCLE-BUILDING WORK
Jim Arness, with sons Joe and Jimmy, picking a stake-net in
Nikiski Beach, Cook Inlet.

Map reprinted with permission from Kathy Haley.

6

Business Startups in the Bush: Kenai, Alaska

We stopped eating to listen. The sound was like racing footsteps on crusted snow. Then there was a thud, like boots thrown on the porch, and the door to the Quonset hut burst open. A breathless young native stared in at us. He threw back his parka hood, revealing weatherworn features that belonged to the wilderness from which he had emerged. He spoke in broken utterances: "That jeep! Whose? Take me to the marshal! There's been a murder!"

Thus began my first night in Kenai. Two hours earlier I had braked my jeep to a skidding halt when a moose of a man wearing bib overalls blocked my way. I explained my presence. "In the village I was told a Pappy Walker might be willing to 'set' me across the river?" The question was uttered timidly because I knew that no sane person would launch his dory in midwinter for a stranger.

"WHY?" he boomed at me.

"I want to hike the beach to Kasilof. I want to check the place out as a possible homesite."

His response was positive: "I'm Pappy Walker, *honey*, and you don't need to see Kasilof." Honey? From a man who could crush me with his bare hands? He screwed his big round face into a friendly grin and confirmed that I heard right: "Honey, I'm about to save you a long cold hike because I can tell you all there is about Kasilof right in here." He pointed to a squatty, drab Quonset hut—the kind that World War II left strewn around amid the litter to be stolen or bought surplus from the government. "And Jessie Belle will fix us some grub," he chuckled. It was settled.

This was my first trip to the west side of Kenai Peninsula. The all-day drive had been harrowing and bouncy. The first half of the trip had been on a narrow roadbed, snowplowed with high vertical ridges that fenced in the moose and resulted in occasional moose-to-windshield face-offs. The last half of the drive had been over an unmarked tractor trail that was traversable only because it was frozen. When I departed early that morning from the old mining town of Hope on Turnagin Arm, I fully expected to encounter some impassable obstacle that would conveniently turn me back to the warmth of our tiny, austere cottage. Instead, here I was standing by the Kenai River, having broken through to a strange land and an even stranger host.

Pappy Walker and his wife, Jessie Belle, had drifted into Kenai from Oklahoma. He was a plumber by trade, but his job as cannery caretaker provided housing and a base for the grandiose plans that would follow in time. Jessie Belle (which was also the name of his boat) was as neat and attractive as the lifestyle would permit. She shared in Pappy's outsized hospitality, but as she set another plate on the table, one could guess that she was annoyed with the regularity of these intrusions. In time, I would realize that I was but one of an endless motley procession of homesteaders, drifters, and fortune seekers who passed their rites of initiation to "the Kenai" at Pappy Walker's.

Throughout the evening meal, Pappy "honeyed" me with the vast and exciting potential of this ugly and dormant little settlement of stranded castoffs. As I drove in that afternoon, I surmised that Kenai hadn't changed much since the Russians departed 150 years ago. Its scattered dwellings were surrounded by the duffel of survival and stacked about as neatly as driftwood on an ocean beach. Pappy foresaw a great future for Kenai, and I drank in his enthusiasm.

With food and warmth added to the camaraderie, I sensed that the Promised Land was near . . . but now here in front of us stood a breathless intruder demanding, "That Jeep! Take me to the marshal! There's been a murder!"

Jimmy Minano, the excited native in front of us, lived alone in a cabin upriver from the cannery. His homesite was near a tidal estuary, which made it a choice location for wildlife and birds. He trapped furs in the winter, commercial fished in the summer, and had ample garden fare to garnish the moose meat. The land was good to him. Recently, he had acquired two homesteading families as neighbors. They were too distant to be visible, but still his lifestyle was affected by their presence. As we hurried toward the village, Jimmy filled me in on how the two men had some "bad blood" between them. Now some of that blood was staining a snowbank where one of them lay—the victim of a point-blank gun blast. The other, the one who pulled the trigger, must be captured before the tragedy enlarged.

Alaska, being a "territory," used federal marshals to administer a minimal level of law and order. The seat of Cook Inlet's "law" was a hodgepodge structure built of frame and log add-ons. Some of its parts resembled an early military outpost. It had a two-room wing with a locking door. The lock, usable or not, qualified it as a jail.

Marshal Allan Petersen and his wife Jetret lived in this shelter of sorts. She was a sensitive and charming woman with a bright mind and the ability to turn on the village's polyglot youth through her school teaching. She had furnished their home with cheery and intellectual gleanings. Its window to the world was a picture card scene of the inlet and Mount Redoubt, a venerable volcano that gave 3-D grandeur to the western horizon. The Petersen's had been in Kenai only a short time but had already filled an indispensable role.

Allan was a stout middle-aged man with a jovial demeanor that would have been fitting for a rector. He was a peace-loving person, and it was readily apparent that having a murder disrupt his evening was not his purpose in taking the job. But murder was too serious an infraction to ignore, and he stirred himself into his official role. Turning to me, he said, "You and Jimmy get a posse in order. Do you mind using your jeep to gather up some men?"

Not at all—I thought—it's what jeeps are for. After assigning the safety of the village to Jetret, the three of us squeezed into my jeep and headed for the two most likely candidates for this sort of dirty business: Al Munson and Odman Kooley. The five of us made an overload.

A short distance beyond the cannery the roadway ended, and the posse, with rifles ready, set off on foot up the trail along the river. Their flashlight beams soon disappeared into the night. I returned to the Quonset.

Pappy and Jessie Belle were waiting up, eager for details. My relay of Jimmy's account was sketchy: It was assumed that

Allan Petersen with "Moosemeat"
John Hedberg

One of the early settlers raised a large family, worked at the cannery at Kasilof, and built a home at what became Kenai pipeline dock site. John Hedberg, known as "Moosemeat John," once shot a moose late in the day. By the time the animal was skinned and quartered, darkness had set in. Too dark to find his way home, John wrapped himself in the moose hide (as in the Hiawatha classic). He placed the fur side inside, and the skin side outside. The night turned cold, freezing the skin side. Friends, concerned for his safety, began a search at daylight and found John, who now was unable to escape from the frozen hide. They cut the hide so John could escape, and the nickname "Moosemeat John" was coined. —James V. Arness

jealousy over one of the wives caused Bill Frank to go to Ethen Cunningham's cabin where he called the man to come outside. Then Frank shot Cunningham point-blank. It was the best I could piece together. Soon the conversation returned to Pappy's favorite subject: charting Kenai's future and mine along with it. Maybe I should open a grocery (I was told that Jones overcharged) or how about a restaurant (Smokey Joe's was not for decent folks) or a roadhouse!

"Hon, what you should have is a fish site!" Pappy spoke with a certain final authority. "I bought mine last year—the nearest one to the river's mouth—and it paid for itself the first season!" Each time Pappy recounted his catch, it grew apace with his excitement: lots of fish, lots of money—lots of "honey"! Fishing was getting hotter and the room was colder. The hour was late and the fire was low.

I sensed that Pappy was near to having my future charted. "What is your name?" he asked, as though it mattered. He would not now, or ever, use it. "Honey, you get a fish site." Pappy didn't hesitate long enough for me to ask how it's done. "Just to get you started, maybe I'll sell you mine. Tonight you can sleep on that cot in the corner."

The next morning, with four wheels churning the snow, my now-deputized jeep and I retraced our route back over the trackless snowscape toward Hope. My mind was spinning as I tried to sort it all out. I sensed that a reckless event was going to change my family's life.

Air View of Kenai, Alaska, Thornton Era

Before reaching home, I was rehearsing how I would break the news to my wife. "Honey (that salutation would usher in many a future episode), we're going to move to Kenai and buy a fish site that will make us a lot of money."

"What's a fish site?" she will ask. Then I will tell my trusting young family that I've never seen one, don't know the cost, and don't know how it's done. Please don't ask a lot of questions because it doesn't matter. Pappy Walker has taken charge of our destiny.

Kenai: The Second Night

Compared with the village of Hope and its seventy or so recluses, Kenai was a boomer. My attempts at describing it to my wife bogged down. Jeanne must see the place before we finalize our decision to move there. And soon, because if I was to be a beach fisherman (whatever that implied), time was short before the coming summer season. So we must make the trip now, in January, even though the days were much too short and the winter weather made it risky.

We left before sunup, hoping to get past the peninsula's interior where temperatures would be the lowest before dark. Lots of things could go wrong in subzero isolation, plus delays by moose blocking the plowed portion of the narrow road. Happily, our jeep now had a rickety plywood cab . . . but still no heater.

In the jeep's back seat, buried under blankets, sat Jeannette, our five-year old, her face masked by the ruff of her parka. It was a parka with special meaning. Before she was born, I had ordered it sewn by an old Eskimo woman of Kotzebue. It was a pullover of unborn reindeer. The ruff was wolverine, a fur that does not collect frost from the breath. It cost me nearly $50, which was real money in those days, but money was no object. It was my baby gift to our first daughter. I wanted her named "Alaska Jeannette." Her first name was my choice, taken from a place I loved. Our daughter's comfort with the name would be long in coming. And we would not be the first parents ever to name wrong.

At the Hope end of the road, snowplows had done their work, but beyond Coopers Landing, it would be a lonely and uncharted trail with the route barely discernible under the winter snowpack. There might, or might not, be a temporary bridge over Moose River, a bad spot to be stalled because it was thirty miles out from the warmer air of Cook Inlet. We must travel with anxiety until Mount Redoubt, across the inlet from Kenai, comes into view. That 10,000-foot volcano, framed in the western sky, would become a treasured landmark in the years to follow. It is a majestic wall-hanging for a region that is short of art work. For small planes coming through the pass out of Seward or winging over Cook Inlet, it is always a welcome sight. You just have to love a beacon you can trust.

Kenai was in hibernation. It's estimated 300 bodies were hunkered down awaiting the return of the sun and the salmon. We took a turn around the village so Jeanne could have a windshield view. There was no life in sight save a few dogs hustling moose. Here and there, plumes of smoke ascending from scattered roofs attested to life beneath. An occasional light from a Coleman or Aladdin lamp beamed through small frosted squares of glass. It was a forlorn sight not apt to induce a young mother to tear up roots. Neither of us spoke, and our silence seemed to ask *leave Hope for this?*

However, there were signs of growth and change like seeds

germinating beneath the surface. A few years prior, the government had constructed a long gravel landing strip and a station for a CAA (later FAA) cadre. New settlers who perceived the salmon fishing economics were filtering in. A few homesteaders were arriving, the vanguard of a WWII veteran land rush. And there was a fish and wildlife agent. Nevertheless, to a newcomer it looked dormant—perhaps as disheveled as half a century earlier. The scattered habitations held tenure on the earth by squatters' right, and meandering fences constructed of whatever materials could be scrounged from the beach or the cannery denoted a haphazard concern for lot lines. The roads through the settlement—both of them—followed earlier paths of convenience and were never straightened because they served the purpose. There were no public utilities.

A mile or so from the village and down a long incline to the river's edge were the cannery and its caretaker, Pappy Walker. He was a robust visionary, a lovable huckster, a legend in the making! For the second time, I halted the jeep in front of his Quonset hut and ushered my little family inside. Mrs. Walker, Jessie Belle, helped unwrap Jeannette, herded us all to the stove, and proceeded to lay out dinner.

Pappy had expected us. A month earlier, he had done his usual missionary job on me and here was his convert back. I was justifiably restless for a change. Hope, with its handful of survivors of the gold era was orderly, solitary, and supine. Kenai, despite its ugliness, was alive, except for one dead homesteader whose murder had been my introduction to Kenai and to the marshal during my earlier visit.

At the time of that first visit, it had been nearly settled. Jeanne and I would buy Pappy's fish site. I had only the vaguest notion of how it worked, but Pappy would train me. As he told it, his site was the best because it was nearest the river mouth. Strangely, this aboriginal occupation had its rules: written and unwritten. The FWS (Fish and Wildlife Service) allowed that a beach gillnetter could set out a maximum of four nets, each 600 feet separated, along "his beach." Every mile, a cannery could drive a trap. This created a fence from the high tide mark to below low tide. What determined these reference points was somewhat legendary. Age-old custom had established that if a fisherman drove his net stakes the first day of the season (as proclaimed by the FWS), it was his site. And for as long as he was driving stakes on opening day, it remained his site by right of succession.

The salmon would arrive in the summer; they would gill; the cannery would buy them; it would credit the fisherman on the books; he could draw supplies to see him through the winter; spring would come, and it's time to drive stakes again. The cannery superintendent was the paternal head of the village. It was a system that worked, somehow.

But it occasionally happened that a fisherman preferred immediate rewards (whiskey or necessary staples) to waiting out the spring, and then he would trade his right to the site. This was generally handled with a handshake or maybe a scrawled note on a tablet sheet. At least, that was the state of the art until Pappy Walker, the plumber, drifted in from Oklahoma and decided on a midlife career change.

Pappy may have been the first person to offer hard cash and lots of it, like $3,000, for the right to fish a beach site. His first season returned his investment and expenses, and now for some reason, he was willing to sell this site—the best one on the beach and a lifestyle he seemed to like—to a rookie who initially wanted only to hike to Kasilof. I was anxious to announce my decision to buy, but the attempt was always deflected. Now I must out with it.

"Honey," he cut me off. "You don't want my site. I have a better deal for you. I think Tom Hicklin is willing to sell. His is better for you. It's north of the Forlands—that's 15 miles or so—and there's no way to see it in winter. It doesn't get as good a run, but there's a cabin and spring and he only wants $600."

Tom Hicklin was wintering in one of the cabins in the village. The one room was all-purpose and tightly packed with the clutter that normally goes in the cellar or the attic. On a table was a single lamp that cast shadows on a demure Indian woman huddled in a corner and working with a needle. Hicklin resembled the old prospectors we often encountered in the interior. He was stout and weathered and warmly dressed to endure the meager heat in the cabin. The formalities were brief. Pappy vouched to Tom that we were good settlers. Tom muttered something that may have been an acceptance of that credential.

The small ruled tablet sheet described an assortment of web (nets for kings and reds), kegs, lines, and claptrap. There was reference to enough beach area to legalize four sets (i.e., 2,400 feet). "Received $600. /s/ Hicklin." He abruptly went outside to a shed and returned with a buoy keg, which he handed to me. "This goes with it."

Pappy and I departed the cabin with the keg under my arm and I welcomed the fresh air. It was done. That simple! I had Tom's word that the "gear" would be there when the snow melted. He had my word that the check was good. I didn't know how to find the fish site; Tom didn't know where to cash the check.

Jeanne and I both knew that life was going to be different, that we were bringing our daughters, Jeannette and Joyce, to the opposite side of the world.

Early the next spring, before breakup, I dispatched a truck-load of our stuff to Kenai, accompanied by John and Ruth Grueninger, part of Jeanne's family clan, as the advance party for the Kenai project. They were great helpmates; they took root and became Kenai stalwarts. Together, the four of us transplanted our Hope folly and named it the "Kenai Terminal."

The Kenaitze People

A few millennia ago, when a land bridge joined our continent to Asia, aborigines crossed over and scattered throughout what is now Alaska. Some settled on the shores of Cook Inlet. A social, religious, and familial order slowly evolved over the centuries. Captain Cook, on his third expedition to find the northern passage, in 1778, sailed into Kenaitze territory, claimed it for Great Britain, and gave this inlet his name.

Russian explorers in search of furs, established Fort Nicholas on the Kenaitze soil, about 1790, and had a habit of coupling an Orthodox Church with their settlements, so by the 1840s they had their distinctive onion-domed church and were telling the natives how to replace their religion, which had worked very well for centuries, with a mysterious hybrid ritual that originated in far-off Constantinople. Thus it was that the native village at the mouth of a glacier-fed river acquired a bit of strange architecture in which to perform incomprehensible rituals to please the Russian Church.

In 1867, the United States acquired a vast territory that the natives called "Great Land" or "Alaska," and in payment thereof the U.S. government parted with $7.2 million, which computes to about two cents an acre and as is so often done by misguided bureaucracies, gave the money to the Russians instead of to the rightful owners. It would be 104 years before this transaction would be rectified. In the interim, the U.S. government was far more considerate of the Russians who were guaranteed an opportunity for citizenship—a benefit the native inhabitants were not offered until 1924.

The natives named their river Kenaitze, later shortened to Kenai. The Kenaitze people were not mindful of property ownership. They little dreamed they might not have sovereign rights to their homesite until in the 1930s, they noticed government surveyors moving through their backyards and trails. They woke up to learn their homes and settlement had been swallowed up by a federal airport reserve. By some arbitrary edict, the land on which they had lived for generations belonged to Uncle Sam. So much for aboriginal rights; more about this later.

Understanding Kenai was a puzzle for this newcomer. Hope, on the north side of this peninsula, was only sixty miles as the crow flies and twice that by the proposed road. However, it was a world apart culturally.

I was intruding into an amalgam of races. There were Russians, left over from the fur trading era; there were Asiatics, mostly Filipinos, imported by the salmon cannery; immigrant opportunists attracted by the bargains in gill net sites; newly arriving homesteaders prompted by a veteran benefit; and most intriguing, the natives who had occupied the area from earlier than Columbus. This human mixing pot had history.

Pappy Selects Our Business Site

Pappy Walker told me I should open a café near the runway. Told me fly-ins had nowhere to wait. I had followed his recommendation to buy a fish site at a location I couldn't view until the ice melted. Why should I doubt him now? True, I knew nothing about café operation. But I already had a good cook in residence, and it seemed since Jeanne was already cooking for four, it might be a good use of her time to just increase the quantity. Also, she was affordable. And thus the Terminal Café was launched.

The location Pappy picked for us was a vacant wood patch at the only intersection Kenai could boast. It was sort of a corner, 100 yards from the gravel parking for airplanes, and it fronted on the settlement's mud/dirt road to an abandoned cannery on the estuary. Inlet boats tied up there to unload when the tide permitted.

The proposed site had one small problem. The government owned it, having included it in their airfield reserve. I knocked on the fed's door in Anchorage and was asked how much area I wanted? I timidly asked for an acre, an answer I would regret. Why didn't I ask for five acres? I would need an acre just for snow removal. My lease from the CAA could be terminated on short notice without cause. What a great omen!

The Consummate Handyman

Kenai was unincorporated, so legally didn't exist. Building permits and inspections unheard of. No one cared what I did or who I was. I had never built anything bigger than our add-on at Hope, but now I was my own *general contractor*. There were a few advantages in the wilderness.

Kenai had no source of building materials. I could overcome that by barging my pile of rough lumber and stuff from Hope. I must time it to arrive about the time the snow was gone. Trees on the site were adequate for sills laid directly on the ground cover. In Hope, I had precut the joists and studs.

But first, I must learn to be an *architect*. I drew the plans on scrap paper. And the specs I carry in my head. For anyone wishing to take advantage of my experiences, here is my checklist:

Kenai had no public utilities, therefore . . .

1. Power must come from our Army surplus 1,000-watt generator. It uses gasoline, which is expensive, and must be turned off when not urgently needed. So we use Coleman lanterns or Aladdin lamps to save the generator.

2. Wiring: I've seen it done. I'll just learn as I go.

3. Temporary garage: We need it for storage and generator to get the noise away from the café.

4. Heating: fuel oil floor furnace. Gravity, of course. Fuel oil stinks and is dirty, but no other choice.

5. Water: a well point hammered into the sandy soil, located in cellar. Pump only when power is on.

6. Cellar: sandy soil is stable so won't need cribbing. Provides a cool pantry, access by ladder.

7. Septic system: That's simple. We dig a hole in the ground, somewhere. We'll figure that out later.

8. Roof: mansard style to permit two upstairs dormitory rooms and the gravity water tank.

9. Toilet and bath: locate on landing, just beneath water tank for gravity feed.

10. Cook range: requires sheet metal hood and stack. I don't know sheet metal. I hate it, but . . .

11. Labor: Salmon fishermen don't want this kind of work, so the labor can come from Hope. Get Bob DeFrance (he knows how to build a good dory) and Jeanne's dad (he'll do it for his daughter's sake) and John will be on hand and vital. (I began to question this solution when I overheard during the roof framing, "How close are these boards supposed to fit? I think if they touch we should nail 'em.")

There: That's all that's required to build a café in the wilderness.

The Terminal Café

The Terminal Café had a counter for eight or ten aluminum stools and a booth. It offered a single menu choice. I was the breakfast cook, and if someone asked to see the menu, he got an ugly stare. Jeanne was far more accommodating.

In our Seattle shopping while on TDY, we had decided on Frankhoma pottery. We wanted some class. Pottery cups hold a lot of coffee and keep it warm. We had blundered into a bad choice. Coffee was dispensed at ten cents with free refills and was our volume leader, of course. Our second big mistake was putting magazines on the counter. Pilots and passengers stuck for weather and homesteaders keeping warm waiting for mail, would loiter for hours. We should have given the coffee free and charged for heat they absorbed.

Bush pilots were often stranded for the night, and occasionally, a large plane (i.e., two-engine prop) was diverted to Kenai because of Anchorage weather, and suddenly we were swamped. Cruel fate usually timed these for near our closing time, and Jeanne, probably already exhausted, would rise to the crisis by opening a canned ham for sandwiches. After our stranded planeload was fed, we instructed them how to turn off the Aladdin lamp, set the coffee pot off the range, and went to bed. In the morning, if Anchorage weather cleared, the place would be empty and maybe a pile of silver on the counter. If the weather didn't clear, they'd be huddled in the booth, on the steps, and on the floor.

Jeanne was more than the only cook-waitress in the village—she was the cutest. So it's a given that she had numerous pets. The most lovable and annoying were the homesteaders. The word was out in the Lower 48 that free land was available on the Kenai. They need only locate their 80 acres, build a cabin, dwell thereon for three years, but with their service time crediting for two years, and presto, they had a patent. Landed gentry, no less. First though, they had some tough times to endure.

These veterans subsisted on meager savings and 52/40, the slang for 52 weekly checks for $40 from the Veterans Administration. They drove mud-spattered, four-wheel drive military surplus castoffs. With great difficulty, they trekked to Kenai, praying the post office would have letters and money. Then to the Terminal Café to warm up. A string of cold-soaked men bundled in GI pants, winter underwear, boots, mitts, and frosty parka would come through our doorway and lower the room temperature several degrees. With our ten-cent coffee and reading matter, we were their "rescue mission." Jeanne and I

Thornton's – Airport & Highway Services

Kenai Peninsula

OPEN from 7am to 9pm   –   MEALS SERVED from 7am to 6pm

--*-*-*-*-*-*-*-*-*-*-*-* a

BREAKFAST..$1.00
(hotcakes or toast, eggs, bacon, beverage

    Coffee and cookies (or breakfast roll).. .25
    Cereal...................................... .20
    Fruit juice................................. .10
    Canned or evaporated fruit................. .25

LUNCH...$1.00
(luncheon entree, vegetable, bread, beverage)

    Chili, with beverage....................... .75
    Chicken hot tamales, w/beverage............ .50
    Soup, w/beverage........................... .50

DINNER...$1.50
(dinner entree, vegetables, bread, beverage, desert)

--*-*

SANDWICHES: (with beverage)

    Peanut butter....... .50
    Cheese.............. .50
    Lunch meat.......... .75
    Ham................. .75
    Pork................ .75
    Beef................ .75

DESERTS: pie - cake - fruit..... .25

BEVERAGES: coffee   .10
        tea   hot chocolate

LUNCHES TO TAKE OUT............. .75

(meals served daily and Sunday, except Tuesday (refreshments only)

Motor Fuel & Accessories   •   Meals & Lodging   •   Transportation Agents   •   Radio Communications

First Menu, July 1948

114

were philanthropists and didn't get credit for it.

The lesson: It's better to donate the coffee and charge for the heat.

Kenai Trucking Was Our "White Water Rafting"

Someday it might become a civilized road across Alaska's Kenai Peninsula, but that winter night it was just two frozen ruts that seldom aligned with the wheel tread. As the loaded truck lurched and struggled ahead, Bob Jacobs shouted over the engine's groaning: "Keep a truck moving and no matter how low the temperature, the cargo won't freeze!"

This assurance laid on me by Bob was about to collide with another arctic oddity: a road glacier. If the thermometer dips low enough, the intense cold will wring water out of a frozen hillside. The run-off will freeze into a glacier across any roadway cut into a mountain or hill. Over this glacier more running water will spread on the top, sometimes only crusting and thereby hiding a trap for the next truck along, which turned out to be ours. Traffic was minimal and help was improbable. Our rear duals, the driving wheels, broke through and sank up to the axle housings. We were in deep trouble. Bob was new to the trucking game. He was shy, lean, and lanky and a fidgety bundle of nerves. These were hardly the qualifications my fledgling business sought for its freighting lifeline. Bob had seduced me into accompanying him on the round-trip between Kenai and Seward. I had only one reason to go—to ascertain if I should give Bob my business. There were better reasons I should not be here. It was midwinter; the road was an unfinished and treacherous trail through an empty wilderness; the truck lacked four-wheel drive; we were rushing our return at the risk of night driving, and my brave wife and young children were alone back in an isolated little fishing village on Cook Inlet.

There on Rock Mountain summit (aka Fuller's Hill) the truck was stuck in a glacier! It was midnight with the temperature way below zero, and Bob asked me to build a fire at each corner of the truck to keep the perishables from freezing while he hiked back to "civilization" to find someone with a rig to pull us out. He soon disappeared down the mountain road, and the sound of crunching footsteps faded away. I was alone in the cold and darkness with only my thoughts . . .

...Now, here on Rock Mountain, the truck is stuck in and on a Road Glacier!

Four fires! With what wood? Right beside the roadway under several feet of snow, of course. And what is the cargo? It's mostly beer for Kenai Joe's roadhouse. Now friendship in the bush is strong stuff. But as for Joe, he was a competitor of sorts to my Terminal Café. As for the beer, I served some of my most formative years in the prohibitionist camp in the Bible Belt. Given these conflicts, a prudent survivalist digs out his sleeping bag. Mine was a "Woods 3-Star" down bag, the best available in those days and tossed aboard at the last moment for just such an occasion: to delay rigor mortis until help arrived.

For those who make it through life safely and sanely, some routine assumptions should be dispelled. One does not "sleep" on the snow, even in a top-quality bag. One squirms and huddles and castigates himself for being in such a predicament. One also reviews the past, preferring it to the future, which may not occur. One curses the cold.

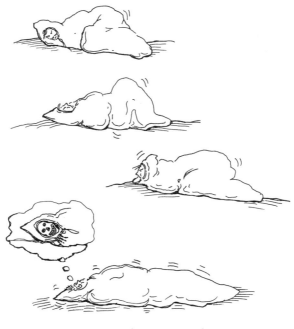

...one does NoT "sleep" on the snow...

The thought of Bob's cargo of beer turning to ice brought a mild feeling of guilt. But then this concern was offset by the suspicions of divine interference. Sixteen years earlier hadn't I stomped Kansas in the name of temperance? Repeal of the Volstead Act had offered "state's option." Dad Winrod and I

...a Carrie Nation Hatchet Job.

had crisscrossed Kansas doing one-night stands exhorting the good people to vote against demon rum.

Winrod was an old German patriarch, the very personification of the brew master ads now on TV. He had been a bartender, with beer belly and mustache to match, when Carrie Nation and her women's troop, including my mother, did their hatchet job on Wichita's saloons. Winrod was running one of these dens of iniquity when Mrs. Nation came through the front door. Now he was born again and doing his utmost to undo his earlier wickedness. He needed a driver and I fit the bill.

We were a team and a sight as we crusaded throughout the state. An eighteen-year-old kid and a Bible-thumping grandfather exhorting Kansas to vote right. The state stayed sober, Dad collected his brownie points in heaven, and I moved west, then north. A glacier too far north! Kansas was getting revenge. I turned my thoughts to the current situation. The night and the cold held on relentlessly. Who would find my frozen corpse?

From deep within my sleeping bag I heard a noise. It sounded like an approaching truck! Probably my ears fooling me, but I must risk the cold and peek out.

If beauty is in the eye of the beholder, then ignore the majestic trees with their snow-laden boughs, forget Skilak Lake in the distance, never mind the jagged mountains, the golden sunrise, the soaring hawk. There are circumstances wherein a rusty winch crusted with icicles on the front end of a grimy Dodge "power wagon" is beauty enough!

The Homesteaders

World War II Veterans were lured to the Kenai by free land. As already mentioned, the word was out down in the Lower 48 that homesteads could be claimed by veterans. It only required building a dwelling and spending one year on the ground. Eighty beautiful acres seemed like a good trade-off for being stuck in isolation in an Arctic environment. These pioneers spent a lot of time in our café while waiting for the mail to pocket their 52/40 money. Forty dollars a week wasn't much, but the difference between eating and starving. They were a hardy bunch, colorful with diverse backgrounds. Each deserves his own book. Two stories should illustrate:

Dewey Magee staked out his claim along the road survey about 16 miles out. He had a pond, which he affectionately named Whisper Lake and crusaded to make the feds designate his water on their geographic maps. Dewey had some experience with off-Broadway acting. He belonged on stage. Had his favorite stool in the café where he loitered over his ten-cent coffee and berated the Road Commission for graveling the road with his topsoil.

On one of my trips with supplies from Seward, I mired my Jeep and its trailer in a frost boil. Dewey came hiking by, saw my plight and helped me unmire.

I said, "Jump in, Dewey, and you can ride in to Kenai."

"No thanks," he replied. "I'm in a hurry."

The Lancashires: Commercial bush planes served Kenai. They were usually met by Phil Wilson driving a station wagon. But come the mud of spring breakup, my four-wheel drive Jeep was needed. I met Sig Krogstad's Alaska Airlines and into the mud stepped an attractive young lady, stylishly dressed in high heels, and three little children. She eyed the empty tarmac, my muddy Jeep, and groaned.

"I'm Rusty Lancashire and these are Martha and Lorraine and Abby. Do you know where to find my husband?" Oh, no—I thought.

I first heard about Larry from Lyle Saxton, road foreman at Moose Pass. He told of a newcomer from Ohio with a Jeep pulling a trailer with a sawmill! It was too heavy to make it up some of the hills and had to be towed.

Lyle said, "He's heading for Soldotna. Miracle if he makes it"

Miles of plowing the muddy road brought us to Larry's tent. Rusty gasped and I could have cried. I didn't ask if she wanted to go back? No, she was as tough as Larry, and she had class. She stayed to become a fixture in Kenai—acted in plays, helped with social programs, knew everyone, became Kenai's first travel agent. Truly a unique lady.

Larry and Rusty constructed a house and barn because they had a "farming" vision. About the time it appeared they may have whipped their obstacles, Larry shot an illegal moose. That's OK. Everyone did, but Larry got caught. That's not OK. He went to Anchorage to work to raise the $500 fine. Rusty was alone in a severe winter.

She was hauling their water from Soldotna Creek in the back of the Jeep station wagon I had sold to them. The water sloshed around, formed a glacier in the back of the rig and Rusty was tooling around Kenai with a few hundred pounds of ice. I took Rusty's glacier into our garage for a three-day meltdown and begged her to move into Kenai with the kids until the crisis was past. She refused. I guess by now she'd become attached to suffering and risk. So I loaned her a Jeep and prayed that her cabin was fireproof.

Homesteading tempted me, too. I put my name in a lottery for veterans and came up winner of an eighty-acre parcel beyond the road, north of Kenai. Jeanne and I debated if we really had the stomach for seven more months of living beyond civilization. No utilities, no road, a cabin to build, for what purpose—to secure a patent on inaccessible woodland we hadn't set foot on? No, we had our fill.

I was doing figure eights over the area with my flight instructor. He yells over the engine racket, "I'd like to have a homestead someday." I yell back, "You've got one." We landed, I told him to follow me to my typewriter. He signed my flight log: 10/16/51—1 hour . . . take-offs & landings . . . *Kitchen;* and I signed a relinquishment on our eighty acres. I presumed it was useless dirt, but oil developers didn't share that presumption. In time, there would be a road past our bog and past a neighbor with a sign unbecoming to the wilds: Union Oil Refinery. The road would be paved!

Salmon Fishing & A-R-C-H-I-E

The newly arrived school teachers—a young couple in the Alaskan outback for the first time—were discovering the difference between theoretical economics and the working version.

Teacher: "Saving a portion of our income is smart planning."

Native Student: "Why?"

Teacher: "So you can buy necessities when your source of money's gone."

Native Student: "Archie takes care of that."

Teacher: "Who's Archie?"

Who's ARCHIE indeed! The new teachers had to learn that in Kenai the basic textbook laws were inoperative. The Thorntons, the newly arrived entrepreneurs, also had to learn new rules for this primitive society.

The cannery was the supreme giver and taker, and ARCHIE was its mouthpiece. He was the superintendent when the cannery was in operation for about five months of the year. The rest of the year he held court in Seattle; except once during the winter he returned to Kenai, and for a single day manna fell from heaven. Kenai's economy would revive. Among the fishing families, especially the natives, a paternal order prevailed. Surpassing the biological father was the cannery father—the source of life's needs. From obeisance or fear, Archie was "the force."

Salmon fishing was an occupation of faith and trust. With the emergence of spring, the cannery awakened from its winter hibernation, whereupon the fishermen launched their dories, revved up their outboards, and steered to the opposite bend in the tidal estuary where the cannery replenished their empty cupboards, supplied fishing nets and gear, and delivered special orders brought from "the states." The charge for this went "on the books" even though the cannery might know little more about the debtor than the purported location of his fish site.

The monster king salmon migrated in June, later the reds, and then the silvers. These wonderful creatures, driven by a mysterious force in search of the stream of their birth, worked their way up the inlet. Instinctively hugging the shoreline, they tangled their gills in the nets that were staked near the low tide. When the incoming tide floated the nets, the fishermen "picked" the nets into their dories and transferred the fish to a cannery scow anchored offshore. Each fisherman had a bin on the scow, and when the tender arrived, the captain logged the number and kind of fish and the value went into "the book." If supplies had been ordered, the tender left them in that fisherman's bin. The charge for those also went in the book.

Come season's end, the fisherman and his kids once again steered his dory to the Libby cannery to reprovision, this time for the winter, and collect whatever money was left on the book. The money was in $100 bills, and these were strewn around the settlement to pay for pent-up needs. Kenai Joe's Bar and the Inlet Bar got their share, some settled accounts with Jones's general store and us, and of most importance—postal money orders to Sears.

With the season behind, the evidence of its bounty could be measured by the big bills. This currency vanished all too soon, and with the winter freeze-up, the village's economy stagnated. Credit was stretched and supplies rationed in the manner of survivors on a life raft, knowing not when rescue might occur, except—ARCHIE is coming.

Rumor built on rumor and eyes turned to the landing strip whenever a bush plane arrived from Anchorage. No later than January, ARCHIE arrived with a satchel of money. The long-awaited day needed no loud speaker. The news permeated the air. Santa ARCHIE would alight from the plane, be immediately surrounded by his supplicants, hustle off to a shelter, sometimes our Terminal Café, and there he doled out money, stintingly, to his many wards eagerly waiting their turn.

Dark would descend before ARCHIE could close his

empty satchel and shuffle off through the snow to the waiting bush plane. The fishermen now were rejoicing in their cabins or the Inlet Bar. Now the Aladdin lamps beamed brighter; tomorrow the kids would chatter joyously on their walk to school. In a few weeks, Sears packages would arrive at the post office.

In a few months, the sun would return, the frost would thaw, the icicles would drop off the eaves, the days would lengthen—all signs that soon the cannery boats would be sighted coming up the inlet. ARCHIE would be back!

The "Non-Scheds"

World War II left our country with acres of surplus planes to dispose of. The marketable ones were twin engine C-47s (DC-3) and C-46s, which was a Curtis version of the DC-3 but larger. It had bigger engines, carried more payload, flew a bit faster, but never shared the adulation of its smaller cousin. They had bucket seats down each side; no heat and oxygen, if any, in a canister near the cockpit.

Alaska, still with meager airline service connecting to Seattle, beckoned to discharged pilots. For a pittance, one of these planes could be purchased and loaded with bodies and goods. They were not certified for regular scheduled flights— hence "non-sched."

They were scary. Slow by today's standards but faster than ship. Because they were not pressurized, they must fly low in turbulent air. These nine- to eleven-hour trips required refueling stops, usually Annette Island and sometimes Cordova. Radio navigation was still primitive, no flight attendant, no heat, no pilot intercom, and no food. Usually, freight occupied the aisle between the seats. It was tied by ropes and sometimes broke loose during rough air. Our family rode these crates. We shivered in parkas and mitts hiding white knuckles. I recall seeing tears running down Jeannette's cheek, my little daughter pleading, "Daddy, will we make it?" Tickets were cheap, air sickness and vomiting included, prayer optional.

Occasionally, these flights landed in Kenai due to Anchorage weather. One such was different. I Jeeped out to meet a C-46. This time no passengers. Instead, a load of ice and stainless steel pans (these were for shipping salmon, and some that disappeared were useful for storing moose meat and bathing babies). Out stepped the pilot, wearing a suit! And his copilot, also his wife. They threw their luggage in and asked to be taken to *the bank*.

"What part of *the bank* do you want to see?" I asked.

"I don't want to see *the bank*; I want to draw money from *the bank*."

"Oh, that's a problem. We only have *the bank* from which we look at the inlet."

"Dammit! What kind of a place is this! Just take me to the hotel."

"Ah-h—that's another problem. We don't have a hotel."

"Dammit!—dammit! I'm here for a week. Where do we sleep?"

"Well, my wife and I have a room over our café. Not much style but keeps the mosquitoes out."

His wife was sweet; he was arrogant and definitely out of his element. Jeanne took an immediate dislike for him. It surfaced early. He didn't know the SOP for our jerry-rigged shower, which was off the stair landing. Water appeared on the floor where it shouldn't. Jeanne's fuse was short. She handed him a mop.

"Clean up that mess." Nothing in the operating manual prepared him for that.

His mission was to buy a planeload of king salmon (chinooks) and fly to the stateside market. He left his wife and took off for several days, bought the fish he needed, and came to our counter to settle his bill. We rented beds, not rooms. A bed was two or three dollars a night. Jeanne charged him for all the beds in their room, three, if I remember. He objected.

"I was gone several nights."

Jeanne was about to boil over when his wife interjected, "Mrs. Thornton is right. You should have told her you'd be gone and she could have rented your empty bed in my room to some other man."

A Jeep Dealer! Me?

Most of the local fishermen had stake net sites along the Cook Inlet Beach, and they reached their sites by dory. This depended on tides and weather. I knew this problem occasioned many a missed fishing opportunity and entailed certain risks.

I eyed my surplus Jeep and wondered how beach-worthy it might be. A good way to find out would be to see if it could traverse the distance to my own fish site, about fifteen miles north of the Kenai River. To succeed would require getting past the "forelands" which was a narrow eight-mile wide passage that squeezed the tidal currents and resulted in dangerous whirlpools. It was vital that a fishing boat going through the forelands know the tides. The shore along the forelands was strewn with boulders.

My assistant, John, and I debated the chances and decided

to strip the Jeep of all excess weight and take the gamble We were apprehensive and nervous . . . but we made it, reaching my fish site and returning. If my Jeep could do it, fishermen along that beach were potential customers for a Jeep.

A few letters to the Seattle area office convinced the Willys people I was worth a try. True, I exaggerated my repair and parts facilities, but in time I could remedy that. Somehow. They didn't ask for pictures.

"Where's the Kenai Peninsula? Have you had any experience?"

"Of course. *I'm an Alaskan*." Suddenly I'm a Jeep dealer with a franchise.

Now some minor details: Showroom? Parts department? Service garage? And bank credit—I didn't know what "flooring" meant. On the bright side, I had Paul Murray, young, good-natured, generous Scotsman, the Chicago drifter who gave up on mink ranching; I have John, a first class mechanic, and I have Jeanne. She looks like a parts store manager to me.

Seward to Caines Head to Scrap Yard

I needed a building fast. World War II was over, but building materials were still scarce, until I stumbled onto the "Caines Head solution." It was a pristine promontory, remote and isolated, beautiful and forbidding. Eight long, long miles from Seward forming an entrance to Resurrection Bay. World War II strategists thought it was just the spot for Coast Artillery guns to protect Seward's harbor. In later time, I learned a Santa Barbara friend, Clark Elliott, had built the barracks; my mission would be to tear them down.

The plan was to buy some of the surplus prefab buildings. Denny Thompson, a soldier-of-fortune-type veteran living at

Seward, had bought the entire camp and was selling the buildings for peanuts—FOB off the edge of the earth. These buildings, called "KD" for "knock-down" were five-foot linear sections—floors, walls, roofs, bolted together. So they should unbolt.

Before closing a deal, I asked Denny how we could get them off Caines Head. He had the answer. Denny volunteered himself as the answer. He knew of a small barge he could borrow.

"How do we tow the barge?" I asked. Denny knew of a little harbor boat that had the oomph of a tug, sort of.

"Who will skipper the tug?" I asked. Denny flew in the war. His experience as an Air Force pilot seemed qualifications enough. He would be the one-man crew.

"How do we load the barge?" I asked. That's no problem. There's a small dock on the north side of the Head. It's in a sheltered cove, sort of.

"What do we need for lifting machinery?" I asked. Nothing. The panels can be manhandled by two or three men. They're not that heavy. (Oh, sure.)

"And how do we get the KD sections across the Head to the dock?" I asked. There's an old 6 × 6 truck left out there by the Army. It still runs. And the road from the camp over the top is not too badly grown over. It's usable if you go slow.

Sight unseen, I bought this totally crazy solution for the materials for our "garage." I needed a crew. Paul Murray and his buddy, Luke Caro, the Chicago veterans who drifted into the Kenai scene to raise mink volunteered. They had already sort of merged into our extended family, and a homesteader named Gearhart wanted work. It was a mission more risky than war.

Things are easier to attempt when there is no plan, no computer printout, no permit, no OSHA, no budget, and no regulations. Just, "Let's do it." We made several trips to Seward by truck (half a day), hoping the weather wasn't too stormy to launch a dory, hoping the outboard motor would run, hoping it wouldn't quit for the eight miles out to the entrance to Resurrection Bay. From there it was open ocean around the point and the hope that the surf would permit a landing on the gravel beach near the buildings.

The building I bought had been a barracks the length of a football field. Twenty feet wide, just right for a row of bunks down each side. So the floor panels were 5' × 10', the walls 5' × 7', each with a window, and we had gable roof panels, 5' × 15', and gable ends, for what purpose we'd decide later. The sills were choice lumber, 4" × 8" × 20' as I recall, and heavy.

The camp snuggled beneath big spruce trees. Deserted and picturesque. South-facing to a gravel beach and beyond were islands scattered about the ocean horizon. Behind, the camp was ringed by low mountains that spilled a photogenic waterfall.

Our little four-man salvage crew settled into a back-breaking routine. Shovel the snowpack off the roof, unbolt, lower to the floor, lift, carry, stack. Plus housekeeping chores. Our water for drinking and bathing was handy in the fire hydrants. Camp cooking is only for survival, and we were too tired to know if what we ate was food or spruce needles.

On one junket to the Head, I took my wife and two little girls so they could savor the excitement and re-create Robinson Crusoe. I hope they were too young to remember the risks—especially one harrowing experience worse than all others, and recounted here only to prove that God cares about fools.

We had been alerted that our beach could have mean swells, but this hadn't happened and so far so good. I felt my crew and my family were entitled to a break, so we loaded into the dory and rode gentle swells to Seward. Stayed for a movie. Bad idea. On our return, we were out of daylight, it was raining, and as we rounded the Head into open ocean, we gasped. All along the bluff was a frightening line of white breakers. The ocean swell of which I had been warned had arrived and the surf had turned wild. We had two choices: return to Seward or hope for the right wave. We opted for an initiation to surfing. Then as we were getting lined up for the least threatening roller, Murphy's Law climbed aboard. The outboard died. We had no steerage. We could only trust to blind luck. A breaker caught the dory, tossed it toward shore, and my crew jumped into the water with a girl on each guy's shoulders, splashed ashore, and set the girls down. We muscled the dory above the wave line and vowed no more R&R in Seward. It was obvious I hadn't learned well from the earlier bout with the Nenana River at McKinley Park. Chalk up attempted drowning #3. We crossed our fingers, praying there would be no emergencies because there was no phone and no road out. Only Denny knew we were there.

Our final campaign was to move the mountain of panels and parts over the top to the opposite side of the Head where the Army's dock faced Seward-ward. The driving tracks skirted a cliff in places, and often the truck rocked scarily, threatening to dump its load to the ocean below. Sixteen truck trips were required. Each was a heart stopper. At the dock, we would load the barge and if lucky, Denny showed up with his makeshift semblance of a tug. Although winter was breathing down our necks, we won the gamble with seven barge trips.

We were loading barge number eight and Denny was standing by. As we topped the crest of Caines Head with our last truckload, we could feel a storm brewing. There were clouds that said *run for cover*. The wind felt like it was coming right off the Harding glaciers behind Seward.

"Denny, from the top we could see the lights of Seward. Let's make a run for it." I reasoned.

"No—I think the wind may lay during the night. We'll wait."

We found a shelter, rolled out our sleeping bags, and worried the night away. In the morning, the wind was howling. Denny coupled his ersatz tug to the barge, and with diesel exhaust whipping into his wheelhouse shelter, aimed for Seward. There was no place on board for passengers, so my crew hunkered under a tarp at the stern, hiding from the wind.

We pitched and tossed and rolled for an hour, and I decided to peek out from the tarp and see if we were getting close. There off the stern, not a hundred yards behind the barge, was the Army dock from which we departed.

"Denny!" I shouted. "Cut the barge loose and save our skins! Right now!" I sometimes wondered why it was called *Resurrection Bay*. I could now believe that if you chanced onto this bay in a rickety harbor boat, the next time you'd be seen would be the "Biblical Resurrection."

Everyone connected to this venture barely avoided being crushed, drowned, or blown overboard. But it was pure adventure in a beautiful spot. And somewhere along the rocky shore of Resurrection Bay, beachcombers are welcome to a fine load of milled driftwood.

There followed some harrowing trucking from Seward to Kenai, and a mountain of KD material arrived. But after all the sweat, strain, and risk, very little of it was used in our garage building.

Scattered about the Kenai landscape, to puzzle the new-era boomers, there must be nondescript panels and structures and platforms and shanties, Army-olive-drab beneath repainting, scavenged creations that probably defy an explanation. Only a handful of us know— it is the scar tissue of an epic boondoggle, a campaign remembered only by its survivors—Paul Murray, Luke Caro, and Dick Gearhart; Jeanne and Hal; and two young daughters—who, in a later era of enlightenment, would probably have been put in the protective custody of the court.

The Terminal Garage

Winter was breathing down our necks, and we needed a garage fast. A concrete basement was necessary for storage, furnace, well, generator, and access to the underneath side of the vehicles we would service. I can attest that a dummy can learn to form up and pour concrete and that it builds strong muscles. The reader probably wants to know how: just borrow a mixer; shovel in cement, sand, and gravel; throw in a bucket or two of water; and wheelbarrow a ton at a time to the forms on planks and dump it. Doesn't that sound easy?

Now change of plans. Paul and I decided that those Caines Head panels weren't going to work. We'd have to go to stick construction. The road to Seward was now fairly usable for trucks; Seward had a lumber yard, and if patient, we could get green framing lumber. Best luck: We had discovered "homosote"—an amazing weatherproof wallboard pressed out of paper. It came in monster sheets, 8' × 14'. Only a half inch thick but unbelievable insulating qualities. When both glued and nailed to studs, it was there for keeps. It had to be shipped in crates from the Midwest and that cost us time, but once on hand, wow! Put one piece in place and 112 square feet has been sheeted. We wrapped the whole building including the roof in just a few days.

Construction always has problems, but some of ours were unique. A truckload of lumber had arrived from Seward, and it needed to be sawed to length for studs. A local chap asked me for work.

"Can you run a Skilsaw? If so, cut these two-by-fours to length." I gave him a list, using symbols to designate feet and inches. I had urgent things to do and left him alone.

He understood inches but not feet and reduced my lumber pile to kindling.

In time, we had a 1,200-square-foot building, parts room, plus a three-bedroom apartment overhead. Our family moved into the apartment with only one half inch of homosote separating us from zero temperatures. Insulation between the studs could come later in our spare time, and some day, not soon, we could hide it with Celotex. The good news! We'd have a bath, sink, and washing machine because Paul's brother Jake had joined us, and those two had learned plumbing at their father's knee in Chicago.

The Kenai Building Supply

The little village had no source of building materials except for what could be begged from Libby's cannery or beach-combed. Well, that's not exactly true. It had me. My operation had piles of KD stuff from Caines Head and the stockpile for my construction. It was inevitable that locals would hang around and ask for a board or handful of nails or something we couldn't find. We were glad to help them out, except it was an interruption.

Strategy huddle: My small crew and I figured if we were stuck with this chore we might as well make it viable. So we erected some of the KD panels beside the café and hung out our shingle. It was one chore too many. Fortunately, a new entrepreneur crossed our path. Stan Thompson and his talented wife, Donnis. They were an important addition to Kenai. Stan needed some action and took on the building materials. He later followed me as commissioner.

Bush Pilot

John was a top mechanic but suffered from migraine headaches, so was short of patience. Our garage had one repair stall plus a drive-over pit. It was generally used for greasing or thawing a ton of ice off the chassis. If John was into a job and needed a part I didn't stock, he was stalled. I had better get it fast or John was gone. Needed parts were available adjacent to Merrill Field at Anchorage. I must buy a plane and learn to fly, and quickly.

I owned a few different planes before I got it right. My favorite was a four-seat Piper clipper. High wing, stick control, tail-dragger, fabric covered, low horsepower, and fuel miser. It could pack its own weight in passengers, baggage, and fuel. I could now have John's parts back in two hours, deliver outboards along the beach, and connect with the dock at Seward. Perfect.

Blazo, Gas, and Fuel Oil

Standard Oil had an Alaska monopoly. I think they were rarely reviled because they were our benefactors. Really? Sure, they supplied our "Blazo"—their trade name for pressure appliance fuel. It was packaged in two 5-gallon square cans in a sturdy wooden box. Kerosene and "case gasoline" also came this way. Blazo fueled our Coleman or Aladdin lanterns or lamps. When empty, the cans had the tops cut off, a limb whittled round and smooth for a carrying handle was nailed across the top, and now primitive man could pack water to his cabin. And use it for the water reservoir. The sight of a Blazo can on the counter or in the corner was part of the décor—just like a bottle of "spring" water in a modern home.

Now the best purpose of Blazo was the wooden box. These were built to last. They stacked neatly. Laid flat they made a dresser and stood on end they were chairs. Those boxes were storage bins and packing crates. Perfect height for bedside table. I never saw a cabin without them and I never saw a Blazo can or box in the dump. We even brought some boxes to Santa Barbara. It was 40 years before they were consigned to the fireplace.

Before the road to Seward was opened, Kenai may have had a dozen vehicles. For whatever dubious reason, we installed two gas pumps, furnished by Standard Oil. They were the type you see in museums with a manual wobble pump and visible bowl that holds ten gallons. We charged five cents a gallon over our delivered cost. Too little incentive to go out in the cold to pump gas, so the customer usually did it—same as thirty years later everywhere—and came into the parts store to pay. It was the honor system. Everyone's windshield was grimy, so we loaned a cleaning rag. We did have water and air at the pump. Occasionally, small planes taxied over to the pumps because one had unleaded gas.

Fifty-five gallon drums should be the logo for Alaska. They were for fuel oil and gasoline and part of the clutter around nearly every store and dwelling. They were everywhere. Such a drum of fuel weighs 500 pounds. I know this because I wrestled them onto my Jeep pickup to service commercial planes diverted to Kenai and in need of the fuel that detour used up. Pumping gas into a DC-3 or C-46, from a barrel into a chamois filter fitted to a funnel by Jeanne is grunt labor. Invariably, this happened late at night at zero temp. For whatever lucky reason. I was spared a hernia.

> **Lesson: Wrestling barrels of gas is not a good career choice.**

Outboard Motors

Beach fishermen traveled and picked nets by dory. The Johnson 9.8 hp outboard had the market cornered. This motor had no shroud, was easily serviced, and any native could fix it, drunk or sober. Every fisherman had a minimum of two plus one for parts. Most were purchased from the Libby cannery. However, in a pinch a fisherman might be stuck and the tide wouldn't wait and he wanted one f-a-s-t. So I stocked these motors and repair parts. My standard response to Jeanne when she wanted to go shopping in Anchorage was to explain that the money she would spend could add several propellers to our inventory. "How do you think I would look in a propeller?" she asked.

There were two methods of salmon fishing: stake net on the beach and drift fishing off shore. I felt if I was catering to the needs of the drifters, as they were called, I should experience a bit of their problems. One season, I hung two 9.8s on the back of a dory, loaded 25 fathoms of sockeye net, and went drift fishing in the inlet, alone. Before power reels there was muscle power. The net was pulled over the stern the hard way. A full-size sockeye weighs ten pounds. I didn't hit a bonanza, but on one pick I landed over 200. That's a ton of fish, and the dory settled alarmingly low in the water. Then I drifted into a tide rip. That's where the incoming and outgoing tides clash. The water can get turbulent, and with less than a foot of free board I was in danger of swamping. I soon knew a bit about tide rips, overloading a dory, and the low price of "reds," circa 1949. It was my fourth unsuccessful attempt at drowning.

Lesson #1: Pulling net by hand can make back ache.

Lesson#2: Near drowning can scare hell out of fisherman—upset the spouse, too.

Surfing with a Jeep

TV commercials in the modern era have shown shiny SUVs frolicking at the edge of the surf. That's one stupid way to seduce a buyer. I once knew a jerk who was delivering a new outboard up the beach to Al Munson. He left Dick Wilson, the owner of Inlet Bar, volunteering to watch the café so he could give his wife a short R&R break. Wanted a family outing so took his two little daughters, too. There wasn't a lot of slack before the tide would come in and cover the drivable part of the beach. They stayed for coffee, the tide didn't cooperate, and on return were forced to dodge waves. Too late. Cook Inlet tides cover the beach in a hurry. Waves sloshed the spark plugs. Engine drowned. These parents, each with a daughter riding their shoulder, waded for high ground. Watched their Jeep disappear beneath the waves.

Author and Piper Clipper With Walter Covich

John and Ruth Grueninger Jeanne, Hal, Jeannette

The Conglomerate

I was the commissioner because the marshal can't function very well without one and because I owned a typewriter, and incidentally, I was convenient because of my parts store's vista of Kenai's activities. I was automatically qualified, and Allan would get the word to President Truman to sign the appointment. I was also the issuer of licenses: car, driver, commercial fishing. Jeanne and I had become a full-service rescue mission. We had the café where frozen travelers could thaw out while awaiting a plane or truck connection and a repair garage where four-wheel drives could thaw a ton of ice and mud from their wheel wells. Hungry? We could feed you. Drunk? We could fly or Jeep you back to your fish site or trap. If one was sick, or worse, mangled by a bear, we had the radio with which to call in a rescue plane. If dead, as coroner I could make it official, and if you wanted to get married, as commissioner I could give you a choice of either secular or religious vows.

As any Alaska native knows, if you swamp your outboard motor in salt water you immediately sink it in a drum of fresh water so air can't get to it. How you gonna dunk a vehicle in fresh water? Well, after the tide receded, the beloved Jeep was towed home and died shortly thereafter from sodium chloride poisoning. Reminded me of a cartoon by Bill Mauldin, the WWII *Stars and Stripes* reporter who best portrayed the mood of the troops. The cavalry sergeant's faithful Jeep has finally given up and the grief stricken driver holds his .45 to the hood, covers his eyes, and pulls the trigger.

Warning: Don't emulate that pitch unless you hate your SUV.

Seward Satellite

Activity increased to where we needed a facility in Seward. We built a structure on an existing concrete base left over from the Army's presence (Fort Raymond). I was flying or driving back and forth frequently to monitor my one-man force named Fred. He was an oddball misfit, common to Alaska. When things at Seward went wrong, which was the norm, his comforting excuse was . . .

"This in time may prove beneficial."

I heard it a hundred times and I'm still waiting.

We had a sale for a Jeep that was in Seward, and I needed a driver to go with me to bring it back. Stanley Wilson was the only local I could finger. He was not a pillar of reliability, but I needed him. At Seward, I handed him the keys, told him to pick up some freight at Moose Pass station, said I'd be behind him if anything went wrong, and I'd be delayed at Moose Pass because I wanted to visit old-time friends, Wes and Ama Laubscher. That's where I was having a snack when Stanley comes knocking.

"Stanley, what's wrong?"

"Damn engineer didn't even stop! That's what's wrong." Stanley had pulled into the station to pick up our freight, stopped too close to the tracks, and the only train of the week hit his front wheel. Now I knew why he was unemployable. All the way back, Stanley mumbled

" . . . didn't even stop. That's hit 'n run."

In that era, four-wheel drives were still somewhat novel, and in selling them, a doubt I had to dispel was the strength of the front-wheel turning knuckles. And this damaged jeep showed vividly that the knuckle had caved and left the wheel pinioned flat on the ground.

Accommodating friends, Lyle and Louise Saxton, lived by the road in Moose Pass and often parked me, so surely they'd love to park my wounded Jeep. The sad sight, now three-wheel drive, got moved to beside the road at the yard. They put a sign on it that every passerby would see:

. . . if your Jeep is hit by a train, the knuckle buckles.

The Road to Connect the Lower 48

Finally, the road connecting Anchorage was open and a two-wheel drive could make it all the way from the States to Kenai—provided it had enough spare tires. Many stretches of the road were far from user-friendly. There were intervals of rough gravel with sharp rocks that were tire killers. Some flats were repairable, but most were casing breaks requiring a new tire. I had an account with Goodyear, and my volume was such that tires were "drop shipped," meaning Goodyear paid the freight as far as Seward. So I foolishly sold tires at the published retail and mounted them free. A motorist from Akron could buy a tire in remote Kenai for the same price as charged in the country's tire capitol. Sunday was our biggest tire day. Also the day Jeanne and I wanted a rest. Anchorage people, curious to see the end of the road, would venture forth and wind up beating on our door with a ruined tire in hand. I was grumpy because I was tired, mad because I had housed us above our business, and knew I couldn't say NO.

"Go away, It's Sunday."

"Hey, come on, I'm stuck" . . .

"I'm tired, come back tomorrow."

"How do you expect to make any money if you treat people this way?"

"I don't need your money. I need sleep . . . Awright, damn it, bring in your tire."

I knew that when this road victim got back home he'd tell his buddies what a harrowing trip and how rude the tire dealer. He wouldn't mention he paid no more when deep into the wilds than in his hometown.

Occasionally, the customer standing around while I mounted his tire would strike up conversation with, "Why does anyone want to live in this remote place?"

"This is a good place to live. Has a lot of action. You just can't see it." But I'm telling myself *out of 100 million Americans, only 400 choose this place.* So this customer's going to think I'm not only ill-mannered but feebleminded.

Lesson: the biblical Good Samaritan didn't get much thanks, either.

And another lesson: don't live in the same building as your business.

Some days it's better to stay in bed. John was the best mechanic in Alaska, but he couldn't put in the hours. I felt I must find a backup. Kenai was not a place to recruit labor.

During a trip to the states for business chores, I recruited a prospect to move to Kenai. He would need a place to live, so we'd build a house behind the garage. It was very basic and went up fast. It was ready for wiring, but I was too busy when a God-sent solution fell in our lap. Paul told me a deaf-mute was stuck out the road with a sick vehicle. After we towed him in, he wrote on a note that he had no money. Could he work it off? He added that he knew a bit about construction.

"If you know how to wire a house, get started and we'll repair your pickup," I said.

His rig was ready to roll, and he handed me a note that the wiring was finished—except, he didn't know how to connect the circuit breaker to the power source.

"I know how—let's go try it out." I connected the wires, threw the switch and no lights came on. I'm puzzled, but he knows. He signaled that *all* the lights must be on. Our new house was wired in series. So we have Christmas tree lights. He tried. And we knew he had too many other problems. We wrote off the repair bill and sent him on his way.

Lesson: Charity can be in many guises.

The New School

Kenai's single school was a big ancient wooden firetrap waiting its turn to burn. Same for all other rural schools in the territory. Our principal, O. C. Connelly, was a talented and motivated professional. He foresaw growth, recognized the inevitable fire, and agitated for action. A village meeting was convened. O. C. displayed a drawing, like an architect's rendering, with his concept of a masonry building that could expand as needed. He contended it would take a lobbyist to bring it to reality. The villagers agreed.

The thirteen colonies went to war over taxation without representation, but that slogan never extended to territorial status. Alaska had a delegate to Congress who couldn't vote, and neither could we residents. We were subject to federal income tax and paid a piddling annual school tax to the territory but little more. Why complain? The feds picked up the bill for nearly everything—except schools. They were the Territorial Legislature's domain. It met annually in Juneau to flex its weak muscles.

Who should go to Juneau? Our ad hoc committee chose Ralph Soberg. He was articulate, head of the local Road Commission, and would have the most clout. As an afterthought, it was felt there should be an alternate just in case, and Hal Thornton was chosen. Ralph's schedule became overloaded with the construction of the road from Soldotna to Homer. Hal was now the designated hitter and was on his way to Juneau with O. C.'s plans under his arm. He knew little about lobbying, but he was motivated.

It was providential that I had a contact in Juneau. Jeanne's school teacher from early Hope days, Jerry Williams, had become a family friend. He had now moved up to a legal assistant for the legislature. I told Jerry my mission. He told me we needed a resolution. He would draft it for me.

The resolution instructed the superintendent of schools to alter the policy of building frame schools that became firetraps. (I wondered why this hadn't been policy years before.) It recommended O. C.'s design, which permitted easy expansion. Most important, if we wanted it to pass, it made the new policy applicable to *all similar rural schools*.

Kenai School
Photo courtesy of Hardscratch Press, Walnut Creek, CA.

"Is it that easy?" I asked Jerry.

"No, your work has only begun. You're staying in the Baranof Hotel?* That's where you buttonhole the legislators. They're busy, always being hustled by constituents like yourself, but you get around that by taking them to lunch and explain Connelly's plan. They're not blind, and they do eat."

For ten days I cornered votes.

"Would you join me for lunch in the Baranof dining room and let me answer questions you might have about the school resolution?"

I badgered, overlunched, and the resolution passed. Kenai got more building than it had dreamed of. More than that, Kenai can take credit for breaking the build-and-burn cycle for the whole territory.

(It was my honor to give the first commencement address in the new school. It was a proud moment. There were eight

* Named for Alexander Baranov, colonizer for the Russian American Co. In 1799, he chose Sitka over Kenai for his new mainland capitol.

graduates, and Jackie Benson, the stepdaughter of Ralph Soberg, gave the valedictory address. This promising young lady moved on to a successful career, and sixty years later I renewed the acquaintance by e-mail. I wish I could claim some credit for her success, but I'm certain she doesn't recall a single thought from my brilliant address. Conversely, I can't remember her valedictory exhortations.)

Kenai Chapel*

Walt Covich and his volunteers worked hard to construct a new chapel. It was a community accomplishment. It was nearly finished, save for some minor details such as a *furnace*, in time for a Christmas initiation. The young people were to present a pageant so, of course, the room was packed. Most kept their parkas, galoshes, mitts, and fur hats on for warmth. I observed that enough people, packed tight enough could bring up the temperature to a tolerable level. While I was toying with that revelation, the marshal tapped me on the shoulder and asked me to come outside.

"Hurry, we have to go to the Road Camp."

"Why me, and what's the hurry?" I asked.

"LeRoy has killed himself with a rifle. As commissioner, you're also ex-officio coroner" That was news to me. I didn't know LeRoy well, but well enough to know he was a handsome, bright kid and stayed out of trouble and sure didn't deserve to die. He was to be in the chapel program. It was a somber ride to the Road Camp. Even more somber when we entered the room where it happened.

---

* For an intimate appreciation of the Kenai Chapel and other early Kenai insights, see *The Dragline Kid* by Lisa Augustine (Arlene Rheingans) (Walnut Creek, CA: Hardscratch Press, 2002).

Wildwood Is Born

Our parts store's large window, looking out on the travel hub of the village was Thermopane. This meant Marshal Petersen could have a frost-free surveillance of the action. He was a steady companion because from the comfort of my store he could survey the town's movement. I might add that he was also our best customer.

On one of those days while the marshal was standing his vigil by my window, he called out with urgency:

"Come quick if you want to see a plane crash!"

The marshal was watching an Air Force C-119, a "flying boxcar," on a long final approach to the Kenai landing strip. Flying conditions were perfect, but the plane was too low and undershot the end of the runway, making it up the slope on the second bounce. The jolt bent both tail empennages skyward. No sheet metal shop would ever put that bird back in the air.

What the marshal and I were really watching was the birthing of a military base. We had just seen the first act of an expensive comedy.

The war might be over, but Anchorage had an ever-expanding military presence with a lot of soldiers stressed out from the rigors of peacetime. Some of these were officers with access to flying craft that could get them to the choice hunting and fishing on the Kenai. Thus the plane off-loaded jeeps and boats and fly rods and officers and all drove off into the outback undeterred by their C-119 with the busted sacroiliac. Well, it couldn't be hidden under a bush, so the wounded critter was relegated to an obscure corner of the airfield, and many a week passed before we saw any evidence that it had salvage value for its owner—the U.S. taxpayer.

"Wildwood Military (something or other)" Is Born.
According to the scuttlebutt in our Terminal Café, there was a newsworthy event from the railhead siding at Moose Pass. It seems that a small military contingent, with a flatbed truck and a monstrous boom rig, de-railed and tanked up at the Moose Pass Pub where a cub bear was kept on a chain to entertain the customers. But the cub was no longer cuddly, and the owner was relieved when the Army chaps asked for him. Thereupon, the bear was inducted into the Corps, loaded into the front seat of the flatbed truck between two servicemen, and aimed toward Kenai.

It's a bit sticky for the driver to hold a truck on a twisty mountain road when a bear sitting next to him wants out. Shortly, the truck was over the edge and down a long bumpy slope toward the Kenai River. It would take a bit of time for the boom truck to rescue its buddy.

The next day, two olive-drab trucks roared past our corner. One was a flatbed with a bear chained to the deck. The trucks continued to the end of the road, which would bring them to the Inlet Bar where the owner, Dick Wilson, presided over the cash register and the storytelling.

The following morning, in our Terminal Café, Dick was at his comical best as he related the plight of the GI cadre.

"They left my bar, piled into their trucks, put the boom truck in reverse and backed the boom right through the General Store." Raucous laughter. Dick continued: "That upset Cecil and Helen (Jones—the store owners), but the Army buddies agreed to repair the damage and promised they'd be around for awhile."

The next official appearance of the monster trucks was less amusing. They pulled up to the side of our Terminal

Café, nudging it as they closed in. Our building had all of the shortcomings of the wilderness, including a feeble foundation. It could support the building, but not a ten-ton boom truck.

"Why'd you park so close to the building? Now you've damaged the foundation!" I was mad.

"We need air for the tires," they chorused as the building creaked and settled slightly askew. "OK, we'll fix it. We plan to be around for awhile."

They located an abandoned Quonset hut near the Road Commission camp and set up temporary housekeeping. Their first priority was to prepare for winter. After that, there was the repair to Jones's store and our café, the construction of a bear pen, and oh yes, salvaging the crippled plane.

No soldier worth his K-rations would try to function without a motor pool. It's the mother's milk of garrison life. So it was only a few days and onto the runway bounced another C119. This one remained intact and was soon disgorging a cargo that included two "weasels"—the coinage for a small amphibious personnel carrier.

With such cute toys, a fitting initiation could only be Cook Inlet. It had sand and waves and tide rips. Oh jolly! Just the test to learn if a vehicle would be proper for a moose hunt. With tracks clanging and propellers spinning they plunged into the surf and beyond.

Submarines! That's what you get with a weasel when the drain holes aren't plugged. For a week thereafter, our village trails were a dirt track marathon with olive-drab trucks pulling two weasels to get the engines started.

With the amount of repair work to be done, there was no choice but to ship in a contingent of tradesmen, which created a workforce requiring cooks and medics and whatever a table of allowance permitted. This called for a regular supply of PX supplies and mail and other creature comforts, without which a bivouac is no fun. C-47s began arriving regularly and our mechanic stood watch, rarely showing excitement until the day when something moved him to shout, "Your wheels are up!" The C-47 threw up a shower of gravel as it slithered down the runway on its belly. The C-119 now had company.

Winter in Alaska is no fun for outdoor repair work, so our burgeoning military force turned its attention to developing defenses against the environment. A bigger location was needed, and finding federally controlled land around Kenai was as easy as pointing. The U.S. Government owned us lock, stock, and moose pasture.

A choice location north of the runway seemed ideal. It was far enough to ensure concealment from the enemy and big enough for expansion. It was also far enough to require more than a jeep trail, so the Corps of Engineers shipped in a construction detail and their equipment was heavy stuff.

Tournapull dirt movers were now showing up. Huge beasts! While standing in front of the Terminal Garage, my insurance agent and I were startled by one of the monsters roaring toward us from the direction of the new camp. What was the driver doing in the village? Ken guessed mailing a letter, but I noted his turn toward the cannery and guessed it was fish scraps for his dog. The road down to the cannery is a modest grade with curves and too narrow for speeding. Braking is not the strongest virtue for a Tournapull. This behemoth was moving too fast as it commenced its descent. The driver's options were all lousy. Luckily the tide was out, exposing a broad slope of bottomless, gooey mud that will stop anything, which it did, but only after shearing off some cannery piling. Well, a monster this size under the cannery, in mud up to its radiator cap, and with the tide due back on schedule, calls for special smarts. Maybe it's in their battle training manual.

Not in Our Front Yard

Kenai in 1953 now had more bars than all other business combined. One had sprouted under our kitchen window. It was noisy at night, but we accepted that with resignation. Now a food service hangout across the road from our front room window had applied for a liquor license. I felt there were already too many places to get drunk. In Alaska, it was rare that a license be denied, but I felt we should try. I enlisted the support of Eldy Covich. She was equally incensed, and others joined us. We circulated a petition, secured a lot of names, and were prepared for the court hearing in Anchorage. On the fateful day, I loaded three determined women, including Eldy, into my little bush plane and took off for Anchorage. Then a cold sweat seized me. *In this flimsy craft I'm flying three priceless wives and mothers across unmarked terrain and Turnagin Arm on a doubtful mission. Their pilot is crazy.*

We presented our petition to Judge Dimond. We each made a forceful statement. The applicant was stunned. Liquor applications were supposed to be rubber stamped. The judge denied the permit and strengthened it by saying as long as he was on the bench it could not be resubmitted. We won! The return flight was a nervous one.

The Merrill Field tower had assigned me a short gravel cross-runway, rarely used and rarely graded. It was a rough and bouncy takeoff and knocked out my radio receiver. If my transmitter was also out, I wouldn't dare complete the flight. I circled the tower, hoped they would receive when I told them my problem. They flashed me a green light. So I nervously climbed out and set course for Cook Inlet. I sweated. I could not breathe easy until I got this trio safely back home. *Lord, please stay beneath my wings.* Jeanne and I had already decided to leave Kenai, so why fight? I guess blocking one more bar was a consolation. I could depart with pride.

My mother belonged with this planeload of women. She would be so proud of us. Fern Randall had marched with Carrie Nation during the saloon smashing episodes in Wichita. The women won and prohibition was their award. Temperance was my mother's passion, and she was a stalwart for the Woman's Christian Temperance Union (WCTU) until the day she died at age eighty-eight. With our foursome, she could have again brandished Carrie Nation's famous hatchet.

Good-bye to the Alaskan Odyssey

Cook Inlet! There it would be—that shimmering reflection with a beach outline as recognizable as the silhouette of a shapely woman. Cook Inlet would never fail to lead me home to Kenai when limited visibility plagued the flight. That wonderful landmark was my homing beacon, ever ready to solve my navigation needs. I recall the force of its powerful tides and cantankerous winds, and I revere the miracle of its migrating salmon. That surging arm of the mighty ocean was truly a mixture of blessings and danger . . . and I miss it.

Fifty years after leaving, I miss Mount Redoubt, the aurora borealis, and the interminable daylight of summer. I long to hear the moose crunching the winter snow outside our window. Most of all, I miss the people—those misfits who fled from a structured society to carve out their destiny in the bush. They were our friends; they framed our lives. Of course, I miss them.

In Alaska during our era, people depended on each other. They lived on credit balances of large and small favors that they willingly gave and might one day need returned. In a land nearly empty of people, "love thy neighbor" is less a pious injunction than a rule for survival. If you chanced on a person in trouble along the trail, you stopped. Another time he or she would stop for you. I miss that.

It was in pre-war Fairbanks that I fell in love with Alaska. Its people had heart. Its winter had mystery. Its economic challenge was open to the newcomers. Fairbanks is where I discovered girls and passed my initiation to adulthood. It's where Jeanne and I began a lifetime journey together. But Fairbanks doesn't dominate my reminiscing. Neither does Anchorage and Fort Richardson where we toughed out military duty and sweated out the end of a war. Nor the serene little community of Hope—our first move after discharge. Hope was as picturesque as a Currier & Ives painting. It was like a perpetual coffee klatch, like camping out, like a romp in deep snow. But it is Kenai that fires my memory. Kenai was raw drama. It was paddle your own canoe. Kenai was a storyteller's bonanza.

"We're moving to the States." Upon hearing of our plans to migrate to Seattle, friends would ask, "Why?" Pappy Walker was firm. "Honey, you stay put and you'll get rich." Marshal Petersen told me the community needed us; Bob and Carol Jacobs thought it was a joke; Walt and Eldy Covich said we'd be back. Would we leave Luke and Paul, John and Ruth, Phil Wilson, the school teachers, the bush pilots, the fishermen, the homesteaders? Why? They were our extended family.

Why not? Living in Kenai in the early postwar years was a dumb career choice. Life in such isolation was a struggle even if we didn't recognize it as such. We were constantly penalized by weather and lack of public utilities. Four-wheel drive was normal with compound gear half the time. There were no shops, no landscaping, and our supply sources were somewhere beyond the horizon. Our settlement of squatters was a hodgepodge. A nonentity. Not a part of anyone's plan and purpose. Kenai just happened.

Our numerous business ventures were accompanied by lots of mistakes and damn long hours. *Pioneering* is a synonym for *primitive*. It is spelled *h-a-r-d w-o-r-k*. That school of hard knocks was a learning experience! I had learned to build structures, learned to fly, to lobby the legislature, to give a commencement address, and to christen a bridge. Our business was at the center of the village activity. We were the tax collector, the U.S. commissioner (coroner inquests included), an unintended source of credit.

Alaska had a way of distorting logic. The living may be hard, but the excitement of living was real. There was an independence (call it struggle), there was a self-reliance (call it stubbornness), there was a freedom that's possible because of the absence of society's restraints. As I write this in 2003, I know that the freedom I recall has now been lost to the bureaucracy that accompanied statehood. Only the primitive era could permit the pioneer mind-set that assumes the right to exploit the land. Alaska had limitless land. And the environment was not something to be saved; rather, it was an obstacle to be overcome, to be endured, to reckon with.

If a man won his battle with the wilderness, if he shot his moose, set out his nets, beat out the storm, built his boat and survived his journey, completed his cabin and stocked his cache, there was a feeling of achievement, win or lose. A man could feel good just being his own person. Wives and young children didn't fare as well.

Jeanne and I agreed on two strong arguments for leaving: Jeannette and Joyce! They were adorable, bright little girls with a future at stake. Here in this homely little fishing village they could claim a nearly exclusive amenity: They had a semblance of a bathroom. They had friends, a dog, a spinet piano, and bicycles. All well and good for youth, but they would be growing up in a dubious social environment where saloons outnumbered all other businesses combined.

While our girls were attaining the ages of six and nine, my attention was woefully distracted. In my frenzied effort to cope with the elements and establish a business from scratch—and another and another—I failed to focus on our growing children.

It's a hard act to be on the run and also be a good parent. "Would life in Alaska always be this way?" It might. The winters wouldn't go away. Summertime's catch-up busyness was a must. My venture-adventuring was addictive. I was trapped and Jeanne with me. There was a third great reason—as yet without a name.

Perhaps in the "States" we could have a baby and for a change connect with its growing up. Imagine! Jeanne and I might pull a parenthood act in a situation where there was leisure time and parks and paved streets. We'd even have utilities. Seductive idea.

There came a balmy fall day in 1952. Jeanne and I gave ourselves the day off. We flew to Kalifornsky Beach and strolled on its bluffs. The birch had turned golden, the inlet was glassy, those volcanoes across the inlet glistened in the afternoon sun, and Jeanne was at her seductive best. There would be another baby, conceived in an idyllic setting and raised in a normal one!

From fall until next summer would be a busy interlude. There would be the targeting for a move to Seattle, liquidating some money, closing out a business, and of course the usual concerns about pregnancy.

It was a clear and frosty March morning when I Jeeped our family out to our trusty little Piper clipper. Jeannette and Joyce were carefully strapped into the back seat while our good neighbor, Phil Wilson, helped my pregnant wife into the copilot seat. Our preheated engine coughed, fired, and slowly nudged the oil temperature needle. We taxied onto the runway, waved good-bye to Phil, revved up, and were airborne over our funny little village still sleeping under the snow.

A fellow bush pilot named Beryl Markham wrote in her book, *West With the Night,*

> If you must leave a place that you have lived in and loved and where all your yesterdays are buried deep— leave it any way except a slow way. Never turn back. Never believe that an hour you remember is a better hour because it is dead. Passed years seem safe ones, while the future lives in a cloud formidable from a distance. The cloud clears as you enter it.

The steady beat of the propeller drowned out utterances, but unspoken emotions pervaded our crowded little cabin. Off the left wing across the inlet were those majestic volcanoes,

Redoubt and Illiamna. On our right, the dawn was just lighting the mountain pass to Seward, a route over lakes and past Harding Glacier along which we had made so many turbulent flights. Somewhere beneath was my eighty-acre homestead in the woods, the veteran's opportunity Jeanne and I had relinquished in preference to seven months of isolated living; never dreaming it was to be part of the Alaska oil bonanza.

Kenai was now behind us and with it the end of an era. Ahead were those nervous ten miles across Turnagin Arm. My attention was focused on piloting our growing family to a safe landing at Anchorage, where a commercial flight would finish the job. Only then could I let my feelings out: feelings of excitement mingled with fear, relief mixed with sadness, the usual suspense—feelings one shares with his wife—expectations that come June, we'd initiate our third baby, the one to be blessed with a modernized environment. She will be a test case on whether a safe and sane launching gives her a better future than our two wilderness-raised daughters. Time may tell.

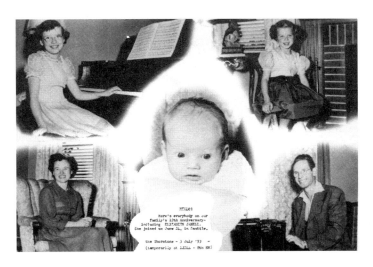

157

7

Return to the Lower 48: Puget Sound Opportunist

Life in Alaska was an entrepreneur's adventure. Kenai was the apex, but it didn't end there. From Kenai to Seattle, so big it was frightening to a wilderness mind-set, so we moved north to a cozy little farming community in the Skagit Valley. We snuggled down among a culture of stable industrious Norwegians. The people were right, the scenery was pleasing, Puget Sound was a playground, the weather was mild but overly overcast. Nearly perfect except . . . There's always an "except." Opportunities for a middle-aged newcomer who lacked a trade or profession were well hidden.

For starters, I tried the insurance business. A more pressing chore was to finish liquidating our Alaska assets. The Terminal Café had been sold on a shaky contract. I found a chicken rancher near Mount Vernon who hated chickens. He had lived in Alaska and wanted to return. He made a quick flight to Kenai, returned, and said, "Let's swap." His property equity for our contract. In two days' time, I found myself in the egg business. He waved good-bye to Jeanne and me, to all his furniture, and to the chickens on the nests. I believe he wanted *o-u-t*.

I knew nothing about chickens other than that eggs were good for breakfast, so I quickly went in search of another trade. This time, it was a dairy farm near Sedro Woolley. The farm came equipped with 25 cows waiting to be milked. I didn't know dairying either, other than that milk is supposed to be good calcium food. This property shouldn't be hard to manage. In Skagit County there was always a Hollander who wanted "millik" cows.

That left our Seward property. It was damaged in the big earthquake of '64 and was nearly worthless. I found a desperate man who was itching to trade his distressed asset for anything. My distressed Seward asset qualified. Result: a partnership in a near-worthless Rambler dealership.

One day my partner walked in to the counter of a business I was tending (overhead garage doors). Dewey said he wanted to take me for a ride in a funny car. Told me we could have the franchise.

"What's it called?" I asked.

"Volkswagen."

I told my partner NO. It didn't have any name recognition. Whoa! I still had a lot to learn.

Dealing Jeeps in Alaska didn't qualify me for the auto business in the Lower 48. Pacific Motors was a tough game. It nearly gave me ulcers, and I was ready to trade it for anything. "Anything" was a "stump ranch," the name for cutover timberland, miles away alongside the Skagit River. It came with a five-acre strawberry crop.

In Skagitland, one quickly learned that for cultivating and picking strawberries, boys are no solution. I offered to employ Joyce's boyfriend, Nelson. He had a prior commitment: "Hal, I'd like to help you, but I have to polish my

Field labor valuable experience for youth

Editor, News-Press: "Strawberry field lark or labor?" Why it's both, plus money, and an athletic contest, too! Your editorial recalled to mind one of the unique windfalls of raising our young family in Washington state.

In the fertile Skagit Valley strawberries were everywhere and the harvest was synonymous with summer vacation. As soon as a kid could convince a field boss that she was big enough to "pick" life took on a new dimension — at last she could join the gang and be in on the action! The strawberry field was "where it's at." And most youngsters — our three girls included — sweat-out the day they would be admitted to the patch.

The first morning always had a choked up goodbye just like the first day of school. And as our little 8 or 9 year old volunteer beginner headed for the grower's bus we suffered all the apprehensions of parenthood. But these concerns ended in proud relief by mid-afternoon when home came a dirty, tired, but contented little waif, eager to recount the excitement of the day and also re-count the punches on the card that spelled how many carriers had been produced.

And shortly our young competitor was telling us of the wonderful ways of the workaday world and the urgency of the harvest and of the discovery of Mexican families who could pick circles around her ("daddy, the father fills two cards before I get one. How can he be so fast?") and she marvels at the way the little shavers in the Mexican family take care of each other. And we're just a bit envious of a family that works together with bonds so firm.

Many a summer vacation had to be delayed because the girls "in the patch" insisted on bulldogging it to the last day of the season to claim their bonus — that meant 10 percent extra pay as a reward for toughing it out to the bitter end.

Thus the season's end meant the satisfaction of winning the contest; it meant a strong body bronzed by the weather; and money in the sock — the kind of money that gets counted over and over because it came hard — and when it "got spent" it must be for something very special!

Happily, as our child matured the volume increased until there came the proud announcement "this year I'm field boss" or truck driver, or whatever denotes success to an eager beaver. But this is not to suggest it was all heavenly. There was the usual grumbling because strawberry fields are not a beautyrest mattress and the weather was not Camelot's. But I've heard bitching over a birthday party, too!

So was it compulsory? Sure, just like catching an early tide for surfing.

Was it hard child-labor? Yes: just like a Scout's 50-miler in the Sierras!

Was it exploitation? Probably the grower was more exploited than the picker on average. At least, more small-fry pickers wound up the season with a spending jamboree in Seattle . . . their fun was certainly more visible.

But now our federal labor act has legislated this opportunity away. And our youth everywhere have been deprived of a healthy and sensible adventure in growing up. For protection against what? Are we saving them from the right to learn how to work; how to earn their own way; how to develop stamina and muscle? All of this so the paid recreation departments will need to provide substitute challenges and time-killers!

My own daughters are now adults with successful careers and homes. But I am again concerned with children-in-summertime as I manage Santa Barbara's low-income housing. And with the "long hot summer" here I wrestle with the problem of what to do with their idle time so they don't annoy the neighbors and mischief doesn't overflow. It is then that my memory drifts back to the Skagit Valley, and I pray:

"Dear Lord, Santa Barbara's such a wonderful place with nearly everything, but couldn't we just have a strawberry patch!"

H. L. THORNTON

motorcycle." It's just as well; girls are much better. Even on a tractor or truck, they're better. I drafted our three daughters and their friend Susan. I can say with pride, these four girls capitalized on this experience. All developed unusual résumés and are now successful professionals and skilled mothers. The results of this career exercise didn't teach me much, but as it did for the girls, it gave me an enhanced résumé.

Speaking of résumés: I envy persons who can describe their occupation with a single word: Farmer. Doctor. Lawyer. Architect. Crook. Our daughter's class once had a show-and-tell about the occupation of their fathers. Jeannette came home exasperated.

"I'm the only one in my class who doesn't know what my father does!"

I tried to smooth it over. I told her I go whichever way the wind blows. I guess that makes me *an opportunist.*

"That's no occupation," she protested.

The dictionary defines that word *as a person who takes advantage of any opportunity to achieve an end.* Our breed find it easy to gravitate together. Such happened with a restless young schoolteacher named Danny. We were both ready for a diversion and hit upon subdividing sixty acres of cutover timberland along the south bank of the Skagit River. Twenty scenic miles upriver from Sedro Woolley. Truly a sleeper.

After studying the merits of the property, we concluded it deserved to be kept as pristine as possible with a major portion preserved wild in perpetuity. We named it Skagitwilde. I'm proud of this footprint we left hidden alongside my favorite river.

Danny's discontent forced him out of teaching, and he went on to be a very successful entrepreneur. Also a philanthropist. If the reader drives along the Skagit (Highway 20) toward the North

162

Cascade National Park, before Concrete watch for a choice spot for a picnic at a sign pointing to Rasar State Park.

The Entrepreneur and "Hardin's Law"

Occupationally, I keep falling out of my groove. There must be a reason I don't stay focused. Why? I believe the reason is "Hardin's Law." I've been a victim of a profound force described by my fellow Santa Barbaran. Garret Hardin a noted biologist, is a wise professor at UCSB. He derides social behavior with observations such as "The Lifeboat Theory" and "Tragedy of the Commons." Even though I know him, I had to discover his answer to my problem in a *News Press* reprint out of the *Wall Street Journal.*

According to Hardin, most anything attempted has a ripple affect that impacts in unforeseen directions. Stated simply, "You can never do merely one thing." Well! I've been afflicted by this ever since early Fairbanks days. At last, I have an excuse for my malady and I know its name. It explains how I got to be a house mover.

There in Skagitland I had without design become a subdivider of innocent vacant land. This anomaly registered with an opportunistic realtor whose energy was momentarily focused on the least promising commission for miles around. Gordon Beck was on my scent and Pandora's box was about to be opened.

Gordon in Burlington was even more displaced than this writer. He had migrated in from Los Angeles with a mind-set for transplanting the LA free-for-all to the Skagit scene. In the search for a living he settled on real estate, and a tougher game was not to be found.

Gordon digressed from our chess game to set me up: "Hal, I know you've done a couple of subdivisions. Would you say that choice land at the edge of town is desirable at $1,000 an acre?"

H. T.: "Maybe."

Gordon: "Would you feel more positive at $500 an acre?"

H. T.: "Yes."

Gordon: "I'm going to get it for you for $400! Sign here." It was everything he claimed. A few acres of cutover timberland at the south edge of Burlington. Easy street access, fertile soil, shady alders and pines, and bordered by lush strawberry farms. It was a sleeper indeed. Of course, cutover timber means a jungle of slashings and stumps and by-passed trees that are less than perfect. Properly done, it could be a park-like setting for half a dozen dreamlike cottages. I would give the subdivision my own name. A mistake. To limit traffic, I would design with a single "lane" ending in a cul-de-sac and that would be its name. A mistake. Someday our own family might live there and the girls' black gelding could browse in our own yard. Heaven!

But first there was much planning to locate a new street, futile attempt to save the trees, and eradication of the stumps. The stumps! There were monsters, five to ten feet in diameter that had been rotting for years but far from surrender. The slashings! A winter's worth of burning. No matter how I juggled the street layout, most of the worthwhile trees were doomed and the stumps escaped. The only consolation was a laissez-faire county sans zoning, permits, inspection, and activists.

Northwest Washington provides a long rainy season, and

I would need it all for the slashing fires to clear the area. In my future there was also a lot of bulldozing and stump blasting. I needed an accomplice with equipment, a powder monkey with contempt for the regulations, someone hungry. I needed Bob Wade. Bob could solve a lot of problems, ignore the system, and could teach me to blow stumps. And soon there were frightened Mexicans in a far-off strawberry field who could attest that I was getting great distance with my dynamiting. Stump after stump and fire after fire and bulldozer after sweat and grime and smoke and mud would eat up the months, but in due time the Thornton Subdivision was finished and waiting for buyers . . . and waiting . . . and waiting.

"It's tough to crack the ice," was the prevailing wisdom. If I could just get the first house up and occupied, the subdivision would come to life. So I needed a pioneer to go first, but Skagitland is not famous for impulse buyers and so I waited. And the weeds grew and I fidgeted.

Hardin's Law struck again. The answer grabbed me out of a newspaper story. Houses along the new Seattle freeway route were being auctioned off. It implied that anyone could buy a house to be moved for $100. Here was a low-risk gamble. All I needed to do was get houses to Lake Union, load them on a barge, tow them up Anacortes Street, plunk them down on one of my lovely lots, build a foundation under it, and sell it to someone who would landscape it beautifully. It was the answer! What could possible go wrong?

So I bought four! At those prices, I could be a volume mover. Not only would this crack the ice for the subdivision, but it should make lots of money, in the currency of 1959.

There were a few minor obstacles, such as the Skagit River. That river has, over the centuries, created a fertile alluvial fan that is the dream come true for most any Dutch farmer. It achieved its mission by weaving its way from the mountains to the ocean like a snake and alternating from high water to low to flood to runoff, and bed hopping. In time, the natives tired of its cantankerous oscillations and built dikes to lock it in place. Thus contained, it was fairly predictable and somewhat navigable by small craft. South of Burlington, it flows under a railroad bridge, and once past the bridge there was an easy ramp over the dike, sort of like a pig stile. With a bit of bulldozing, this could be made traversable for the dollies used to support houses in migration. Yes, the trip from Seattle to Culdesac Drive was doable, maybe.

The railroad bridge was a worry. If the river was low, the barge's tug would have insufficient draft, and if the river was high, the bridge wouldn't clear. And all the while I was measuring from the bridge to the water, the highway department was hustling me to get the houses off their right-of-way. Two of the freeway houses were a story and a half. No matter how I measured bridge to water, they were going to be scalped getting under. One house was single story and should have no trouble squeezing under but only if the river was low. Hardin's Law was haunting me.

An alternate plan was badly needed. That's how I stumbled into the saltwater solution.

Puget Sound is wall-to-wall waterfront. Granted, there were not many locations suited to beaching two—yes, it needed two because the barge would handle two—two errant floating houses. And not every waterfront community welcomes a pair of period-piece misfits into its architectural collage.

The criteria for a suitable nesting spot was formidable. The elevation was critical, likewise the tide currents, under-

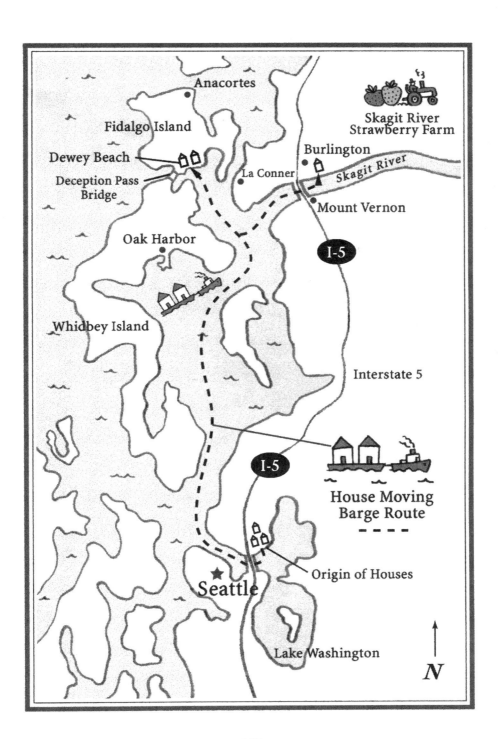

Anacortes

Fidalgo Island

Dewey Beach

Deception Pass
Bridge

La Conner

Burlington

Skagit River
Strawberry Farm

Skagit River

Mount Vernon

I-5

Oak Harbor

Whidbey Island

Interstate 5

I-5

House Moving
Barge Route
- - -

Origin of Houses

Seattle

Lake Washington

N

water obstacles, ground slope. The odds of finding such a spot were astronomical, but it existed, it was for sale, and we owned it within a week.

The barge would ride about six feet above waterline, so I needed a beach bulkhead of concrete to a height matching the barge deck, and the bulkhead would have to be submerged at high tide enough to give the barge floatation. Landward of the bulkhead, there was an elevation of eight or ten feet to a level area with a few worthwhile trees. I could bulldoze basements, moving the excavated material behind the bulkhead and thereupon have a support for the dollies. With the houses in place, we would simply pour basement walls and lower the houses into place. It sounded simple enough.

There would be the gamble on calm weather, on the tide being right, on the arrival time from Seattle to match the tide, and on the barge lining up with the elevation of my bulkhead and with the basement holes. This project had some contingencies.

"Do you think our daughters would be good at concrete work?" I asked Jeanne as we stood atop the bulkhead staring across the water. She gave me a dirty look. The nervous time had come. The tide was starting to rise against the base of the bulkhead, and we were searching the horizon for any speck resembling a tug and barge. In time, we saw more than a speck. It was an apparition! We were not prepared for such a bizarre spectacle as two steep-pitched roofs bearing down on us from high perches. These disembodied ghosts, once torn from their root had lost whatever pride and function they gave to their neighborhood. They were dead ugly, and I wished they could be sent back.

The tide was in. The tug captain was lining up on the

bulkhead and now cut the towline to change his craft from a puller to a pusher. There was a creepy interlude while the barge and its outlandish cargo meandered aimlessly on the gentle swells of the bay—and then it all came together.

There they sat on their cribbing in their basement nests. The odds had been nearly impossible and we had beaten them. We were going to have twin waterfront houses on Dewey Beach. There would be up and down fireplaces, a patio connecting the basements to the bulkhead, steps down to the beach, and our boat anchored in front.

"Girls, there's quite a bit of work there, and I'll be occupied with it all through the summer. Wouldn't it be neat if we made a family vacation on the beach? We could move back when school starts." It all made good sense: summer on the bay, a scenic fairyland, our children learning a trade, great physical conditioning. What a time of growth! Our children would love it. We'd all love it. A "concrete" vacation!

Concrete! There are always problems with concrete. It requires forms. Concrete is impatient. Once in the ready-mix truck, the clock is running. Once out of the truck, it is heavy. Backache heavy. It is also unforgiving. When it sets up, your mistakes are "set in concrete."

The days and weeks commenced to make a pattern. The early part of the week was for forming up. Thursday was pour day, Friday was cleanup, Saturday was form stripping, and Sunday was for fun. Then another week closed in.

There may have been times when the girls pretended that concrete Thursdays were not their favorite career pursuit. Indeed, they even resorted to subtle hints. Jeannette would announce an urgent date back on the mainland, Joyce would often disappear down the beach, and Janell would get Adrian

Joyce on the Bulkhead

(the boy next door) to take her in his rowboat beyond earshot. True, there was a bit of absenteeism with this crew, but in time the job was finished.

The summer was loaded with guests. Our boats made frequent runs through Deception Pass, and the crab pot was boiling in the fireplace as often as we pulled our traps. We lived by the tide's ebb and flow and feasted on scenery.

Come September, we would move back to Burlington and even live on Culdesac Drive. A friend, Don Nevitt, had now completed the first house. We could rent from him.

The single-story freeway house made it under the railway bridge with inches to spare. It ultimately joined the company of custom-built homes. As I look back, it's inconceivable that a chess game could lead to such a tangled web of complications, a chain of events that would take a year out of my life.

I can't remember if I won the game. When I complained to Gordon, his retort was, "Hal, it's your own fault. You seem unable to do merely one thing." He was echoing Garrett Hardin.

Steelheading Is Not for Me

The Skagit is one of God's great creations. This river starts in the snows of the Canadian Rockies. South of the border, it flows into two hydroelectric lakes of spectacular beauty. It then meanders to Puget Sound near LaConner. Over the centuries, its rich silt has built the alluvial fan that attracted the Scandinavian and Dutch farmers who rate it next to heaven. Indeed, its children revere it like motherhood, and if they ever leave they usually return like metal to a magnet.

This river was a 200-yard walk across strawberry farms that bordered our Burlington house. From its bank, I could watch the natives at their favorite activity, or more accurately nonactivity, which is steelhead fishing.

Steelheading is to Skagit Valley as moose hunting is to Alaska. More than a pastime, it's a devotion, even an addiction. To become properly addicted requires a tolerance for crummy weather and a low excitement threshold.

This style of fishing is done from an ugly little boat with a shacklike shelter against the wind/rain/snow. When in use, the boat may appear to be lifeless, but the stovepipe out the roof will have a plume of wood smoke, which confirms that inside is a fisherman and perhaps a buddy warming hands grasping a cup of overbrewed coffee.

The boat will be anchored over a secret hot spot, the knowledge of which is vitally important. Somewhere near the bottom, a cherry bobber is doing its job, or more likely it is snagged, and it is highly improbable that steelhead will strike today, or any day, but it matters not because from the time he caught his first steelhead, the fisherman was hooked for life.

Many times I strolled over to the tie-up landing with drizzle or rain blowing in my face. I thought perhaps if I greeted the dumpy little boats delivering their devotees back to land, I might get the hang of it. But instead of asking to be included in the sport, I more often asked myself, *Is this the way you want to retire? Is this to be your reward for aging?*

A voice inside told me that surely somewhere the sun is shining and the air is warm and one's cherry bobber is visible above the murky bottom.

Unless I found that place, my retirement is apt to be chilling and damp and the river would be my companion. Search I must, and alone because my family would not support anything smacking of a move. Moving to Hope, then to Kenai, then leaving an impressive brick home in Seattle had been my choices. Coming to this valley had been my choice. The family distrusted my choices. They were content. I was not.

I needed a cover for my search, and circumstance sent one. I was momentarily in the auto business, and there was a repossession in Porterville, California. From there, I could route down U.S. 395 to San Diego and meander up the coast, checking out popular areas such as LaJolla, Laguna Beach, and Carmel.

It all came together when I stood at the railing around the clock tower atop the Santa Barbara Courthouse. Ten minutes surveying the red tile rooftops of the city and I knew: *This is it!* What a revelation!

After forty years of wandering in the wilderness, God/fate/luck has taken me to the top of the mount and showed me the PROMISED LAND. On the two-day drive back north to Skagitland, I rehearsed how I might break the news to the family. Should I tell them that it's God's will? That He feels He made another mistake by sentencing me to a life of drizzle? That if I ever intend to find my career choice, time is running out? This won't be easy. Jeannette is happy at the University of Washington at Seattle, Joyce is happy with her high school buddies, Janell is happy because her horse loves her, and Jeanne is happy if they are happy.

I must simply take the blame for stopping our south-bound migration a thousand miles short of Valhalla. I would tell my family, "Santa Barbara is small, the way I like. It has an exciting mix of people; it has movers and shakers and rich philanthropists; the Pacific Ocean provides climate control; it is insulated from Los Angeles by a barrier called the Rincon. It is where I want to be, and now I want to rectify my mistake. So I plan to move."

The response spoke to me loud and clear through a female phalanx. **"We are NOT moving!"** While waiting for them to come to their senses (it would take seven years), I continued to search for my occupational identity. It didn't make me rich, but it sure expanded my résumé.

The Syndicator

Some friends wanted to pool their funds to buy a sizeable pea farm located along the Swinomish Channel near LaConner. I volunteered that I had a grasp of syndication. They didn't know that everything I did was self-taught. It came off well. Everyone was happy. One more for my résumé.

The Self-Taught Landlord

A smart man named Nickerson once wrote a book, *How I Turned a Thousand Dollars into a Million in My Spare Time.* I had spare time, for sure, and I could use a million. Nickerson's strategy was to buy a small property, leveraged to the hilt. Upgrade, raise the rents, trade up, and keep leveraging and trading and bingo. I was too impatient for steps one to ten, so started at eleven and leveraged into a brick building, near the center of the city. Problem though—that city was seventy miles away. I moved the family out of Seattle five years prior. It's a cinch they wouldn't move back. So weekly, I commuted to my investment. Who else would do the maintenance for such low pay. Now I knew Nickerson's secret. It didn't net us a, million but it taught me a bit about women tenants. A dear old lady knocked on the manager's door. She was worried. If our building toppled into the freeway excavation, her fifth-floor apartment would be on the bottom. My disdain for I-5 may have had its roots in that moment.

Whidbey Mobile Home Sales

I smelled an opportunity for which I needed some vacant land near Mount Vernon. The ideal location was occupied by a mobile home sales. So I bought the business to get it off the property. What to do with this inventory? I chanced to meet a Navy noncom at Whidbey Island's Naval Air Station. Curley was a likable huckster and knew a lot about selling mobile homes to Navy families. I moved the business to Oak Harbor to be near his duty. I provided the bank credit, Curley made the sales. I wanted to preserve our capital, he liked to spend it. We were a team. . . .

When Jeanne finally released me from captivity and we moved to Santa Barbara, I gave the business to Curley and rented him the land. He ran sales up so high he was awarded a Bahama vacation. He achieved this volume by seducing bad credit risks. It was ingenious! Curley generously gave the trip to Jeanne and me and he crashed within the year. Too much creative financing. If I could have that rent check back I'd gladly forego the Bahamas. In the '90s, Curley could have risen through the ranks with Enron, World Com, or Global Crossing. A plunger with real charisma. They come in all shapes and sizes.

Education for me has come the hard way. But occasionally a good lesson pays off. I now knew that cleaning up after a move-out from an apartment requires a painter and carpet layer and lost rent, whereas a mobile home park vacancy can be redecorated with a rake and shovel.

The daughters all love horses, so they bring their families for a Christmas party at a Tucson Resort ranch, 1983.

Shifting Gears

Comfortably settled in Santa Barbara, I gave thought to some unfinished business: college. It's thirty years late, but if I can stay awake . . . My involvement with Adult Education led to activities with Santa Barbara City College and what better place to try for a degree. Cap and gown—here I come.

First, a student should ascertain a major. SBCC had a course just for that purpose. Cal Reynolds was teaching career choices. At the end of the session, we were given a scan sheet for a computer profile. If we would disclose our temperament, our preferences, our skills, and our gender, it would identify our best occupational chances. That's a mystery I had wondered about all my working life. At last I would know. I opened the results with eager anticipation:

"The subject did not specify gender. LAWYER is indicated if subject is female."

I know a lot of lawyers and I like them. I don't even tell "lawyer" jokes. That makes me different from most of my friends. And I've done a bit of my own legal work. (Yes, Bill and Randy and Des and Arch, to name a few, have all told me that a layman who plays at being a lawyer has a fool for a client.)

My lawyer was drawing up a living trust for us. I told Joe I wanted to apply a unique concept for disposing of our estate. He agreed, it was *most unique* but saw nothing wrong with it. I felt it was so superior to the traditional approach that it deserved a book for the benefit of humanity. I would write it.

One thing leads to another. Hardin's law again. As any fool knows, the first step in writing a book is to learn something about your subject. If I'm studying estate planning, what better classroom assignment than the super-rich: Rockefeller, Ford, DuPont, Getty, Hearst. I was delighted to confirm that they could not take their wealth with them, no different from me, and much of it survived them as awesome attractions in the public domain. This discovery deserved a book for the benefit of humanity. I would write it. As with a bird dog chasing rabbits, this is more fun. Estate planning can wait.

I can think of no better travel treat than tracking down the legacies our movers and shakers have opened to the public. The airlines were wooing senior travel to fill seats and tickets to any place in the country. Fares lower than $100 and instant reservations using stand-by. I left a car on the East coast, and as often as I got the urge, I shuttled off to check out another spectacle. Sometimes Jeanne, family, or friends went along. I was like a kid in a candy shop.

Traveler's guide to Monumental Treasures in the U.S.A. (Museums, Monuments, Mansions) has not made the bestseller list. Self-published books rarely do. Because it's out of print, is my explanation. My daughters tell me it's great. One of my bridge friends gifted out free copies to her alumni group and said they liked me and my book. Agents have been slow to catch on. No matter, because I collect my royalty whenever I encounter someone who says "I remember you. I visited _____ because of your book!" It's the best investment I ever made.

Glacier Bay, left to right. Back row: Kate Delimitros, Courtney Jerge, Tom Delimitros, Hal, Jason Delimitros. Middle: Dan Wright, Joyce Jerge, Kirsten Jerge, Rose Lewis, Jeannette Delimitros, Jeanne, Riley Lewis, Philip Jerge, Janell Lewis. Front row: Randall Lewis, Sarah Lewis.

8

The Call of the Wilderness: Revisiting Alaska

Geologic survey crews were in and out of the Terminal Café. They liked Jeanne and regularly complimented her on her cooking. It would have been far better had they shared with her that they were doing oil exploration and it looked promising. They were tight-lipped. In 1957, four years after we packed it in, Richfield Oil's well north of Kenai on the Swanson River, launched the Alaska oil epic and the territory would change forever.

Statehood followed oil by one year. I always felt that territorial status had two big advantages. The Feds paid the bill for nearly everything. We had no territorial income tax or property taxes. At one time, in the early '50s, our legislature tried to impose such a tax, but it was self-assessed and most of the stubborn settlers either cheated or balked and it was repealed. Second, we had a very skinny bureaucracy, and it was inevitable that with statehood, Alaska would immediately duplicate most of the agencies and offices that sprouted over time in established states. So a lot of freedom might be lost in exchange for meager political power in far-off Washington, D.C. However, with the mother lode of oil, it is obvious that statehood was the way to go, and I'm pleased that it was President Eisenhower's privilege to sign the bill. So in retrospect, it's lucky indeed that statehood preceded the oil bonanza because it's a sure bet the Feds would not have shared the bonanza.

It was 1953 when our little family left Kenai safely in the hands of the Army, but I returned occasionally just to be sure. One such trip was spur of the moment. I was sitting beside John Johnson during a board meeting of our church. I was bored and restless and sensed that John felt the same.

1960: "Let's break out and fly to Anchorage," I whispered. "We could buy a car, visit the Kenai; you could shoot a caribou and we can drive down the Alcan. I haven't covered it since it was finished."

Two days later, we were on the plane. Buying a car in Anchorage is easiest in the fall. Short-termers with money from a decent season have no inclination to return to the Lower 48 by *that road,* so they depress the market below what a car will bring in the States. An insurance adjuster sold me a Ford retractable hardtop.* It had been slightly damaged, but repairing in Anchorage was a formidable problem. This design marvel had eleven solenoids to put the hard top in the trunk. Serviceman's nightmare and a car buff's dream.

Our drive from Anchorage down to Kenai was a delight with mountain sheep, bear, and moose standing near the road as if to say *welcome back.* When we reached our old business corner nothing looked familiar. We turned onto the road north along the inlet. Gee whiz! Pavement!

* Ford made them for only two years—'57 and '58.

Wildwood

In a few miles, we came to a professionally done sign proclaiming "Wildwood Station." I turned into the drive and came to a guard gate manned by an MP wearing white gloves, matching leggings, and helmet. *Good grief! What have they done to my wilderness?* The guard wanted a reason for my entering his fraternal domain. "Just looking" was not good enough, but I had already seen too much. My WWII experience filled in the blanks. I knew there would be a command HQ, a QM supply, a PX and commissary, officer and non-com clubs, medical, engineer. Possibly even a contrived mission.

We continued our drive, aiming for some important friends out of the past. I only need find "Arness Road" and I was sure Jim and Peggy would feed us and invite us to throw our sleeping bags on the floor.

Blas Garza's recollection of Wildwood: As I recall, the 71st Infantry Division Band stationed at Richardson Army base near Anchorage was invited (or ordered) to go to Wildwood Station in the Kenai Peninsula in order to entertain the troops stationed there. We were informed that it was an outpost type of military installation and that there was not much in the way of entertainment for the troops stationed there. Our mission was to play for a military "inspection of the troops" parade and later on, a concert.

The whole operation was sort of "hush-hush." My friends and I understood that we were not to ask any questions. We surmised, however, that it must be a secret base used for spying on the Russians. We never found out for sure, but that made our mission more "secretive," and since we were flown in on DC-4s weren't quite sure where we were.

Wildwood Air Station was sort of rustic, surrounded by forests and wilderness. We felt sorry for the personnel stationed there and counted our blessings. The troops there did treat us like VIPs, and we truly felt appreciated.

My job? I was an alto saxophone player, and that's all I did during my eighteen-month tenure in Alaska (1954–1956) . . . just practicing, playing for the constant military and town parades in the area, including the Seward Marathon Race Celebration, concerts, recruiting shows, and the weekly radio show: "The U.S. Army Presents . . . (ta-ta-tah-tah-ta-ta-tah!) . . . the 71st Division Army Band . . . (drum roll)"

> — Blas M. Garza, Ed.D., school administrator and professor, California Lutheran University

---

This 1960 trip was enriched by a déjà vu incident. Driving the Richardson "Highway," we arrived at Paxson's Roadhouse. In my early days, it had been a favorite destination for grayling fishing. The old log landmark was gone, replaced by a nondescript tourist trap totally lacking the rustic charm of a respectable roadhouse. Here is the terminus of a new roadway connecting to the Anchorage-Fairbanks Highway near

Denali Park. A caribou wasn't important to me, but for John it would be a happening. We turned off the hard-surfaced road onto this road. It was bumpy, gravel with chuck holes, and challenging just like the good old days. It sits astraddle of the Alaska Range. A sign warned CLOSED FOR WINTER.

"John, I'm nervous with this two-wheel drive, but let's inspect this road for a few miles. We can do a 180 if it looks scary." It soon did, and I intended to turn around when I saw a Jeep station wagon approaching. The driver looked familiar. It was John Sume and his wife, Ruby, in a vehicle I had sold to them in Seward many years earlier.

They told me that Denny Thompson was flying in hunting parties with his Super Cub on floats. He was based at a lake twenty or so miles behind them. They volunteered to go back so we would have a rescue if we got snowed in.

"I haven't seen Denny since our Caines Head folly," I said. "We have a lot to talk about. Would you lead us to Denny's camp and stick with us until we're out of here?" Alaskan friends will do that.

Denny had several hunting parties scattered around the hills. He volunteered to fly us to a caribou migration route as soon as he retrieved his clients. In the meantime, we bunked in his tent and Ruby cooked for us. The second night a howling wind awakened us. I called across the tent:

"Denny! I'm worried about your plane. Are the tie-downs secure?"

"Don't worry. This tent will go first."

We spotted a caribou herd moving across the crest of a hill, heading toward a lake. Denny landed on the lake, let us off and promised to pick us up later. John shot a medium-sized bull; we butchered it, packed it to the water's edge, and waited. We had brought no sleeping bags or provisions. Winter was breathing down our necks. There was no wood or brush with which to build a fire. Stars were out, but there was no moon. Long after dark, we heard the throb of a plane. Before we could see it, the Super Cub taxied up to where we stood at the lake's edge. This workhorse plane comes with two tandem seats. Floats are an added load. We were three and a caribou plus its rack, which Denny tied to the floats. No wonder this plane is Alaska's favorite.

Strange thing about night flying. There is enough light from the stars to make a lake shine like a mirror. Denny flew past half a dozen lakes until he spotted the silhouette that matched his base lake. One hundred or more feet above landing, the shine disappears. Then it is white-knuckle time until you feel the floats settle onto the water.

The Sumes escorted us back to the Richardson Trail, and we thanked them with a hindquarter. They were going south to Seward. We set course north to Fairbanks, overnighted with Red (my Alcan buddy) and Gladys, and braced for the long ride back to Skagit County.

Approaching Big Delta, I made a prophetic observation: "John, you've seen all the wildlife Alaska has with one exception." As we rounded a curve, we were halted by three buffalo blocking the road.

The settlement of Chicken is a historic option when driving the Alcan. There we had dinner at one of Alaska's few remaining authentic roadhouses. At the Yukon ferry landing, I told John if he'd piss in the river he would be one-third of the way to qualifying as a "sourdough." He declined, and it's just as well because he could never meet the other two requirements.

We crossed the Yukon on a ferry that landed us near Dawson City. It was my first opportunity to visit Robert Service's ghosts.

> There are strange things done in the midnight sun by the men who moil for gold;
> The Arctic trails have their secret tales that would make your blood run cold;
> The Northern Lights have seen queer sights, but the queerest they ever did see
> Was that night on the marge of Lake Lebarge I cremated Sam McGee
>
> — From *Spell of the Yukon,* by Robert Service

As we blissfully cruised down the Alcan, enjoying beautiful fall weather, comfortable in a jazzy car with which I expected to make a windfall profit, I was reminiscing in my mind the changes since my wartime drive in the opposite direction. Near Williams Lake in British Columbia, while on the outside curve of a paved highway, driving cautiously because of school children on the shoulder, an approaching car with driver asleep drifted slowly across the center line.

"John, we can either save the car or save the kids." To save the kids, we took a sideswipe.

1998: My grandson, Philip, wanted a taste of Alaska, and I obliged with one proviso. He must stay until he "knew" the territory. When we stepped off the plane at Anchorage in 1998, the *Daily News* headline told us with a dollar sign that Prudhoe Bay has oiled the economy. "Your Dividend from the Permanent Fund: $1,540."

Alaskans have rewarded themselves with an annual divvy up of the oil money. As of 1998, the fund had over $25 billion stashed away, dispensing its earnings annually. It is off-limits to state spending. Starting in 1982, the fund has paid off like a slot machine to every qualified resident, including infants. Philip started his residency clock, should he decide to go for the oil windfall.

After 44 years, I was back to witness the miracle unleashed by oil. Hope had not changed, except its population had doubled, to 150. The state had been lavish with a new school at a cost of $3 million. I did some quick math and concluded that the fifteen or twenty students could easily retire on the earnings from a nest egg that size.

Grandson, Philip, at Hope

And what of Kenai since my previous visit? Near this hapless little collection of huts of my memory, the first oil was discovered. Platforms were planted in Cook Inlet, a refinery was built out the north road, and easy money has paved the streets. They have names, even sidewalks, lighting, and landscaping. Whoever heard of landscaping in Alaska? Kenai also has a supermarket and an air terminal.

The money must have flowed like a gusher because at a meeting of the Kenai City Council, the discussion centered on what to do with $30 million surplus in the treasury. Mayor John Williams took me on a tour to show me his latest coup—a training school for statewide firefighters. By now my eyes were glazed. The little native village of my memory had joined the big league. I was in shock.

Returning to an old haunt can be risky. On the site of our primitive café where homesteaders soaked up our heat while stretching a ten-cent coffee for hours, now in 1998 sits the Paradisio, where we dine on a gourmet dinner. Across from the site of our gas pumps (the village's only supply in the '40s), is an impressive visitor center. Fishermen who sold their ten-pound red salmon for fifty-seven cents in the '40s now sell by the pound and they are capitalists. Homesteaders who fought mud and mosquitoes and isolation and persevered until their land patents were in hand are now millionaires. They will long be remembered because the highway signs are a roster of their names.

Alaska of my era was populated with self-reliant "characters." Who else would inhabit the woods without utilities, roads, and stores? Jim and Peggy Arness are a prime example. Jim, a Cook Inlet boat captain of the '40s, created a shoreside pier for the oil platforms at a spot deemed impossible because of Cook Inlet tides. Carol Anderson, the Covich's daughter and her husband, Jim, treated us to dinner at the Paradisio. Carol was our daughter's favorite friend. Her brother, David is also a Kenai resident and is married to the daughter of Senator Ted Stevens. So Kenai has an unofficial lobbyist in high places. Carol and Jim live beyond civilization, near the homestead I opted not to prove up on. That's a blooper for which I don't need a reminder.

I wanted my grandson to meet the ultimate homesteader, Rusty Lancashire. It was not a happy encounter. She was now bedridden. We were greeted by her daughter, Martha. We visited with Rusty, but the old fire was missing. I hugged Martha and we drove on. *Thank God for daughters,* was on my mind. It was a prayer I've uttered countless times.

Other favorite pioneers are too numerous to mention. These rugged individualists are rapidly leaving the scene. They are irreplaceable. I miss them.

Discovering how Wildwood had transformed was worth the trip. Even with the military, waste occasionally becomes too ludicrous to hide. And on rare occasions with big government, a token retribution occurs.

In an earlier chapter, I wrote how in the late '30s the Kenai natives were mugged by the Feds. A survey team for the CAA (now FAA) encircled their ancient village and pronounced by edict that it was now government owned to provide a reservation for the airport facility. There was no mention of due process.

Martha Lancashire Merry with Philip

With the passage of the Alaska Native Claims Settlement Act in 1971, Congress tried to give the natives some form of restitution. To be recipients required the creation of tribal entities. Our friend George Miller led his Kenaitze people in a sort of endurance game against big government. George and his people came away with the biggest prize imaginable—a deed to Wildwood Air Force Sta-

George Miller—Receiving the Deed to Wildwood

tion from the government! The whole kit 'n kaboodle! March 1974. It's next to impossible to close a military operation, no matter how useless. This time was the exception. The Indians stuck it to the cavalry.

Two Exiles in the Back of the Bus

A travel itch attacked me in the '80s. Like Ferdinand Magellan, I felt I needed to circle the globe. Unlike Magellan, I chose the northern route through the USSR, which meant Siberia, and that permits a side trip to a most unique lake.

Natasha's tour duties were at rest and now our guide was relaxing beside me on the bus returning our group from Lake Baykal to Irkutsk. For a change, she would ask the questions and in better English than mine: "What prompted you to cross Siberia to visit us?"

"I feel that once in a traveler's lifetime he needs to prove to himself the earth is not flat. Seriously, it was curiosity about your railroad. And nostalgia. When I saw the telegraph tripods I knew I was revisiting permafrost. You see, I, too, have lived in the arctic. Our cabin sat on permafrost. I've been stuck in the mud of a spring thaw, and I know why wood is stacked near the back door. What I'm seeing is reminiscent of Alaska when I went there in the thirties."

Natasha's interest quickened. "Did you stay long? Were you forced to go?"

"In a way I was forced. Our country was in an economic depression. I was fresh out of school and unemployed. Lots of other young people were in the same fix. Work could be found in Alaska, so I shipped north. I felt secure, so stayed fifteen years. Why are you in Siberia?"

"Mr. Thornton, it sounds like we have a kinship. You chose Alaska for the same reason my husband and I chose Siberia. Economic freedom. Here our pay is higher, our housing better, and the vacations longer. How was your housing in America's Siberia?"

"Sometimes grim. My wife and I learned to build our own. We started married life in a log cabin, similar to many we've seen along your railroad. Often we lived without utilities, and I should add we sometimes froze our butts. Since most of our friends were in the same fix, it was easier to be content, so we took it as par for the course—that's a bourgeois term, isn't it? With World War II, our housing got even worse until I made sergeant. How did your parents fare during the war?"

"They didn't. Our house was burned. I was raised by an aunt. But tell me more about your Alaskan exile. Surely you could have left had you chosen?"

"Yes, but not readily. In the early stage of the war, my wife was evacuated by the Army because I was a key employee. I endured a lonely year before I got a work permit to transfer to the states and rejoin my wife and see my newborn daughter. We still had housing troubles, so out of desperation we returned to Fairbanks where we still owned our little log house. We toughed it out, and as often as we could save enough money, we took a trip to the lower states to thaw out. Natasha, do you get vacations?"

"Of course. And we don't have to wait two years to save enough money. Ours are free, three weeks a year. We go to the Crimea. It's a Black Sea Resort with warm sandy beaches, balmy breezes. I think you would love Yalta. Do Alaskans get warm vacations?"

"Sure, well maybe. Natasha, could you and your family leave if you want to?"

"It is possible, but I'd run the risk of not getting another job this good. And our daughter might not have as good a school. Would you excuse me? We are nearing our hotel and I must make the announcements."

Phil Wilson and the Feds

One thing I hoped to see in Kenai is a memorial to Phil Wilson. It is deserved. He was the key to creation of the Kenai Township. After the CAA hijacked the settlement for a "Federal Reserve," somehow Phil knew he and other native had rights. He had the tenacity to pursue their claim, wresting ownership away from the Feds.

Phil and Fiocla had several children. They were in and about our place and played with our daughters. Now I could visit with one of their sons I chanced to meet at the King's Inn Motel.

Could I ask you some questions? I see you're driving an expensive pickup. Do you own one of the nice homes I've seen?
"Yup."

I know the Alaska Natives Claims Settlement Act (ANCSA)

signed in 1971, was a landmark change in Federal attitude. You natives came out of the Statehood shuffle with a big chunk of land and a billion dollars. You fellows must have learned a bit from seeing what happened to the Native Americans in Colonial days? "Yup"

I read where you Natives got about a tenth of the land. Does that mean 44-million acres? "Yup"

Well,. Congress is tough, so I presume Ted Stevens was working for you? "Yup"

Did I hear the loot got parceled out to thirteen Native Regions and your Cook Inlet Region has annual revenues of maybe $200 million? That's big business! So the money must have been wisely invested? "Yup"

As I hear there were only 80,000 Alaska Natives when ANCSA was signed and your district has only 6900 members? You must all be getting fat dividend checks? "Yup"

Wilson, I've enjoyed this visit and I've learned a lot. May I quote you in my book? "Nope"

Phil Wilson's little daughter, Phyllis, now grown and charming, is the proprietor of her own business. When she took Philip and me in tow, I felt honored. I told Mrs.Bookey a memorial to her father is needed and I'd be happy to chip in. I hope someday to get a solicitation.

This trip's mission was accomplished. I left the grandson in Anchorage to fend for himself. Philip Jerge is smart. I doubted if he'd make a sourdough but I knew he could survive. When my plane climbed out, returning me to the lower forty eight, Mount McKinley came into full view. Such majesty! I sort of wished I was staying with Philip.Returning to an old haunt awakens emotions of what should-have-been. My overly busy Kenai lifestyle deprived me of many encounters more important than making a living. Fifty years late, I am enjoying two authors/poets/composers I barely noticed as Kenai kids: Jackie Bemson, the step-daughter of our Road Commission boss, has helped me with editing and pictures; and Arlene, the daughter of our Kenai postmaster, has graciously permitted me to borrow from her book,[*] sentiments to conclude this chapter.

Alaska . . . a beautiful but frigid mistress:
She would test you, she would take you
She would bend you and would break you
As she beckons with here tantalizing song
She would steal your dreams and haunt them
'Til you swear that you don't want them,
Then she'd cast you out and back where you belong.

But oh, my friend, the glory,
As you undertake the story
That unfolds, and taste the challenge of each day.
You will know when life is ended,
Though you're broken, or you're bended,
That you've lived a life somewhere along the way!
                    Lisa (Arlene Rheingans) Augustine

---

[*] *The Dragline Kid* by Lisa Augustine. (2000) Hardscratch Press (Jackie Benson Pels) Walnut Creek, CA.

Part Two: Preface to Gospel of the Wilderness

A ndy Rooney, Art Buchwald, Garrison Keillor, and Dave Barry are my inspiration. Curmudgeons all. I wish I could match them. They all have their special way of showing their annoyance with the system. They have the media to go public with it. I have only this book. Even though I am lucky in a thousand ways, I have every bit as many annoyances as these celebrated writers

Recently at a bridge social, a friend surprised me with "I

Persevere for sixty years and a few of your family and friends will drop by

thought you were a Republican!" She has known me for a long time and thought I was a Republican? I can't let these rumors circulate. Neither am I a Democrat. I am registered Independent, but in truth *I'm a political agnostic,* hopelessly out of the mainstream. I need to go on record.

I literally began life in the ministry. I was born in a parsonage. A parsonage in Kansas. That's Bible Belt country. With that distinction, I feel entitled to sermonize. Or, quoting Snoopy, another author of note, "I'm writing from a sense of need. You can't just sleep all day." I have been warned that if I turn this book into a pulpit, astute readers will conclude what my editor tells me: "Hal, what you want to do won't work." Well, just to disprove her, I will sign off with a happy ending.

for an anniversary potluck, June 2001. Photo by Peggy Jo Love House.

My values and priorities are important to me. Peace, the environment, religious tolerance, overpopulation, resource sustainability (overconsumption), and the importance of family—advocating for these concerns is my "Gospel of the Wilderness." Call me a liberal if you must, but I claim to be a conservationist—a conservative who wants a decent planet for his heirs. I don't think I stand alone in this.

Like Andy Rooney, yes, I'm a disgruntled curmudgeon. "That claim is fraudulent," says Maryellen Kelley, a program manager for our Adult Ed classes. She specializes in seniors and refuses to accept that old codgers are irascible. She teases me with a paraphrase from Yeats: "Hal has an abiding sense of tragedy which sustains him during temporary periods of joy."

If only I could be famous, my sermonizing could draw a bigger audience. Never happen, so I'm resigned to obscurity. Happily, there's another way I will achieve fame—the progeny route. Jeannette and Joyce and Janell must have our genes. These three surpass us. They have blended their genes with their spouses', and to our delight, we have grandchildren we think will be geniuses. This bloodline will be extended exponentially, and it seems logical there's a miracle down the line. It should work the same as dynamite. As the DuPonts have demonstrated, by mixing the right three inert ingredients, you get a blast. So someday in the far-off, I may acquire vicarious fame because of my descendants.

Thus dear reader, even though the following pages project a wilderness seen through the mind of a skeptic, a message of hope intrudes. If this ancient pessimist is optimistic, who can doubt?

9

Family: The Ultimate Security Blanket

The Creator has given us humans one fundamental social group that is cohesive and more prone to love than to fight: Family!

Family is a cooperative that a person can trust. The mating instinct that results in family has been universal for all of recorded history. Without a family, a person has been cheated; with a family, a person is blessed. I am one of the lucky.

Upstairs in a "parsonage" was my maternity ward. It is where I was born. This was the term for the minister's housing and was usually next door to the church. So it became an extension of the church. My family (I had one older sister) ate, slept, and recreated church.

"Christian" was the label for dad's church, which is confusing because all Protestant churches think they are Christian. There were and are distinctive differences. The Church of Christ was better known as "Disciples," or in Father's case as "Camelites," named for Alexander Campbell who had a divine revelation. This persuasion believed communion must be served every Sunday and baptism must be by immersion. At age eight, father called me to his study, told me I had reached the "age of accountability." He gave me a sobering discourse, then asked if I felt ready for baptism. I decided yes, father immersed me in front of the congregation, and presumably my sins were washed away. So officially I'm "saved" or "born again."

My father's church study was a library of theology, history, and geography. I had access to the wisdom of the era, what little there was in the '20s, but of course I was too young to benefit.

Lifestyle for a Midwest Bible Belt preacher's kid meant two Sunday services, prayer meeting Wednesday night, weddings and funerals, and Bible study in between. Plus, the preacher's kid had to wash the communion glasses, distribute the hymnbooks to the pews, and check the water in the baptistery.

Until after World War II, most kids did chores. We split firewood and carried it in, carried ashes out, pumped water, hoed the vegetable garden, fed the chickens, and ran to the store. It didn't leave a lot of opportunity for mischief, but it wasn't all bad and was on-the-job-training.

Kids sat on the curb chewing grass, speculating on whence came babies, played hockey on skates in the street, bicycled into the country, strolled along the river, and hiked on the railroad tracks. For spending money, we delivered papers and/or sold them on the street; we prowled the alleys in search of any junk that would sell. We were the forerunners of recycling. Supervised play had not been invented. Before television and computers, time was consumed by chores, invent-your-own-game, and hiking to school.

Both of my parents were gypsies by nature, and travel was my fringe benefit. We crisscrossed the country, visited national parks, and learned a lot about Model Ts. Mother did. Father read the Bible and prayed for the flivver while mom patched a tire or hiked for water for the radiator.

Family life during the '20s and '30s was austere by today's standards, but since most people were in the same boat we didn't think of ourselves as "poor." My father took me to baseball games, we never missed a circus, and ministers were given movie passes. Movies were safe because there were no X-rated movies, no obscenity, and no computer-generated violence. My worst and only sin might be to sneak into a movie because I lacked a dime. It's forgivable when Douglas Fairbanks is playing *The Black Pirate* and I have spent all my money on Hershey bars.

A church lucky enough to call my father got two for the price of one. It was not unusual for the pastor's wife to fill most, or all, of the church voids. My mother, the product of a work ethic Midwest family, was dad's crew. She played piano, was song leader, taught a Sunday school class, arranged socials, and was the janitor. If my father was away, she filled in at the pulpit. And why not? She was ordained, and long before the feminists marched. The only thing lacking in her job description was child rearing. So she was less than perfect.

As role models, I can't knock my parents. No smoking, drinking, gambling, profanity. My sister and I were as pure as Ivory soap.

There were no Jews or Catholics in our orbit. I well remember when an itinerant crusader used dad's church for an anti-Catholic pep rally, showing graphic slides of torture during the inquisition. It should have been X-rated. My innocent mind was imbedded with a torture chip, and I lived many a nightmare before I accepted that Catholics are very possibly decent people, even though they couldn't go to God's exclusive Protestant heaven.

Parsonages were the antonym for permanence. That suited my dad because he favored changing churches until he found the perfect climate. One of his short stints was Santa Maria. It is in Central California and separated from Santa Barbara by only seventy miles and the Santa Ynez Mountains. Had he only known and nursed the Model T over the pass, his search could have been over.

We lived in a cozy and cloistered social environment. Just your semi-normal and semi-happy parsonage dwellers. As a pastor, my dad was personable and persuasive, with the result that my parents had a host of friends, many who would travel to the next county to hear a sermon they had heard before. Had TV been invented, dad had the potential to be a Billy Graham or a Robert Schuller—except my father heard God tell him to go ballistic on prophecy. My daddy took the Book of Revelation on the road, and thereafter Armageddon was in, homemaking was out. It was an easy abandonment because his home was in heaven. A good career went to waste.

It took me years to get my father's influence out of my life—both his lack of permanence and his religious dogma. It surprises my wife that I have clung to the same Santa Barbara dwelling for thirty-three years, and it is where I intend to end my life. It is a home that enshrines our reunions, festive occasions, and memories. I wish everyone could have such luck.

Jeanne and I married in an era of simplicity. When living is austere, when the future is scary, when children are the top priority, staying together is the best option. During our marriage startup, the role of each spouse was well defined. We were guided by tradition. I went to work in the morning to make a living to support the home. My wife also went to work. Her trade was *homemaking* and Jeanne concentrated on home. When I arrived from work, she gave it a special feeling. It worked for sixty-two years. I'm sure that when both spouses are employed, the priorities change. I'm sure it is far more difficult.

The Creator could have done better for the unlucky and could have remedied a complication that befalls those of us who were lucky. I'm not complaining. I just think one vow in the wedding ritual could be improved. "Till death do us part" is a bum arrangement. There should be a better way. How easy it would have been for the Creator to dispatch us out of this life together. No, unless it's a car accident or a cruise sinking, we depart alone, leaving the remaining partner to cry over the vacant chair, clean up the red tape, empty the closet, adjust to going solo, and return to the relationship wilderness. God has the power to save us from this sorrow. Except, as most of us discover the hard way, if you fix one thing, something else breaks. God may know that, too.

The lines from *Fiddler on the Roof* are set in concrete on our veranda: "Sunrise, sunset, swiftly fly the years. One season following another, laden with happiness and tears."

Jeanne and I have a family that is an ecumenical mixing pot. It defies explanation. My wife has Methodist roots. Our first daughter married a son of Greek immigrants with Eastern Orthodox tradition. I have observed in the Soviet Union the firm grasp this church holds over its adherents, but it came unstuck for Tom Delimitros, a self-made Harvard MBA, successful in venture capital. Jeannette and Tom appear to be on the fringe of Presbyterian worship but never discuss doctrine with me. Their children, Jason and Kate, also have the subject on mute.

Joyce Jerge, our second daughter, was given a Lutheran twist and a tryout year at Pacific Lutheran U. Then she married a doctor with solid Roman Catholic roots. I see no Catholic residue showing with this mother and her three children. Courtney, Kirsten, and Philip show lots of independence and individuality. They are competent to decide what religion works for them without missionary help from this grandfather.

Our youngest daughter seemed to have no religious propensities. She married an ultra-successful man of Jewish parentage. Imagine my amazement at seeing my gentile maverick ushering her three children through the Temple's rituals. Rosie, the youngest of the three Lewis children, has just now attained Bat Mitzvah. It was her thirteenth birthday and qualified for this rite of passage. Not exactly true. She qualified by learning Hebrew. Jeanne and I, with our entire family sitting in the front row, are hearing this granddaughter read parts of the Shabbat service in Hebrew.

It is a proud moment when the Rabbi calls on siblings Sarah and Riley and all of Rosie's cousins to surround her as she opens the Ark so the Torah may be removed. As the Rabbi invites us grandparents to join the procession that carries the Torah through the congregation, our emotions are profound, and more so because we're walking on ground donated by the paternal grandparents. We sense that we are saluting a long tradition, an ancient history.

As Rosie reads from the Torah and is draped with the tallit shawl, she is proclaimed a daughter of the Covenant. It's our third time to see one of the Lewis grandchildren declare their commitment to the tradition and respect for the family. It is their transition from child to adult. No, let's make that semi-adult. I'm not comfortable with their taking on the baggage of adulthood—not yet, please.

Come evening, the ceremony is capped by a party the likes of which I haven't seen in Christendom. Janell and Randall, and their friends, sponsor an extravaganza. Professional merrymakers pour on the hilarity. Rosie and the rest of our grandchildren are somewhere in a laughing, jumping, dancing jamboree of fifty or a hundred youths of all ages, plus as many parents. Near the bedtime hour, the announcer clears the floor so we ancients can also dance, and we do. There are no fights, no drunks, no rowdiness. It was a love fest from start to finish. Mazel tov! Shalom!

As I watched our three daughters and our eight grandchildren (including Jason who had just revealed that Nicole is carrying our first great-grandchild), I'm asking myself "Did Jeanne and I launch this!"

Bonuses keep coming! This year Jeanne and I did a travel workout to witness the statewide Geography Bee. Riley, our fourteen-year-old grandson, came in second and won a globe and a check, compliments of the National Geographic Society. (I occasionally come in second; if it's in a field of two. But Riley won in a field of ninety-eight.) It was another proud moment. My kids are my easy claim to achievement, done vicariously. Since my parents were geography wise, I want to believe some of that filtered down through the genes. It's just a fantasy.

Weddings have been on my mind since a box office smash, *My Big Fat Greek Wedding.* It brought to mind a local happening reported in the news as a $5 million wedding. This was when dot-com high rollers were raking in a blizzard of money generated by Wall Street. I wasn't invited, even though I was a stockholder in the company that made it possible (My ten-cent stock in the groom's bankrupt company has now dropped to two cents. I told my broker to hold because it is bound to go lower.)

Recently, our granddaughter Kirsten married Phillip, a companion of several years, after an engagement of nearly one year. It was a beautiful production. Friends and relatives came from far and wide and made loving and generous contributions. There was just a lot of hugging and kissing, and the spirit of the party ran its true value through the roof, so I concluded the $$-budget of a wedding is not an accurate measure.

My friend Larry was a guest. He has had a lot of experience, so I ask if he thought a $5 million wedding was a happier event than Kirsten and Phillip's.

"Hal, it doesn't work that way. Hugging and kissing at a rich bash can get one's pockets picked."

It is just another illustration of how to be rich without working for it. I got my fair share of hugs and kisses at this family wedding, and for an ancient grandfather that's priceless. Daily, my life is enriched by family, and also by friends. They are all my benefactors.

When a guy proposes to a girl, having children and grandchildren is not what is on his mind. I proposed to Jeanne sixty-two years ago and the memory lingers of how terribly I muffed it. (I daresay, a multitude of guys can say the same.) Had I been mature enough to comprehend the gravity of marriage, had I been rational with 20/20 foresight, had I rehearsed . . .

I would start with singing "Love look at the two of us, strangers in many ways . . ." Then I would come on with —

The disclaimer: *"Jeanne, I confess it is long past the hour you are due home and my rented car is hopelessly stuck in this mud hole, and we are stranded in an Arctic wilderness. You are thinking I'm a stupid jerk with a lot to learn. I have no roots. We know war clouds are gathering. I'll probably need to join up. This will not be the last mud hole."*

Next the soft sell: *"Despite the tough times, I foresee enough good times. If we face life together, the good times will over-shadow the bad times, and if we are lucky we will outlast the war and my mistakes and someday I will get it right."*

Now the clincher: *"If you will marry me, we will love each other and keep each other safe and warm. We will face the world together. We will parent a family! And if we persevere, with the help of our children and our grandchildren **we will climb a stairway to the stars.**"*

The life we've lived has turned our hair white.

10

God's Wilderness: The Gates of the Arctic

Wilderness appealed to those bored or disgusted with man and his works. It not only offered an escape from society but also was an ideal stage for the Romantic individual to exercise the cult that he frequently made of his own soul. The solitude and total freedom of the wilderness created a perfect setting for either melancholy or exultation.
— Roderick Nash,
Wilderness and the American Mind

Alaska's natural wilderness was a physical challenge to those who ventured near. It was severe but surmountable. And in the '30s, it seemed limitless. However, when the Pilgrims arrived on this continent, Massachusetts had seemed inexhaustible, as did the Louisiana Purchase. At the time of the '49 gold rush, California seemed inexhaustible.

Often I've been asked how I feel about the oil intrusion in Alaska. Friends know I'm an environmentalist and Alaska-smart even though I'm out of touch. I cop out on this with a disclaimer:

"When I lived in the territory, the wilderness was not something we protected. More likely, we felt it was an obstacle to overcome. It made life austere. When there's more of it than you can comprehend, you tend to shrug it off. But wake up. Folks my age can remember when Yosemite and the Grand Canyon were lonely places. In a short half-century, most of our great attractions are suffocated. Humans wall-to-wall, always with a sprinkling of litterbugs and graffiti nuts.

When there were only a billion humans and the Japanese didn't have money for travel, one Yosemite could entertain all comers. My parents and I could gather at Camp Curry's amphitheater with seats to spare and listen for "Let the fire fall!" Now, in a world of 5 billion humans, the fire does not fall. Too much risk, too much liability, and it pollutes. When population quadruples and money is plentiful but there is still only one Yosemite, we humans overrun the place. The problem is not with wilderness. It is *population*. I must discuss it with God.

"God, You've created a big problem. When You told Noah and his sons to be fruitful and multiply and fill the earth, You must have been out of Your mind! Do you realize what You've done?"

"Harold, I don't understand. I gave the command to only eight people. I envisioned a fertile little valley of farmers where everyone had his own vineyard and it was wine and roses. Read Genesis 9:3. The narrator tells how good it should be."

"Good Lord! Have You heard of exponential growth? You're supposed to be omniscient. You must have known there would be 5 billion people and counting. They all want to live near the fleshpots. And fight for elbowroom. They all want cars. Our cities have become the parking lots from hell. The streets are plugged. We're not allowed to drive along the Grand Canyon rim. Road rage is us."

"Oh! Really? That bad? Why haven't your systems put a cap

on growth? I admit I didn't foresee that medical tech would keep people from dying. As for cars, I gave each human two legs, well designed for walking. Incidentally, you shouldn't be cell-phoning when driving."

"God Almighty! Can't You see this traffic isn't moving."

It did not seem possible to threaten the Alaska wilderness in the '30s. In the entire interior, along the Yukon, along the Alaska Railroad's 400 miles from Seward to Fairbanks, there were fewer than 11,000 humans, native and white. Now Fairbanks alone has four times that population and Anchorage a quarter million, not counting military. Who can guess the future? Who can guess continuing population buildup? What impact on the wilderness? One can be sure most of the males intend to shoot a moose or a caribou. There will be RVs and campers along every hot fishing stream. And Mount Denali's peak will need a comfort station and an oxygen refill concessionaire.

The following speech, attributed to Chief Seattle, expresses a dedication for this planet. The Chief didn't say the words for which he gets credit, but we can be sure it mirrors his feelings—and speaks for devout environmentalists:

> The President in Washington sends word that he wishes to buy our land. But how can you buy or sell the sky? The land? If we do not own the freshness of the air and the sparkle of the water, how can you buy them?
>
> Every part of the earth is sacred to my people. Every shining pine needle, every sandy shore, every mist in the dark woods, every meadow, every humming insect. We are part of the earth and it is part of us. The perfumed flowers are our sisters. The bear, the

deer, the great eagle, these are our brothers. All are holy in the memory and experience of my people.

This we know: the earth does not belong to man, man belongs to the earth. All things are connected like the blood that unites us all. Man did not weave the web of life, he is merely a strand in it. Whatever he does to the web he does to himself.

One thing we know: our God is also your God. The earth is precious to Him and to harm the earth is to heap contempt upon its Creator.

Gates of the Arctic

President Jimmy Carter consummated the greatest single act of wilderness preservation in world history when, in 1980, he signed the Alaska National Interest Lands Conservation Act. This protected 100 million acres of federal land, including Gates of the Arctic[*] National Park and Preserve.

This park is bigger than Delaware, Massachusetts, and Connecticut combined. If there is a genuine wilderness left, this is it. The government did something smart. This park will not be geared for spectators. You might call it user-*un*friendly. There will be no marked trails, no warning signs, no food services, just limitless space, the way God made it.

Gates of the Arctic has a few thousand visitors a year. Most go in by floatplanes from Bettles. They have bears for companions, the Brooks Range for a climbing challenge, tundra for aggravated hiking, and numerous rivers. One being the John River. Should these hardy explorers decide to

[*] See "Gates of the Arctic," by Jon Krakauer, *Smithsonian*, June 1995.

float down to the Koyukuk River they can visit the site of our trading post (1940 era; described in Chapter 3). Jeanne and I will not be there to greet them, but had we decided to wait it out for fifty years, we could have been the outfitters for a needy tribe of backpackers.

If Gates of the Arctic becomes congested, there's an alternative piece of wild land in a trackless retreat named Wrangell-St. Elias National Park and Preserve* in Southeast Alaska. Its 13 million acres ranks it the biggest spread in the National Park system. Mount St. Elias reaches heavenward 18,000 feet, the second highest peak in the United States. (It may be visible from your cruise ship if the weather is perfect.) God and His weather have placed this national park off-limits to tour buses, motor homes, and vandals.

It is interesting to speculate on gold mining versus conservation in early times. Imagine an EIR (environmental impact report) for placer mining. The planning director wants a recital from the developer:

"First, we strip away all tundra. It's worthless. Sorry. That lets us get to the topsoil. We call it overburden. It's no good, so it gets sluiced away. Somewhere. Maybe into a river. Sorry. Now we deal with the permafrost. This gives employment to young bucks[†] strong enough to drive "points" to thaw the permafrost. Gotta do it. It hides the gold. Next we divert a creek into a dredge pond. How else to float a ship full of machinery? Now the dredge will clank along, throwing the tailings behind. Tailing piles sort of break the monotony of

---

[*] See *National Geographic*, March 2003.
[†] Young men from the Lower 48 regularly converged on Fairbanks in the spring, hoping for a job with "F. E. Company" (Fairbanks Exploration) in their placer fields. The job was hard work and paid ninety cents per hour.

tundra. Once we get the gold, we sell it to the government and it's buried again in Fort Knox. So the gold is sort of recycled—underground to underground. Make sense?"

"When you finish with the site what do you do?"

"We move the dredge to the next claim and start over again."

Pat, one of our bachelor group in Fairbanks, was a rep for a wholesaler. He needed to call on Martin Slisco's roadhouse in Wiseman and invited me to join him. We were 150 miles north of the Arctic Circle, flying over an expanse so vast, so impassable, so useless. The bush pilot agreed to return for us at an appointed time. He told us it would be after dark, so when he buzzes the village, some of the Natives must set out Coleman lanterns to mark the landing strip.

"How will you find this place?" I ask.

"It's easy. I'll follow the Koyukuk (River)."

Before the days of FAA and VFR navigation, terrain provided the flight vectors. Alaska has so many landmarks it is easy for a pilot, plane or boat, to home in. Weather permitting. Bush pilots were akin to the wilderness and respected its dominance. A book by Harmon Helmericks titled *The Last of the Bush Pilots*[*] describes vividly the men who have made a legend of wilderness travel. Helmericks hop-skipped around the Brooks Range and frequented the landing field for our John River Trading Post—however, it was many years after we surrendered to economic reality. He describes Alaska as we remember it and lived it, a time before jets and pressurized cabins and flight attendants.

---

[*] *The Last of the Bush Pilots,* by Harmon Helmericks (New York: Alfred A. Knopf, 1969).

> There is just one hope of repulsing the tyrannical ambition of civilization to conquer every niche on the whole earth. That hope is the organization of spirited people who will fight for the freedom of the wilderness.
>
> — Robert Marshall, 1930[*]

Any library contains countless volumes on early Alaska times and on the impact of the wilderness. These are writers far better than I. Here are a few of my favorites.

John McPhee's *Coming into the Country.*[†] This book is part of a trilogy. Book one focused on the northern tree line, the second book is about urban Alaska, and book three covers the interior bush country. This trilogy is a compilation of stories that first appeared in *The New Yorker Magazine* in 1977. The writer foresaw the importance of conservation.

Tisha: The Story of a Young Teacher in the Alaska Wilderness.[‡] Anne Hobbs's true story as told to Robert Specht is an adventure full of energy and ideals. Anne treks across the northern tundra to become schoolmarm in the remote gold rush settlement of Chicken. The winter was a problem, of course, but not as serious as racial prejudice. A lone white woman in a man's world beyond the edge. What a challenge.

This Was the North[§] by Anton Money with Ben East. It would be easy to call Anton a crazy Englishman, staying out

---

[*] Marshall was an urbanite, howbeit wilderness lover, instrumental in shaping federal policy in the '30s.

[†] *Coming into the Country,* by John McPhee (New York: Farrar, Straus and Giroux, 1977). Text originally in *The New Yorker Magazine,* for whom McAfee is a staff writer. Twelve previous books published by Farrar, Straus and Giroux.

[‡] *Tisha: The Story of a Young Teacher in the Alaska Wilderness,* as told to Robert Specht (New York: St. Martin's Press, 1976).

[§] *This Was the North,* by Anton Money, with Ben East (New York: Crown, 1975).

in the midday sun. Gold lured him into the Yukon wilderness. In 1923, he made his way up Canada's Stikine River to hell-and-gone in the backcountry. Anton and I have a bit in common. Both of us had the itch, fled from civilization, and found young wives. We both won the consolation prize. We both struck it rich, not from gold but by retiring in a choice place. I persuaded Anton to entertain our Rotary Club, hoping my friends would assume my experiences were as death-defying as Money's. Anton lived through a dozen flirts with early death in the wilds but survived to succumb in the comforts of Santa Barbara.

> Yet we're hard as cats to kill
> And our hearts are reckless still
> And we've danced with death a dozen times or so.
> — From the "Rhyme of the Restless Ones"
>   by Robert Service

*Wilderness and the American Mind** by Roderick Nash (another Santa Barbaran), is a broad view of conservation and ecology that relies heavily on most of America's best minds: Henry David Thoreau, Aldo Leopold, John Muir, Robert Marshall to name a few. William O. Douglas said it best:

> This book is a mandatory prelude to any modern treatment of conservation problems. It does not purport to tell us where we go from here. But it tells us how we got where we are and the nature of the forces that have driven us pell-mell toward a leveling of the wilderness.

---

* *Wilderness and the American Mind,* by Roderick Nash (New Haven, CT: Yale University Press, 1967).

Don George handed me the book, *The Island Within*. It is set in Alaska, a place with which my friends readily connect me. Don knows I'm a curmudgeon in need of venting and that Richard Nelson's book *The Island Within*[*] would calm me.

A few years ago, at La Casa de Maria Retreat Center where I had served as executive director for 28 years, I met David Brower. He was the fiery voice of the Sierra Club, and I had invited him to participate in a conference that was asking the question, "How can we change our thinking from linear to holistic." Like my friend Hal Thornton, David loved to look at "what ifs." The eternal questions that have a way of stimulating thought. David also had this way of hooking me by saying, as he paused, "If you would just think about it for a moment" and then he would pause again to make sure I had.

When I gave Hal the book *The Island Within*, it really was intended to give him the experience of pausing and remembering how truly remarkable his time in Alaska had been. It was his time to grasp the wonders of nature. And Hal, if you just think about it . . . it worked.

— Don George, administrator, theologian, and philosopher

The story contains good headline stuff: sex (a buck courting a doe), violence (an ocean storm lashing the coastline), and adventure (climbing a mountain). In Nelson's pages, the whole stream is alive with salmon: schools and clusters of them, whirling in the deep ponds and swimming with their backs half exposed to the shallows, all working to hold their places against the current like birds flying into the wind.

The book Don handed me has a bit of harassment: "The

---

[*] *The Island Within*, by Richard K. Nelson (New York: Vintage Books, 1991).

eagle is perched in a treetop at the woods' edge, and two ravens swoop around it like songbirds harassing a hawk. It glares up and threatens with opened beak, then launches out over the water. The ravens shadow along, diving against the eagle's back." I'm reading about the problems of society mirrored in nature.

Don has given me a book that doesn't even have a plot! I knew I wouldn't get far in it but randomly glanced at an inner page: "Timber slugs are the gentlest and most peaceful of creatures, slipping silently along on saturated stomachs, sensing their way with stalked antennae, feeding on the forest's loamy decay. They epitomize the cool jungle wetness of this place—soft clouds, dark as evening, damp as mist, bellies full of rain."

When the headlines leave me dismayed, I pick up *The Island Within*. It transports me from the insane society that entraps me to a natural-world order where miracles are commonplace and violence makes sense. I have several friends who suffer frustrations similar to mine. I hope they'll find their own island within and also want to pass it on.

> Whenever the light of civilization falls upon you with a blighting power . . . go to the wilderness. . . . Dull business routine, the fierce passions of the market place, the perils of envious cities become but a memory. . . . The wilderness will take hold of you. It will give you good red blood; it will turn you from a weakling into a man. . . . You will soon behold all with a peaceful soul.
>
> — George S. Evans (1904)

216

11
Man's Wilderness: Peace, Politics, Prejudice, and Parents

"Wilderness: an extensive area that is barren or empty, a waste" (American Heritage Dictionary). Preferable: Woods in which it is easy to get lost.

Alaska's natural wilderness was a physical challenge and it was surmountable. Life therein was too busy to prioritize the really big challenges. We moved stateside and took a broader look at the world. Now I perceive that human society has wilderness in many disguises, each far more formidable than Nature's Wilderness in Alaska.

Relationship Wilderness

The human need for a special someone to be with is a first priority. Very few individuals wish to hike alone the pilgrim trail through life. The Creator installed in most all forms of life the mating urge, and there seems to be no antidote for it. For those who are lucky, it is a fateful blessing, and for those who are not lucky, it is a nagging hunger.

How do I know this? Not from experience. I sometimes

read the personal columns in the paper: men seeking women, women seeking men, lonely souls seeking someone, anyone. Urgent messages that say, "Find me, I'm a great person!" For the unlucky, the search within the human wilderness is aggravating and endless. John or Jane Doe must believe the right person is there, waiting to be found, also searching, also lost in the multitude.

The Divine Omnipotence has installed in all living creatures the instinct to mate. How much better if it had given humankind a built-in homing radio that would identify and lead to the perfect companion. The lucky find romance by some chance of fate. Some of the unlucky nearly succeed sometimes, then have to start over, and over. They lose precious years, the lawyers cash in, the courts assess the losses. Others among the unlucky keep searching. It is not fair. I fault the Creator for not devising a better system.

I am convinced of one fateful reality: Not everyone finds someone they can grow to love and make love with. It is such a very random chance. Those who do find that other person whose being kindles the fires of passion, those who know beyond doubt that a mate will be there through life's trials and triumphs, the ups and downs, the ins and outs—they are indeed lucky. If they're luckier still, they realize how lucky they are, and spend their life protecting what they have.

Ethnic Wilderness

Human history is awash in man's injustice to man, and much of it is ethnic strife. The Holocaust is the most ghastly injustice in modern memory, and the Nazis were the worst, beyond compare. Hitler's blind hatred of the Jews deprived Germany of some of its finest scientific minds and skilled craftsmen. Only a maniac could do what Hitler did. The Russians are guilty of pograms; the Spanish were brutal to the Incas and Aztecs, to the Jews and Muslims; the Turks tried to exterminate the Armenians. What made the Japanese so brutal? Not only to the U.S. troops as attested by the Bataan March and their POW camps but also to their fellow-Asians. The record of atrocities confirms that abominable behavior knows no color lines.

It is sad to review our own country's history. The United States should be above ethnic abuse because of our origin. The noble words in the Declaration of Independence and the protections of our Constitution are testimony to our good intentions. Something went terribly wrong. Whether from misguided manifest destiny or wartime hysteria, our country has at times trampled on the rights of ethnic outcasts. Our so-called Christian nation felt entitled to inflict genocide on the natives of the plains, on the natives of Florida, and then our guns went global.

When I drive Highway 395 to Mammoth, I stop at a sign marking Manzanar where 10,000 Japanese were imprisoned because of wartime hysteria. It is a painful reminder that World War II was an excuse to incarcerate 120,000 Japanese, many of them second-generation citizens, none guilty of impeding the war effort. False assumptions by the commanding officer of the Western Defense Command fed a widespread resentment of Asiatic intrusion on the West Coast. Prejudice spawned a groundswell of ethnic anger that culminated in Executive Order 9066, signed by President Roosevelt, February 19, 1942. Can one signature deprive 120,000 innocent people of the protection of our constitution? Yes, the mob psychology of war inflicts lamentable behavior.

At what cost-benefit, this Japanese punishment? The building of ten internment camps was a drain on our labor and material. We squandered an estimated $80 million. We fed, housed, guarded, and forced idleness on producers of food that would have nourished our own defense workers.

Forty-six years expired before our country admitted this imprisonment had been a mistake of terrifically horrible proportions. It was wrong, and those still living were entitled to restitution. The language of Congress's Civil Liberties Act of 1988 carries a message to bigots, to racists, and to future leaders:

> These actions were carried out without adequate security reasons and without any acts of espionage or sabotage documented . . . and were motivated largely by racial prejudice, wartime hysteria, and a failure of political leaderships.
>
> For these fundamental violations of the basic civil liberties and constitutional rights of these individuals of Japanese ancestry, the Congress apologizes on behalf of the nation.

This belated act of contrition was signed by President Ronald Reagan, August 10, 1988.

The $20,000 restitution didn't match the immensity of the wrong, but it was an important symbolic token and more than the British did for the French Acadians of Nova Scotia,* and we can be sure it is in bold contrast to what Tojo, Hitler, Stalin, or Mussolini would have advocated.

---

* When their region was ceded from France to England by the Treaty of Utrecht, French landholders, hard-working farmers and craftsmen, were unwilling to swear allegiance to a British king. They were expelled in 1755 under the pretext of "imperial defense." The heart-breaking story is told in Longfellow's *Evangeline.*

Now terrorism has justified a new hysteria, and again our government has rounded up ethnic "suspects." Some may be a threat, but some are innocent. They are guilty because they look like Arabs, think like Arabs, and worship an Arab God. It is infringement on their rights, reminiscent of Manzanar.

Semantics lesson: When we do it, it's called "detainees in resettlement camps." If the enemy does it, we call it "prisoners in concentration camps, deprived of their basic human rights."

Our United States condoned slavery through a long succession of presidents and Congresses. A bloody war couldn't end the hypocrisy. Another century elapsed before Congress would declare that discrimination based on race or color was wrong. But it seems impossible to legislate tolerance.

Jeanne and I encountered prejudice in Alaska where I would least expect it. "This book will take you right down memory lane," I warned Jeanne as I handed her *Tisha—The Story of a Young Teacher in the Alaska Wilderness*. The story revolved around the village of Chicken, an odd collection of cabins where Anne Hobbs battled racial prejudice, a problem more severe than the weather and isolation.

It was 1927. Racial prejudice caught teacher Hobbs unprepared. Surprised us, too, in Fairbanks. Savages they were born and savages they should remain. Within sight of the territorial capitol building, there were "No natives Allowed" signs.

"Illegal aliens" are fighting words in California. We can't live with 'em, but without 'em who would do the dirty work? Most of them come from Mexico. At the end of World War II, Mexico's estimated population was about 20 million. Now it is estimated over 100 million. This teeming population sees abundance across the border, so they do what comes natural, and they bring their culture with them. After arrival, they

This Is My Song

Words: Lloyd Stone, 1912– , © 1934, 1962 Lorenz Publishing Co.
Music: Jean Sibelius, 1865–1957, arr. © 1933, renewed 1961 Presbyterian
Board of Christian Education

FINLANDIA
11.10.11.10.11.10.

have children. Lots of children.

Our polyglot, light-skinned race should remember that not too far back in history, California was Mexico and we were the "illegals." Their border patrol was asleep and our guns were better. We brought a foreign language, a more aggressive culture, and we overpopulated their land. Now they're getting even.

Finlandia by Jean Sibelius has words by Lloyd Stone that echo the lament of broad-minded humanists whose vision reaches beyond artificial boundaries. **I would that it could be our national anthem.**

Political Wilderness

To me, this is the wilderness of perpetual darkness. It could make Greek theater: black comedy, tearful tragedy. I fail to see a great difference between the direction our country drifts, whether controlled by Republicans or Democrats. What I do see, and with great clarity, is that special-interest money and lobbying have a dominant role in government. They elect and re-elect. Our founders would be aghast. They might also be chagrined could they know their cherished government would set its first priority on being the greatest military force in world history while short-changing its citizenry with a grotesque health care program.

Albert Einstein: "I am convinced that . . . the very domain of human activity most crucial to the fate of nations is inescapably in the hands of the wholly irresponsible political rulers" (from a 1932 letter to Sigmund Freud).

Our Constitution was good for its time, but times change.

It did not foresee the domination of political parties and the divisiveness they cause. It did not foresee that re-election would become a stronger force than a congressman's conscience. It did not foresee that television time would replace the campaign stump and money would sway the outcome. The Constitution did not foresee that the "party" power could turn the elected representatives into reluctant rubber stamps. It did not foresee that my mailbox would be cluttered with pleas for money to support remote campaigns across the continent.

The framers covered their bases with the Bill of Rights and the amendment process. Could they have dreamed of the mayhem to result from an amendment that can be twisted to allow lethal guns for crime sprees? Could they have dreamed that the electoral college would become useless and yet a strategy to thwart a majority choice?

The Tikkum Community* is advocating an Amendment to the U.S. Constitution that would require "social responsibility" by any corporation receiving contracts for work in the public sector. Such companies would be required to prove a history of social and ecological stewardship. I believe the amendments to our Constitution are totally silent on the regulation of corporations and yet these giants are the ruling force in America. Isn't that strange?

Another malfunction of our system is obvious in a book by a Santa Barbaran, who functioned within the inner circle of Truman and a Senate Majority leader.† He writes "In the atmosphere of the Senate, I became more and more conscious of how difficult it was for any President to get the majorities he needed for high achievements." More disheartening is his

---

* Tikkum is a Hebrew word which means healing and transformation.
† *Harry Truman and the Human Family*, by Frank K. Kelly, Capra Press, 1998.

observation "The fires of McCarthyism—which burned up the reputations of many good men—had started a conflagration of suspicion which was beyond the power of the Senate to control." The writer bemoans "I was deeply disturbed when (his boss, the Majority Leader) permitted McCarthy to hold the floor for six hours."

This morass is too incongruous (good word) for me to handle, but Gene Kelley, a Santa Barbara scholar and wordsmith, has composed an Affirmation of Independence as it would read if our Declaration's grievances were framed against today's infringements on freedom. It is serious food for thought.

Religion Wilderness

The Israelites are not alone for time spent in the wilderness. I, too, have wandered. Inconsistencies in the Bible and misbehavior by sanctified leaders have perplexed me. For my student preaching, I had a sermon taken from the book of Joel. It was titled "Redeeming the Years the Locusts Have Eaten." (This homiletic exercise may have prompted the dean to toss me out.) Religion-locusts ate a lot of my years.

In pondering my retreat from fundamental religion, I realize that although I left the faith, the faith didn't leave me. I tried to believe. I also wondered. How can religion thrive in our era of technology and reason? When we sent a spacecraft to the moon, we pretty much eliminated a locale for heaven. We know from reading history that there can be no room left in hell. And yet, fundamentalist religions, whether Christian or Islamic, are the fastest growing.

Many of my friends are professing Catholics and presumably subscribe to ecclesiastic dogma that, to me, defies logic.

The disturbing thing is that most of these friends are smarter than I. When John Kennedy, a Catholic, became our president I had to rearrange my prejudices. He was brilliant, and had charisma to spare. So who's crazy?

Why God Is Here to Stay. The answer may be in a recent book by neurologist Andrew Newberg titled *Why God Won't Go Away.** The author contends that the human species' brain is hardwired to experience the reality of God. The rituals of religion—any religion—satisfy a thirst. Supplicants find strength by being surrounded by fellow believers. The mass is social communion. A church service is a pep rally. The attendee may not believe but needs to be surrounded by fellow worshippers. It's a phenomenon that has, throughout history, engulfed most of the world population.

This compulsion to worship cannot be ignored. Its energy is evident in the countless temples it has created. When I see an ancient mosque in Istanbul, I'm seeing an Islamic miracle. In my mind's eye, the Salt Lake City Tabernacle is a Mormon miracle. I see a miracle at the Mother Church of Christian Science. St. Peter's in Rome is a Catholic miracle. The new Cathedral of Our Lady of Angels in central Los Angeles is . . . well, let's admit that $190 million buys a lot of holy ground.

In my teens, chauffeuring for my evangelist dad, I did countless hours of prayer meetings, so I had honed the praying skill. I've prayed in more states than most eighth graders can spell. There was the time back East, I was smitten with an adorable high school sophomore. I was too timid to tell her I loved her, so I prayed the Lord would give me the courage.

---

* *Why God Won't Go Away: Brain Science and the Biology of Belief,* by Andrew Newberg, Eugene G. d'Aquili, and Vince Rause (New York: Ballantine Books, 2001).

God let me down. Oh, Margie wrote to me in Alaska, but the separation was too much. Fifty years later, my wife and I and a pair of joyriders were tooling about New York State. We were going to Watkins Glen anyway; Marjorie would be living near our route, so I wanted to pay a return visit. I polled the car's occupants:

My wife: "That is NOT a good idea."

My niece, Jo: "That is positively the stupidest . . ."

My friend, Nelson: "How else will you know if she waited?"

I followed Nelson's brilliant conclusion. Should have followed my wife's advice.

My friend Dan knows very little about prayer meetings but he knows a lot about women. I asked Dan, "Can you imagine how hard it is to court a girl in prayer meeting? No wonder she didn't wait for me." Dan had a good answer: "Hal, it's God's doing. He knew Marjorie belonged in New York's Chemung Valley. You didn't. God knew Alaska girls are more your type. Just trust Him; it's what I do."

Twenty-five years after I abandoned my pursuit of the "ministry," I was president of a Lutheran congregation. There came a Sunday when the missionary we supported in Nagoya, Japan, reported to the church on his work in the "fields of the Lord." At a dinner in the church basement, I had opportunity to query him on the effectiveness of the "work." He reported that there were at least 1,000 Christian converts in Nagoya. "And just how many Christian missionaries of all persuasions?" I asked. He thought a long time and came up with "165." What futility! Peter and Paul, the two earliest missionaries, did better than that alone, with no financial base, while hiding with their converts from the emperors in the catacombs. It should be factored in that Peter and Paul were preaching a pure gospel, whereas our missionary was trying to sell a doctrine that had been tampered by nineteen centuries of human interpretation. Our Lutheran emissary had in effect told me that God doesn't support our foreign missions in Japan—that maybe God is content with whatever the locals are practicing. Otherwise, the conclusion is that God has failed. I don't buy that.

I cannot reconcile the wonders of the universe and creation, the miracles of life, and the diversity of fauna and flora to a God that can fail. My God is too big and too powerful to be concerned with denominational proselytizing. My God shouldn't be saddled with ecclesiastical dogma. If I shed the man-made creeds and icons, the idols and hypocrisy, will I not restore God to a size I can truly believe in? If that makes me an agnostic, let the record show I'm a *believing agnostic*.

My escape from fundamentalism evolved slowly. It was certainly nudged by the credibility stretch of the Old Testament. Those myths would make a TV sitcom, with adultery and incest, child abuse and murder, animal sacrifice and theft, often ordered by a peculiar God on the mountain or in the bush. One of the most erotic—in Genesis—concerns God's own pet, Abraham. He and Sarah were not having much luck with a male heir, so Sarah approved of using a surrogate, her Egyptian slave, Hagar. (This would be an absolute no-no in Jerry Falwell's pulpit.) Well! This eighty-year-old messenger of God sired a son, Ishmael, the father of the Arab tribes.

Thirteen years later, Sarah got with the program and along came Isaac, progenitor of the Israelites. After which, with two mammas living with one papa in the same household, jealousy raised its ugly head. Isn't that a familiar plot? Haggar was shipped out, Sarah died at age 127, and Abraham had to be the sexiest dude in all of Canaan because he found a new wife and had six more children. It is little wonder he died at age 175. My own view is that a guy that old trying to raise six kids is a case for protective custody and we are not surprised that it spawns a lot of subplots. Those ancients in the Bible were a bit kinky. I believe their sit-com would go prime time.

On a Mother's Day TV program, I heard a mother being lauded, and she answered by saying she raised her children according to the Bible. I wanted to scream, "Lady, you haven't read the Pentateuch!"

"Almighty God, when I read the scriptures purported to be Your word, I get confused. For example: in Genesis 12:12, Abraham is in Egypt and lies about Sarah being his wife. Fourteen chapters later, in chapter 26:6, it is Isaac, instead of Abraham, telling the same lie about Rebecca. Did the narrator have dementia?"

"Harold my boy, you know how these slips get past the proofreader."

Sometimes I have trouble reconciling God's plan with what I read in the papers. In the broadest sense, we and our president, the Taliban and the Iraqis, the Vietnamese and the North Koreans, and all the children of Abraham, are distant cousins.

"God, it's me again. Excuse me if I seem confused: Why did You put most of the oil under the Arabs? You must have known we lovable Christians would own most of the cars? So now we have to buy oil from those Arabs who we don't like?

"Harold, don't blame me. It was the French and English who parceled out the territory. A lot of mistakes followed World War I."

Nothing in the scriptures about OIL and it's such a vital subject. I have a Jewish friend; he's cynical but might have some answers. So I asked Mort, "Isn't it a bit weird that you

Jews claim to be God's 'chosen people' and not a smidgeon of oil?" Doesn't the evidence show the United States is really God's favorite? He gave us a big and beautiful land with lots of oil under it, we have cars and money to waste, and a war-making machine like you can't believe. Isn't that proof that God loves us more than anyone, including you Jews?"

"Hal, don't ask me to apologize for God. He gave me the good sense to be an atheist."

A Unitarian is more apt to have analyzed this puzzle, so I laid the same question on Mark, he had the answer: "It's a good question. You can be chairman of a discussion group."

Abraham's lineage can be blamed for big mischief. We get the Crusaders slaughtering Turks who retaliate against the Armenians, the Ottomans butchering the Eastern Orthodox, the Puritans burning witches, and the Catholics inquisition-ing everyone. In this new millennium, is it any surprise there are suicide bombings in the Levant?

Would an all-knowing God create such a fighting family? Does He not know that innocent women and children are vic-tims? Does God condone terrorism and the waste of war? To me, the evidence is convincing: The Creator has a hands-off attitude.

Dale Lindsay Morgan, astute pastor of St. Andrew's Pres-byterian Church, Santa Barbara, has the following thoughts on this premise:

"Hal has called this chapter, 'The Wilderness of Man,' quoting the dictionary definition, 'an extensive area that is barren or empty, a waste.' But son of the church that he is, Hal also knows that it was in the wilderness where the great leaders of the Jewish and Chris-tian scriptures encountered God. Jacob met God the night he ran away from home (see ladder of angels, Genesis 28); Moses met God the day he took his flock "beyond the wilderness" (see burning bush, Exodus 3); for forty years, the Hebrew people met God in the wilderness as they wandered in search of a promised land (see pillars of cloud and fire, meals of manna and quail, drinks of sweet water from the rock throughout the book of Exodus; while you're there don't forget to look up the Ten Commandments given, ditto, ditto, in the wilderness!); and through forty days of "temptation," Jesus clarified his call in the wilderness where he was led by the Spirit after his baptism (see early chapters of Matthew, Mark, and Luke). The prophet Muhammad, founder of Islam, was a wilderness shepherd boy in his youth; as an adult it was in a desert cave that Muhammad heard an angel dictate the Qur'an.

"A most observant man (he's my friend, so I know), Hal has chronicled in this chapter the various wildernesses through which we wander in our postmodern, postbiblical, world. Like the real thing, these cultural wildernesses can be barren places, filled with thorns and thistles. But like the wildernesses of scripture, they are also the places where we, following those spiritual heroes who have gone before us, come to know our need for divine guidance, where we acknowledge our thirst for salvation (this good word's not just reserved for "olde tyme" tent meetings), where we sense, in its vastness, how puny we are. The wilderness, in short, is exactly where we encounter God. The wilderness is not "barren or empty, a waste." It is the place where God waits, where God calls, where those who listen may be empowered to change the world.

"You think the Creator has a hands-off attitude? Wait 'til God lays holy hands on you!"

The pastor and I can certainly agree that God is Great. Who can tour the awesome Cathedrals of Europe and doubt God's energy? St. John the Divine in New York is divine, indeed. The National Cathedral in Washington is inspiring. The Mosque at Cordoba, so large that it can encase a Catholic

Church, is w-o-w! The Bahá'í Temple at Evanston is a place of reverent elegance, and the St. Louis Cathedral is a monument in mosaic. St. Isaac's Cathedral in St. Petersburg is an impossibility, and the list is endless. Whence comes this amazing energy? So many sects. So many Gods. So many miracles!

Flower Drum Song is one of my favorite musicals. It starts with Mei Li singing of "One Hundred Million Miracles." I join Mei Li in the belief in miracles. I have a long list:

Computers, the Internet, and e-mail

A tiny hummingbird at our feeder

A monster Boeing 747

A 5,000-year-old bristlecone pine and a redwood

Jeanne's flower garden and our drought-resistant oaks

The human anatomy and modern medicine

The 1812 Overture in the Hollywood Bowl

The Wurlitzer at San Sylmar Treasure House

A salmon returning to spawn in its birthplace

An astronaut walking on the moon—and my
    seeing it on TV

The energy wrapped up in a tiny atom

The aurora borealis

The human brain and the heart that ticks endlessly

Machu Picchu, Easter Island, the Ch'in Dynasty

Our spinning planet in orbit, this good earth!

And the most dazzling miracle of all, which is with us constantly and is taken for granted: the reproduction of life, especially human life—the miracle of conception, of gestation, of birth—and if it commences with sexual passion and fulfillment, it becomes a breathtaking miracle!

Parental Wilderness

I'm a double-dipped-preacher's kid. Both parents were ordained. My mother graduated from university in an era when women in the pulpit were a rarity. My father became obsessed with Bible prophecy and decided to take it on the road. He heard God upgrade him to "Evangelist," heard Him say Jesus would be returning in the '30s. That took care of any need for housekeeping. The "saints" in the churches where meetings were scheduled would house and feed the evangelist and his wife. It was a commonplace substitute for money—theirs and ours.

"Oh, incidentally, our son may be with us. He helps us in the work. You'll like him." Yeah.

Thus, upon leaving Bible college I was a nomad. My father sincerely believed I was called to the ministry by God. My dad had no hesitancy in pushing me into the pulpit. If I protested my lack of a message, he insisted that God would put the words in my mouth. Yeah.

"You lost your job because the plant closed? Just keep the faith. God will provide."

"Your fields are dried up and the dust storms have buried your fences—let us pray for rain."

"And the bank is foreclosing? God sees their wicked ways. He is merciful and just. Amen."

"You have cancer and may die? Praise the Lord. He heals the body and enlivens the spirit."

"Your children are troubling you—just teach them the scriptures—hallelujah!"

"Any other problems? Let this idiot kid from Kansas help you."

This immature dropout was behind a pulpit, telling "the

faithful" the way of life and salvation. He had not witnessed death, heartbreak, depravity, or violence. He knew nothing of child abuse, dope, and alcohol addiction. As for sex? Only what my parents had taught me—you guessed it.

Why, I now ask, would God put a green kid behind a pulpit? Subsequent experience tells me that God knows how to find qualified ministers.

Let me speak for many of my generation, an era before counseling and enlightenment: Many of our parents did the best they knew, but what they knew was damn little. I'm certain I'm not the first adult child to conclude that my parents needed a course in parenting. It is the more inexcusable for my parents because they were ministers. Furthermore, I'm irritated because both of them were blind to the social injustices of society. I grant that ignorance has always abounded, but ordained and with college degrees?

As I look back, I am contrite. My father should have been ashamed. Such arrogance. Since those years, I've done some penance and wish I could do more. I should look up those audiences and apologize—if I knew what cemetery. When I was a teenager, I had the answers. Seventy years later, I have questions.

I am only one of a multitude that did not belong in a pulpit. Ernest Hemingway, in *Adventures of a Young Man*, tells of approaching an editor of a New York paper to secure his first job. He tells the editor he wants to write.

The editor asks, "What will you write about?" Hemingway says he wants to write about life.

The editor's reply was, "How can you write about LIFE before you have lived LIFE ?"

12

Return to the Bible Belt: Ozark Beauty and Bombast

After a sixty-year elapse, I returned to Ozarkland, showing my wife where I was heaven bound at Central Bible College. I muse that since my departure the school has sent into the fields of the Lord two notable ministers with charisma to spare: Jim Bakker and Jimmy Swaggart.

That college had a dress code, a decorum code, and an abstinence code. The dormitories were sin proof. We entered virgins and departed virgins, and that is certainly a worry our parents were spared. I might, with luck, sit beside a female student while driving to a rural church for ministerial practice. If so, the conversation was not geared for making out. The dormitory dining tables were coed—more literally, "cofed"—and chaperoned by an upperclassman. We guys wore suits and ties, even to breakfast, and the girls wore blue uniforms—dresses, of course, with big red bow ties. Sort of cute, but not sexually stimulating.

Contact with the opposite sex was tightly rationed. With the year's single exception—Christmas vacation, with most students gone and rules relaxed—I was able to strike up an acquaintance with a gorgeous Italian brunette. She was my only Christmas present during a lonely campus-bound holiday. No embracing, just conversation, but a relief from monastic living for ten days. A monster bully who laid claim to Josephine heard about it when he returned from vacation. He worked me over. I didn't get even a kiss and I was beat up. Such was my romancing at Central Bible College in the '30s.

An hour's drive south of Springfield is Branson—an entertainment phenomenon perfectly suited to these hills (described in Chapter 13.) Discovering Branson's College of the Ozarks was a treat. It is different. Students at this college work for their tuition. Hence its nickname: "Hard Work U." Central Bible College where I attended also required the students to pitch in and assist with campus chores in lieu of tuition. It was good for us and we learned some practical skills. The school raised cattle for milk and meat. My on-the-job-training qualifies me as a meat-canning specialist. (Confuses anyone reading my resume.) Visiting the College of the Ozarks campus, I speculated: Just imagine the benefit if this work program were applied to California's universities. It could eliminate the state's budget deficit. Too sensible. There's bound to be a law prohibiting something as dangerous as honest *work*.

Those attending service in the College of the Ozarks' Williams Memorial Chapel will be impressed by a throng of well-groomed attentive students, youngsters to make any parent proud. It is a spiritual experience. The campus has a charming restaurant, also staffed by the students, and open to the public. As I enjoy my dinner, I'm prompted to indulge in a bit of remorse: *Hal, you missed the school where you might have belonged by only seventy miles, and now it is too late.*

This visit was also a return to *Shepherd of the Hills* country and a memory I can do without. In the Bible college era, a carload of us students needed a visit to this famous area. We rushed the spring season, went swimming in the White River, and I paid with pneumonia. This did not help my grades.

This corner of the Ozark hills (no Californian can bear to call them "mountains") claims its fame from a best-selling book by Harold Bell Wright,[*] written at the turn of the century. In my early youth, we lived our fiction with Wright and Zane Grey. Their books could be found in every midwestern home.

It is no coincidence that the shepherd of the story was a minister, hiding from a trauma. He had come from the big city, seeking atonement amid a rural and uneducated society of hill dwellers eking out an austere existence from their rocky soil. (One year of my early schooling was living with an aunt on a farm near Neosho, west of Springfield, and I can state from experience that the Ozark rocks are a hard field to plow.)

The minister-turned-shepherd sends us this message:

If thou art worn and hard beset,
With sorrows, that thou wouldst forget;
If thou wouldst read a lesson that will keep
Thy heart from fainting and thy soul from sleep,
Go to the woods and hills! No tears
Dim the sweet look that Nature wears.

The shepherd adds, "I never understood until now why the Master so often withdrew alone into the wilderness. There is not only food and medicine for one's body; there is also heal-

---

[*] *Shepherd of the Hills,* a novel by Harold Bell Wright, 1907, Grosset and Dunlap.

ing for the heart and strength for the soul in nature. One gets very close to God . . . in these temples of God's own building."

Deep in these Ozark hills there was, and still is, a pocket of innocence and simplicity. Churches were, and still are, plentiful, mostly Baptist and Pentecostal. One of our college courses was "personal evangelism." It presumed that our peculiar dogma was right, those who disagreed were wrong, and lucky for them, we could lead them to salvation. We invaded these hills for our homework. It was an easy stand for us students to buttonhole sinners:

"Brother, are you saved? It says right here in these scriptures that God wants you to come to him through Jesus" No? "Brother, let's kneel and pray for God to open your eyes . . ."

Christianity has blossomed all over these hills, including Eureka Springs, just across the state line into Arkansas. It is a charming little city with lots of tourist appeal. Topping its attractions is a "Passion Play" modeled after the famous Oberammergau. This is the creation of Gerald L. K. Smith, a minister and noisy bigot who spread hate over much of the Bible Belt in my days, meaning the '30s. Smith's associations were colorful, if not always noble. They ran the gamut from William Pelley's Silver Shirts (ultra-right) to Dr. Townsend (politics of the left) to Father Coughlin (social injustices) to Governor Huey Long (God's gift to Louisiana).

Behind the Passion Play's outdoor amphitheater is a towering statue of Jesus with sixty-five-foot outstretched arms. "Christ of the Ozarks" sort of shadows the granite block below, which marks the Smith finale. His bones are there and God only knows where his soul went.

Remorse is my reaction as I stare at this monument. I am reminded of my work for one of Smith's fellow pulpiteers, the reverend Gerald Winrod. These two reverends had much in common: a shared first name, a pulpit from which to sanctify their anti-Semitism, and always, Roosevelt hatred.

Winrod was invited to Germany in the mid-'30s. He claimed to have met with Hitler, returned a convert. His Defender Publishing Company in Wichita spewed out hate books and tracts by the zillions. His favorite targets were handed to him by President Roosevelt. One of FDR's strategies for attacking the country's economic crisis was enlisting a select cadre of highly qualified leaders, dubbed the "Brain Trust." Several of them were Jews. Each was quickly targeted by Winrod as a threat to our country, and each was the subject of a book or pamphlet exposing a "conspiracy." These diatribes were joined by the *Protocols of the Learned Elders of Zion.*

I ran the mimeograph (the forerunner of the Xerox), cranking out hate letters to scare the loyal supporters to fund the battle against evil demons in government. I carted tons of this garbage to the post office. I knew the bombastic bigotry was wrong. I was a green, tongue-tied kid. I should have sounded off. Where was my voice? Where was the voice of my parents? These two ordained ministers remained silent. Many of us can track our silence and our biases to our in-house teachers. I should echo Frank Sinatra's line—"Regrets, I have a few . . ."

(Until after the war and the full impact of the Nazi's purge became known, anti-Semitism was a force in our country. It had broad support. Politically, it was too hot to handle. This will be a surprise to the postwar generation that is attuned to "civil rights." After the horror of the Holocaust registered on the general public, the cry went up, "We can't believe it. We never dreamed. We didn't know." But the White House knew, the State Department knew[*], the War Department knew, most of the Cabinet[†] knew. There are myriad conjectures as to why it was not publicized and why the power structure opted for inaction until the military liberated the camps.)

My evolution from fundamentalist to agnostic has been fueled by distortions. Increasingly, I ask myself, *Would an intelligent God send His message to the world via dogmatic Bible-thumpers who expound their intolerance and warped judgmental condemnations from pulpits behind which is an image of Jesus, a teacher noted for love and mercy?* I wince when my TV surfing stumbles on a self-appointed charlatan prancing across the platform claiming he or she knows what God is demanding of us, what God is saying. Giant orators with shrunken minds seem able to clothe their vituperations in Christian garments to hypnotize their listeners. Dogma and intolerance should be confined to a soapbox on the street corner.

Protestant services ask us to join in reciting the Apostles Creed. Jesus didn't give it to us, so whence comes its validity? Like the disciple, Thomas, I'm a doubter. Better if the creed could be documented. Better if it addressed modern needs. The affirmation below used by Unitarians is a creed I can endorse. It has relevance for the 21st century.

WE BELIEVE in the freedom of religious expression. All individuals should be encouraged to develop their own personal theologies, and to present openly their religious opinions without fear of censure or reprisal.

[*] *Haven* (Random House, 2000). Ruth Gruber's account of shepherding 1,000 Jewish refugees to Fort Oswego, New York, a token relief arrangement by President Roosevelt.
[†] *The Conquerors: Roosevelt, Truman and the Destruction of Hitler's Germany*, by Michael Beschloss (New York: Simon & Schuster, 2002).

WE BELIEVE in the toleration of religious ideas. All religions, in every age and culture, possess not only an intrinsic merit, but also potential value for those who have learned the art of listening.

WE BELIEVE in the authority of reason and conscience. The ultimate arbiter in religion is not a church, or a document, or an official, but the personal choice and decision of the individual.

WE BELIEVE in the never-ending search for Truth. If the mind and heart are truly free and open, the revelations that appear to the human spirit are infinitely numerous, eternally fruitful, and wondrously exciting.

WE BELIEVE in the unity of experience. There is no fundamental conflict between faith and knowledge, religion and the world, the sacred and the secular, since they all have their source in the same reality.

WE BELIEVE in the worth and dignity of each human being. All people on earth have an equal claim to life, liberty, and justice— and no idea, ideal, or philosophy is superior to a single human life.

WE BELIEVE in the ethical application of religion. Good works are the natural product of a good faith, the evidence of an inner grace that finds completion in social and community involvement.

WE BELIEVE in the motive force of love. The governing principle in human relationships is the principle of love, which always seeks the welfare of others and never seeks to hurt or destroy.

WE BELIEVE in the necessity of the democratic process. Records are open to scrutiny, elections are open to criticism—so that people might govern themselves.

WE BELIEVE in the importance of a religious community. The validation of experience requires the confirmation of peers, who provide a critical platform along with a network of mutual support.

— David O. Rankin

It is this layman's contention that God's message deserves wisdom and objectivity, honesty and conviction. The pulpit should be used for comfort and inspiration. I am content believing God knew what was right when He allowed me to be ousted from that Bible college. God knew I would not be a happy camper, and more important, congregations deserved better.

Bat Mitzvah for Sarah Lewis, June 2000.

13

Grumpy Ol' Sourdough: Taxes and Traffic, Prayer for the Planet

A lot of things bother me. *If there's a GOD, why isn't He just and fair?* If we've been blessed, life is good and we are lucky. What about the majority on the earth who are *not lucky?* Why should being born in the wrong place and/or at the wrong time destine a baby to malnutrition, no medicine, and ravishes of war? Where is the fairness? Funny way to run a planet.

There is no justice when some of us have long lives and stable environments while others are cut down in their prime. Some of us get off this earth peacefully, without pain; others are sentenced to lengthy illness and suffering. So—some of us got better genes than others? Something is wrong with this picture.

As I near life's finish line, I have much to like and enjoy. But I'm troubled when I ponder the inequities that befall human-ity. The human scene has never been a level playing field. That isn't fair. Time for a heart-to-heart with The Creator:

"Listen, GOD, I'm a veteran of a war with a staggering death toll of 50 million humans. The fundamentalists preach that you're a God of love, so where is the love thing?"

"Harold, I was blind-sided. I never dreamed that most of the German race, presumed to be smart people, would support a madman's atrocities. These were ultrareligious folks, so who can I trust? Yes, I made a colossal mistake. I feel terrible. Do you have any other problems?"

"Of course. Lots of them. Back to Hitler. There were 40 assassination attempts on his life. You failed to assist in a single one. What in hell were you doing?"

"Harold, I'm proud of the planet I created. I like it the way I made it. If I made a mistake, it was in creating man. And woman. You'll have to deal with it. Over and out."

I don't understand our Cuba policy. Our government doesn't like our next-door neighbors because they abuse human rights. But we like Saudi Arabia. I guess that means we like oil better than sugar and cigars. Maybe we're peeved because the Bay of Pigs was a fiasco. Forty years seems a long time for a nation to carry a grudge. Vietnam was a much worse fiasco, and we got most of that venom out of our national psyche in less than thirty years. Our government needs a psychotherapist. The international world should call the police, like we do for domestic quarrels, but I guess the CIA would respond.

Obsession With War. "Foreign Relations" should be renamed "Foreign Squabbles." Of all of the sacred cows that have desecrated the landscape of history—be it by moderns or ancients, by the USA or other world powers, be it the past or the present—no delusion is more revered than mankind's obsession with war. The waste and human suffering and destruction that have been justified in the name of "national security" or "manifest destiny" or *"lebensraum"* or "orders from God-on-high" is beyond measure.

History is my best subject. That's how I know war is unhealthy. Generation after generation, nations and tribes and religious zealots have opted for arms and destruction as the preferred way to communicate. There are no winners.

"National defense" should be renamed "national aggression." "National security" is the U.S. catchall that legitimizes mining the harbors in Nicaragua; destroying Panama to capture our CIA's own man, Noriega; squandering mega-billions in Vietnam; dispatching fuel-guzzling bombers to fly about the planet.* It is all necessary for "defense." If our military napalms a native village a hemisphere away, that is also "defense." The collective "we" are safe and snug at home while thousands die from our arsenal. These are humans like ourselves, people we know little or nothing about, people who also want to live to see their grandchildren.

It seems probable that the explanation for mankind's militaristic behavior is that a sizable percentage of people worldwide—mainly the males—*like* war. The chiefs in our power structure like the arms race. It is profitable. We have become hi-tech military hardware addicts and would have economic D.T.s if it were withdrawn.

Albert Einstein and Sigmund Freud Agree. This painful accusation is supported in a series of letters (1931–1932)[†]

* To site an airbase in the middle of the Indian Ocean, the U.S. sponsored the displacement (by the U.K.) of an indigenous native community from the island of Diego Garcia. It is a hemisphere away, 10,000 miles from our nearest shore. Is there no limit?

† From *Einstein on Peace*, edited by Otto Nathan and Heinz Norden (New York: Schocken Books, 1960, pp.186–203).

wherein Einstein asks Freud, "Is there any way of delivering mankind from the menace of war? . . . How is it possible for a small clique to bend the will of the majority who stand to lose and suffer by a state of war? . . . How is it these devices succeed so well in arousing men to such wild enthusiasm, even to sacrifice their lives?" Answering his own question, Einstein commented: "Only one answer is possible. Because man has within him a lust for hatred and destruction."

Freud's answer from Vienna was almost a resignation: "Why do we, you and I and many another, protest so vehemently against war, instead of just accepting it as another of life's odious importunities? Because every man has a right over his own life and war destroys lives that were full of promise; it forces the individual into situations that shame his manhood, obliging him to murder fellow man against his will; it ravages material amenities, the fruits of human toil, and much besides."* (*Much* in 1932 translates to *everything* in 2003 nuclear parlance.)

Einstein and Freud seem to have confirmed my worst fears. Yet the human instinct for survival may be strong enough to enforce a transformation. As we evangelists put it, "The first step toward salvation is to confess that we're sinners."

Santa Barbara County is beholden to "defense" for spending a ton of money at Vandenberg—the West Coast launch center for missiles. On occasion, organizations to which I belong take me on tours of the center. Our indoctrinator contends that this military base is in the business of peace. It

---

* By the time this exchange was published in 1933, under the title *Why War?* Hitler, who was to drive both men into exile, was already in power, and the letters never achieved the wide circulation intended for them. The first German edition is reported to have been limited to only 2,000 copies.

makes test launches of Minuteman missiles designed to carry nuclear warheads. The Reagan administration dubbed them "peacekeepers." I am perplexed. I have three questions: "What is peaceful about a nuclear warhead? What purpose is served in spending $50 to $75 million to test a weapon we know we dare not use? If we can't use it, what matters if it works?"

I am not alone in this conviction. President Eisenhower said it better in his speech to the American Society of Newspaper Editors, April 16, 1953. An excerpt is reprinted below:

As president, Eisenhower ended the Korean War and presided over eight years of calm prosperity. The record of his administration is on display at the Dwight D. Eisenhower Library in Abilene, Kansas. It is a place every American should visit, but few will because it is off the usual traffic pattern. That is unfortunate because folks miss the "Place of

"Every gun that is made, every warship launched, every rocket fired signifies, in the final sense, a theft from those who hunger and are not fed, those who are cold and are not clothed. This world in arms is not spending money alone. It is spending the sweat of its laborers, the genius of its scientists, the hopes of its children...This is not a way of life at all in any true sense. Under the cloud of threatening war, it is humanity hanging from a cross of iron."

Meditation" where they can see carved in stone, the wisdom of this president who warned that a military-industrial complex was taking control of our country. So we have had that insight since the '50s.

General Omar Bradley stated, "We have grasped the mystery of the atom and rejected the Sermon on the Mount. . . . Ours is a world of nuclear giants and ethical infants. We know more about war than we know about peace, more about killing than we know about living."

General Douglas MacArthur, in his famous speech to the United Nations at the Ambassador Hotel in Los Angeles, "War has become a Frankenstein Monster to destroy both sides. . . . If you lose you're annihilated. If you win you stand only to lose. . . . The billions spent in mutual preparations for war would abolish poverty in the world. . . . The next great advance in the evolution of civilization cannot take place until war is abolished."

Terrorism is the new science of war. It was perfected by Arabs who brought down the World Trade Center towers, but before that tragedy, it has been an on-going way of life for Israel vs Palestinians, or vice versa. A fireball Rabbi, Michael Lerner, is advancing a drastic solution: "We need to free ourselves from those parts of religious systems and national myths which generate an attitude of superiority, chauvinism, hatred, or war. Safety and security for all. Our individual and societal well-being depends upon and is intrinsically linked to the well-bing of everyone else on the planet." The Rabbi believes that both Israelis and Palestinians are responsible for the current mess, both sides can do something to end it. Palestinians should follow the nonviolent path of Martin Luther King, Jr. and Mahatma Gandhi. Israel sould end the

Occupation, share Jerusalem, and provide leadership . . . to provide reparations to Palestinian refugees.

Santa Barbara's Nuclear Age Peace Foundation resonates my feelings. Its mission is "to advance initiatives to end the nuclear weapons threat to humanity, to foster the global rule of law, and to build an enduring legacy of peace through education and advocacy." That is an advocacy I can salute. If patriotism must be equated with war, then I'm out of step, right along with Eisenhower, Bradley, and MacArthur.

Misadventures of a Semi-Happy Man

Channing Pollock was a respected playwright and author who wrote a book titled *The Adventures of a Happy Man*. This book was written during the Great Depression when life was austere but simple. Pollock states, "I must admit that I have never been unhappy a whole hour in my life!" He also says that when asked to give five principal reasons for his state of mind, he was able to jot down fifty-one reasons in a short ten minutes.

Well! Since his time, I believe there's been a drastic change. I think I can update his list and identify fifty-one experiences Mr. Pollock never endured. Check these for starters:

1. Pollock never tried to get across LA on the freeway or out of Toronto at rush hour.

2. I'll bet he never needed to get through to the phone billing on their toll-free number.

3. Did Pollock ever try to mail a package at the PO at Christmas time?

4. In the Depression era, I guess he couldn't fly, so he didn't lose his baggage.

5. He never had to open vacuum packaging with his bare hands!

6. Never lost his computer hard drive or his car in a parking garage?

7. He never had to find a hardware item in a clerkless store.

8. Never tried to park at a Southern California beach on the 4th of July?

9. I'm sure Pollock knew a dozen service stations that had air and water.

10. Did he ever try to sign into an emergency ward?

11. You can bet that Pollock was never in a recruit camp for the Army.

12. Pollock has quite a bit to say about romance. I wonder what he knew about divorce?

There was a Santa Barbaran who was a Pollock soul mate. Vernon Johnson, who barely survived a bomber crash in World War II, is quoted as masking his troubles with, "There is no such thing as a problem." Vernon took his wife and eight children around the world in an old transit bus. His wife wrote a book* telling of daily breakdowns. He could stay sane because there's no such thing as a problem. If my transmission went out in the center of Rome as happened to the Johnson family, to me it would be a damn big problem. Wish I could have known Vernon better.

* *Home Is Where the Bus Is,* by Anne Beckwith Johnson (Santa Barbara: John Daniel & Company, 2001).

Lament of the Ancient Taxpayer. Income tax time irritates me! I've saved my 1940 U.S. tax return. It's a single yellowing page. Readers in 2003 won't believe; sixty years ago, the tax was 4% of income, which was the same as "taxable income." In 1940, there was a 10% defense tax add-on. For me, it came to $4.40. Total tax = $53.92. If you're one of those cynics who think taxes always go up, hear this: The next year, 1941, the rate dropped to 3%, and the defense tax was dropped. Total tax on an income of $2,368 = $69.00. (I guess I rounded it in my favor but wasn't audited.) This was filed the year I married. I expended about fifteen minutes, and as you can see, I typed my return neatly. Somehow in that far-off past, the Feds were able to operate on 3% of my gross income, and if there was a deficit I wasn't aware. For nonbelievers, I'm reproducing the form (p. 242). Look it over at the risk of your tears wetting the page.

To the affluent young of the new millennium, my wages must appear as that of a peon in a Third World country. Actually, my 1941 job in Fairbanks paid well. I was newly married, and there was no need for my wife to work. We started without a nest egg but were able to buy our own log home and make the monthly payments of $50. Our honeymoon house was primitive but had electricity, and I busied myself putting in plumbing, paying cash for the materials. My experience provides a budget tip for those overextended: Occupy your evenings crawling beneath the floor and you will save on movie tickets.

Those days are far off in the past. Now I ponder a worktable covered with 1099s, K-1s, canceled checks, paid receipts, tax advice columns, and organizational guides from my accountant. January 15 used to be an easy deadline to meet,

FORM 1040 A

TREASURY DEPARTMENT
Internal Revenue Service

UNITED STATES
INDIVIDUAL INCOME AND DEFENSE TAX
RETURN

FOR GROSS INCOMES OF NOT MORE THAN $5,000 DERIVED
FROM SALARIES, WAGES, DIVIDENDS, INTEREST, AND ANNUITIES

(NOTE.—If you are engaged in a profession or business (including farming), or are a member of
a partnership, or had income or losses from the renting or sale of property, use Form 1040)

To be filed with the Collector of Internal Revenue for your district on or before March 15, 1941

1940

**COPY TO BE
RETAINED
BY
TAXPAYER**

PRINT NAME AND HOME OR RESIDENTIAL ADDRESS PLAINLY BELOW

Harold L. Thornton
(Name) (Use given names of both husband and wife, if this is a joint return)

901 Cashman St.
(Street and number, or rural route)

Fairbanks   Alaska
(Post office)   (County)   (State)

IF YOU NEED
ASSISTANCE IN
PREPARING THIS
RETURN, GO TO A
DEPUTY COLLECTOR
OR TO THE
COLLECTOR'S
OFFICE

QUESTIONS

1. What is your occupation? _____

2. Check whether you are a citizen ☐ or a resident alien ☐

3. Did you file a return for any prior year? _____ If so, what was the latest
year? _____ To which Collector's office was it sent? _____

4. Are items of income or deductions of both husband and wife included in
this return? _____

5. State name of husband or wife if a separate return was made, personal exemption, if any, claimed thereon, and the Collector's office to which it was sent:
_____

Item and Instruction No.	INCOME			
1. Salaries and other compensation for personal services. (From Schedule A)		$ 2330	50	
2. Dividends				
3. Interest on bank deposits, notes, mortgages, etc.				
4. Interest on corporation bonds				
5. Other income (including income from annuities, fiduciaries, etc.). (From Schedule B)				
6. Total income in items 1 to 5			$ 2330	50
	DEDUCTIONS			
7. Contributions paid. (From Schedule C)		$ 75	00	
8. Interest paid. (From Schedule D)				
9. Taxes paid. (From Schedule E)		5	00	
10. Other deductions authorized by law. (From Schedule F)				
11. Total deductions in items 7 to 10			80	00
	COMPUTATION OF TAX			
12. Net income (item 6 minus item 11)			$ 2250	50
13. Less: Earned income credit, either (a) or (b). (See Instruction 13)				
(a) If item 12 is $3,000 or less, enter 10% of such item		$ 225	05	
(b) If item 12 is more than $3,000, enter 10% of item 1 or 10% of item 12, whichever is smaller, but not less than $300				
14. Personal exemption. (From Schedule H-1)		800	00	
15. Credit for dependents. (From Schedule H-2)			1025	05
16. Balance of net income taxable (item 12 minus items 13, 14, and 15)			$ 1225	45
17. Income tax (4% of item 16)			$ 49	02
18. Less: Income tax paid at source on tax-free covenant bonds		$		
19. Income tax paid to a foreign country or United States possession. (Attach Form 1116)				
20. Balance of income tax (item 17 minus items 18 and 19)			$ 49	02
21. Defense tax (10% of item 17)			4	40
22. Total income and defense taxes due (item 20 plus item 21). (See Instruction E as to payment of tax)			$ 53	92

NOTE.—In order that this return may be accepted as meeting the requirements of the Internal Revenue Code, the data called for
herein must be set forth FULLY and CLEARLY.

16—16468

then it was April 15, and now it can extend into October. And all the while, the estimates must be confronted. The time thus spent could be better used reading the sports section.

Time is running out for those born in my era. The clock is ticking on my life, and I resent giving up part of it each year to placate a wasteful government. For those who wonder why the Feds can't operate on 3% of your income today, the answer is simple: *Pork barrel budgeting is designed to devalue the dollar and move the tax rate up. And up. And up.*

What if my epitaph should read, "Here lies a frustrated taxpayer who was mugged."

Damn Traffic! Santa Barbara is a choice place, but it has its share of blemishes: The gate wasn't closed after we moved in, so the "south coast" is overloading with people. We all were happier when our town had few traffic signals and easy parking. Parking! Those my age can remember when nobody drove around the block searching to stash our cherished wheels. Santa Barbara lets us park free, even in our parking garages, which are smog generators. So are drive-up windows. I believe both should be illegal.

There was no freeway when the view from the courthouse tower seduced me to move to Santa Barbara. Now an overloaded Highway 101 allows LA-to-San Francisco commuters to swamp our hideout. Of course, all Californians have vehicles. It's their birthright to hit the road to God-knows-where. When I moved into our home, the highway whispered. Now it roars. Will it get worse? Of course.

Once upon a time I was the family authority on vehicles. After all, I had experience as a car dealer. So I asked my granddaughter, "Courtney, why is your new car a SUV?" She told me her male friend picked it out for her. He wanted her in a safe car. "Gee whiz! He must be a prize!" I told her there's no such thing as "safety" in Los Angeles.

SUVs annoy me. I don't understand their popularity. I queried my friend Thaddeus.

"Hal, guys like big because it unleashes their aggressions. Mud-bogging is a guy-sport. Cool, man. Drives Smokey nuts."

"Tell me, Teddy, why the four-wheel drive, especially in California?"

"That's easy—the TV commercials show the fun of hanging on a mountainside and fording rivers, so you gotta have four even though there's no river for a thousand miles."

"Ted, that explains the guys, but what of the women?"

"They need big rigs to armor-plate their six or eight kids."

"But I thought family size was dropping—to one or two. What's with so many kids?"

"Women like to be prepared. If they have six kids, they'll be ready."

I dare not expose my SUV attitude because I don't want my daughters and grandkids on my case. A granddaughter in Manhattan walks or uses the subway, so Kate gets a gold star.

Lord Almighty! "Cars control our lives. We can't live with them or without them. They're a blessing and a curse. What can we do?"

"Harold, you have Amtrak and Metrolink. You can walk or bicycle. You can roller-blade. Better yet, you can stay home where you'll be safe. Have you thought of that?"

New Technology Bugs Me. My grandkids were smarter than me by the time they got out of grade school and they can write better than I. Most grandparents can say the same. These kids were weaned on computers, so it's no big deal. They felt I should come into the twenty-first century, and

I don't want to go the other direction . . . I'm already in the fast lane.

they bought me a computer to force the issue. Riley was seven at the time. His assignment was to teach me. But he's impatient with slow learners. I'm begging for help from him while his five-year-old sister, Rose, looks on.

"Riley, you're going too fast. You've got to explain what you're doing."

No response.

"Come on, Riley, please. Just answer my questions."

Riley: *"Why don't you listen to Rose? She's trying to tell you."*

When Sarah was ten she popped into my den and asked, "What's that?"

"It's a typewriter. It was my closest companion in the CCC and the army," I explained.

"What does it do? May I use it?"

Grandson Jason's wife has laid a challenge on me. I tried to give her a fancy desk planner. She told me she had something that worked better. It is a technological marvel that fits in the hand, no bigger than my billfold. Better than a "Palm Pilot," it's called a "BlackBerry." I asked Nicole what it cost. She didn't know because her company gives them to department heads, but she estimated $300. (Jeepers, when I was in the office equipment business, $300 would outfit the entire office.) Nicole gave me this laundry list of its skills: calendar, address book, alarm clock, e-mail, calculator, notepad, "to do" list—and it does it all in an instant, while updating her office computer at the same time. ("Hal, is that enough factual regurgitation?") In other words, this brain substitute does everything but shop for the groceries. I asked Nicole to program my week:

Mon: Complain to phone company about stupid bills.
Tues: Complain to bank about unfair service charge.
Wed: Complain to governor about waste in state budget.
Thurs: Complain to Congress about waste in fed budget.
Fri: Complain to HMO because everyone does.
Sat: Complain to wife because spouse expects it.
Sun: Ask minister to speak loud enough to be heard.

This new helpmate is going to improve my efficiency and free up my time. Time that can be better used for letters to the editor and reading obituaries.

God-Awful Justice. Our courts and the tort system create more problems than they solve. Litigation is a growth industry. If I'm addicted to tobacco, I can sue the industry, collect big time, and continue to smoke. If my addiction is gambling, I either get rich and the government collects taxes or the bankruptcy court forgives my debt. If I'm addicted to alcohol,

I can buy all I want, drive a car until caught, and make a fool of myself. But woe and beware if I'm caught with dope, marijuana, or hemp. My property is confiscated and I'm sent to prison, a prison the state can't afford. Prison has some advantages. If I need a heart transplant it's free, plus I'm in line ahead of private customers because the State is afraid I'll sue. Is anyone in charge of this asylum?

Pillow Talk. Even with the perfect spouse, there are bumps in the road. We have problems:

Jeanne: "How many times must I ask you to quit using the good silver to . . . ?"

Hal: "So I bent the damn spoon. We have seven that aren't bent. How many do you need?"

Jeanne: "These are my wedding gift from my parents. I want them used right."

Hal: "No—they're *our* wedding gift. We live in a community-property state. We can split the set."

Jeanne: "Shut up."

Hal: "Honey, be reasonable. They've lasted for sixty years. Do you plan to take them to heaven when you die?"

Jeanne: "And I wish you wouldn't belch when we have company."

At the rate I'm moving, I will be 90 when this book is re-edited for the umpteenth time. I can only wish that Jeanne will continue to be there for me, whatever my age. But *age* is not the issue. What is crucial is the stage of life when it takes two to function. There comes the time when it takes two to hear, two to see, two to monitor traffic, and two to figure what the movie just said. Our memories will fail, and each may have to remind the other where we're playing bridge. To have a spouse or trusted companion to lean on is a blessing indeed.

To be without that helpmate—I hope I don't have to find out.

What of the Future? Beginning this new millennium, I have reason to be grumpy. I wish I could leave my eight grandchildren a safer world. In the past century, human society has survived some narrow escapes. For thirty years, our country and Russia gambled that mortals with their finger on the button wouldn't make a mistake with our nuclear arsenal. Our face-off threatened to annihilate mankind. It was high noon at the OK Corral. We start this century with terrorist attacks and saber-rattling responses. Despite the enlightenment of the new millennium, the world seems more inclined for violence than for peace. More inclined for terrorism than for negotiation. We refuse to heed Gandhi's warning: *an eye for an eye and the world goes blind.*

I think maybe my wilderness is behind me. Old age does have its consolations. If a "senior" can cope with the physical and mental limitations, contentment is a fringe benefit. Of course I'm not content with this societal behavior, which I know I cannot change, or with injustices and inequities, which I perceive as needing heroic remedies. I am content with those things I feel able to touch: my family, my friends, my home, and my town—it is going better than I ever expected. Better than I deserve.

Our daughters phone to ask if we're OK. And thank God for our grandchildren. I hope they know how to save human society. While their grumpy grandfather retreats into the past, their generation must deal with the challenges of the future. *Good luck, kids.*

14

Enjoying the Bounties of the Benevolent Rich

In the capitalistic world, gurus who offer seminars on asset accumulation lecture on the strategy of getting rich the easy way, as opposed to years of toil. It is done by "leveraging" with other people's money. It works beautifully for persons like Donald Trump. For Trump it is easier than robbing banks because he knows how to find the "other people" who have the money. The Donald knows their unlisted phone numbers.

For those of us who don't have such a handy phone book, I have a fallback strategy. We can very easily *enjoy* the way the OPM experts spend their money. For example, I can escort my wife into Trump Towers, ooh and aah at the décor, eat on the patio, and watch Mr. Trump's devotees come and go. It gives me a rich feeling. Also causes me to wonder: Are the truly rich the ones who have the most, or are they the ones who need the least?

I am one of the lucky rich. I admit it. Up the coast a bit, I have a castle loaded with baubles that would make kings and queens covetous. This property was willed to me by the Hearst family. They even made a deal with the State of California to take care of it. The Parks Department does a terrific job.

Much of my art is stashed down the coast at the Getty campus. I inherited it from John Paul Getty. He never saw it, poor guy, but he thoughtfully arranged to have it protected and tended. J. Paul even provided undercover parking. I really appreciate that.

Getty and the Hearst family wanted these treasures to be shared by the public. That's how I struck it rich. If it's public domain, my name is on the deed—as is everyone else's. My co-owners are legion. They're rich and poor, camera toters and note takers, Asians, Africans, and Australians, Latinos and Europeans, Canadians, too. All are welcome.

This is only a part of my vast holdings. However, my portfolio has value only to the extent to which I seek it out and enjoy it. If California slides into the ocean, some of my best properties will be lost. If the ice cap melts, Vizcaya and my Ringling art treasures in Florida are goners. But Mount Rushmore will still be high and dry. The Carnegie at Pittsburgh is safely inland. My legacies are well dispersed across the nation and are in good management hands. Someone is paying the bills, I guess, because I never see them.

Getting rich never seemed an option for me and was never my goal. I was content to survive comfortably. However, there came a time I realized I was indeed rich, and it was as easy as adjusting my thinking. Wrestling with business ventures in the Alaska wilderness was a misguided strategy. How much easier to seek out the public legacies that dot the land. This route to richness is available to everyone who is motivated to simply feel rich. I call it *my gospel of vicarious wealth*. (I borrowed the idea from Andrew Carnegie.) I urge the reader to apply it.

The Rich Can't Take It When They Leave. I believe this is a universal truth. If they can't take it, they must have left it here on earth. That's where I live. All over the land, there are the creations of movers and shakers. Overachievers have crafted big monuments. Many of them are in the public domain; most are open for people like you and me. I call them our "legacies."

To claim the creations of the rich and mighty, all we need is the ability to enjoy. I was so excited over my discovery, I wrote a book describing 36 attractions, coast-to-coast: *Traveler's Guide to Monumental Treasures.*[*] I am not satisfied with the book because it was printed before I could include some late discoveries. I describe them here as an illustration of the delights available to everyone. If someday I revise the book, these will be included.

Another reason I wasn't satisfied with the book: I had no Alaska attraction that fit my criteria. On a 1998 return to Alaska with my grandson I discovered the Alyeska Resort Hotel; a year later, with wife and two daughters, Chena Hot Springs.

The Denali North Star Inn, mile 248.8 on the George Parks Highway, 11 miles north of the Denali Park entrance, is an apparition no traveler should rush past. It is huge, out of touch with its surroundings, and obviously has a story. After the visitor reads its history, there comes a gasp, "I can't believe this!"

This inn was moved to its present location from—here's the unbelievable part—Prudhoe Bay, 610 miles north. However, before that, it was housing at Endicott Island. When it was no longer needed, it was acquired from British Petroleum by its present owners and moved over the Beaufort Sea by way of an ice road to Deadhorse where it opened as a hotel in 1990.

---

[*] Self-published. Hal Thornton. 1990. Now out of print.

In 1994, the North Star Inn was moved again, 610 miles in the winter, one module at a time, using 150 semi-truck trips, to Healy where it would be construction housing for the Healy Clean Coal Project. It is surely the biggest rolling hotel on earth.

As I scanned the pictures on the wall, I inquired. "I know a bit about this moving game. Who was crazy enough to buy this monster and attempt such a move?"

"That's him in work clothes," the manager told me. I knew I must meet Bernie Karl.

Chena Hot Springs was this wild man's current preoccupation. I remembered the old roadhouse north of Fairbanks. In my time, it was a day's drive by dog team. Now it's an hour on asphalt. We were having dinner at the resort, eating opposite a very messy family. They left and a hulking chap in coveralls took to the cleanup. He didn't fit the busboy role.

"Are you Bernie Karl?" I asked. I was face-to-face with the ultimate entrepreneur.

Karl's Chena Hot Springs Resort is a testimony to his free-enterprise spirit. Currently, it offers a new lodge, meals in a rustic relic out of the past, mineral baths, horseback riding, an excellent landing strip, in process of enlargement. Why? Karl plans to have his own little air service to bring guests, mainly Japanese, from Anchorage.

The northern lights are an important amenity of the resort. That arctic phenomenon makes it a favorite with the Japanese visitors who believe a baby conceived under the aurora borealis will be an exceptional child. The September night we were there, the northern lights came out and the Japanese hastened to their rooms. It gave me a nostalgic itch.

The Alaska of my memory is history. I can't bring it back and shouldn't if I could. It is no longer relevant. It is over. Oil money brought modern progress. Gone is the struggle with wilderness and lack of utilities, gone are the washboard roads, the mud, the frozen ruts and austere living; gone is salmon that sold by the fish instead of the pound. And gone is the cabin fever for which the only cure was the ten-day trip to the "outside." Gone is an era when it wasn't even fantasized that Alaska would someday have a *classy resort hotel at Girdwood,* a tiny settlement opposite Hope on Turnagin Arm.

Alyeska Prince Hotel near Girdwood. Annual snowfall at this ski resort averages 560 inches. Nine lifts start near sea level—at only 250 feet elevation! That's almost ground zero. Imagine an hour's drive from Anchorage to ski slopes and on a paved road!

The Alyeska Prince Hotel is the best and the only choice. You may be sure it's the best when you discover your room has bathrobes and slippers, iron and ironing board, shaving mirror, hair dryer, heated towel rack, and in-room safe. These are features that speak of quality, and I could list even more.

The resort is there because of Chris von Imhof, a German with ski resort smarts. He first came to Alaska in 1963 and served as tourism director in the new state. He was hired by Alaska Airlines to run their small resort at Girdwood. Imhof had a vision of something grander, and this led him to the Seibu Group of Japan. He convinced them; they responded with $200 million in capital investment and put Chris von Imhof in charge. The Alyeska Prince Resort is his baby. From the moment a guest arrives until departure, there is a sense that the friendly staff has been drilled by a true professional. Alyeska makes me feel special.

Grandson Philip and I checked into the Alyeska Prince Hotel for five nights. Philip was exploring for a job. I was

Breakfast at Alyeska— L to R, Joyce, Philip, Jeannette, Walt and Eldy Covich, Hal and Jeanne

Philip With Alyeska bellhop

reaching for a chapter for my travel book in case I do a second printing. I felt overwhelmed at the change sixty years had wrought with my pioneer territory. No more wilderness deprivation. We are camping in luxury with hot running water, elevators, telephones, and climate control! I could do my moose spotting from the comforts of a tram as I rode to Seven Glaciers gourmet dining.

I took Philip to Alaska with a one-way ticket. It's the same way I arrived. He stayed a year and fulfilled the requirement. A year later, I returned with Jeanne, Jeannette, and Joyce (his mother) to see if he had succumbed to the call of the wild. No—basketball was his first love; snow and cold were not.

Branson (Missouri)

Every senior who is in tune with the fun-and-games world knows Branson is a must. The problem is that Branson is not on the beaten path to anywhere. It snuggles down in the Ozark hills of southern Missouri, an hour south of Springfield. Tour buses are the popular option, and droves of white-haired and bald ancients arrive under the umbrella of guides, mostly from Midwest points within one or two days' drive.

Branson happened without a plan. A loosely defined genre of entertainers coalesced around a fascinating cave that would become "Silver Dollar City." And shortly, these meandering hills became the flip side of Las Vegas. No naked dolls parading on these stages. No dirty jokes. Of course, no gambling. The Branson brand of theater is as pure as your mother's parlor.

When Jeanne and I aged into the lure of Branson and bent our travel habits to check it out, we struck pay dirt! Regis and Kathie Lee were doing their TV show from the Grand Palace (seats 4,000). We connected with two performances. For reasons I don't understand, the TV public either hated or loved their show. I belong to the latter. (Kathie Lee alone was enough reason for me to tune in. Her TV commercials, prancing the decks of Carnival Cruise Lines, are stuck firm in my memory. This charming lady in her wind-blown sun dress, alluring me with "if they could see me now," gives me a vicarious cruise.)

Well, back to reality. Branson is famous for more theaters and amusements than you can visit in a month if you attend a different one every day. Unlike the Las Vegas strip, they are scattered, mostly along "76," a two-lane winding road. This overloaded highway is often bumper-to-bumper, and when we first visited, it had no pedestrian crosswalks but also didn't need them. We quickly learned that to cross, one need only step forward and traffic would stop. Did this really happen or am I dreaming?

It is quite common that visitors on conducted tours will be ticketed for two shows daily. Popular song-and-dance artists provide a menu of Mother, God, and Country. It ranges from Andy Williams, Glen Campbell, and Bobby Vinton's Blue Velvet Theatre to Shoji Tabuchi's violin (Branson's most popular). Silver Dollar City is the site of the famous caves. It has expanded into a full-blown amusement park and deserves a half-day minimum.

Sport fishing is easy because Table Rock Lake and Lake Taneycomo make this a water resort, thanks to dams on the White River. The Ozarks are a rock formation that leaks wonderful soft spring water. In my childhood, I hiked along spring-fed streams, finding a spring any time I was thirsty. The water was cold enough to chip the teeth and so pure and soft, the thirst was unquenchable. I presume some health department has now put up a warning sign to encourage the thirsty to drink Coke or Pepsi or carry expensive bottles of exotic water labeled "Mountain Pure" and usually drawn from some public supply. We're overcivilized and have lost some of nature's blessings.

The roads around Branson are like spaghetti, so the visitor needs a map, and you'll note on the following page a reproduction of the map you'll need. You also need a schedule of the shows. If you don't require nude and dirty jokes, Branson is a delight.

San Antonio's Paseo del Rio (Texas)

Rivers are magnets to settlers. Also to songwriters. Water is most useful, and rivers are full of it. They are handy to travel along, do the laundry in, and carry away the pollution. They draw population and commerce, and occasionally they go dry, but more often they flood and sometimes drown people. If fifty people drown, as happened to San Antonio in 1921, the citizenry is apt to say, "Kill the river." Happily, this city is lucky enough to have had a handful of visionaries. The river was saved, beautified, and with a thousand trees added, the meandering walk is a delight.

From ugly river to lovable park required a dream. Architect Robert Hugman did the dreaming. This young architect, then recently graduated from the University of Texas at Austin, called on the city fathers to turn a "sow's ear into a silk purse." Hugman's dream is more remarkable if we try to imagine the attitudes of 1929. A few months after Hugman sprung it on the town fathers, the stock market crash sent shivers through the land.

The Hugman dream reached for the moon. It had sight— a charming meandering walk lined with flowers and cypress trees. It had sound—the songs of waiters and of mariachis and of waterfalls. It had smell—steaks broiling, pizzas in the oven, magnolia blossoms. And it had motion—gondolas gliding, water flowing, children flitting. It had lovers strolling.

The dream didn't become reality without struggle. It took crusading and money and community cooperation. The depression-borne WPA launched the initial construction, and its director has the Arneson Theater named for him. It required the gamble of hotels and businesses to reverse their front doors to face what previously had been their "out back."

Hugman wanted River Walk to be right for gondolas and purposely shallow. Its uniform three- to four-foot depth makes drowning improbable. It also tempts canoeing romancers to dunk their dates, for laughs or squeals—either cements relationships or destroys them. There are thirty-one stairways designed by Hugman. No two are alike. There are 17,000 feet of walkways of numerous designs and materials.

Many boosters contributed to the River Walk, and perhaps it might have found reality without Robert Hugman. But he was the driving force from its earliest concept until the dream was in place. After ten years of crusading, he was appointed architect for the project. It was a commission of short duration but enough for him to set the guidelines. The River Walk dominated his life. It was his quest; it is ours to enjoy. I call it charming.

Palm Springs Tram (California)

There are desert dwellers who suffer from heat. The sight of snow sets their glands abuzz. A young electrical engineer in Palm Springs knew these feelings . . . and while driving toward Banning, in view of San Jacinto's snowy crest, Frances F. Crocker started dreaming.

While sweating the Palm Springs heat, he pondered the how and wherefore needed to bridge the gap that separated his below-sea-level habitat from that lofty snow. Without guessing the form or magnitude of his 1935 fantasy, Crocker launched the "eighth wonder of the world."

The tramway constructed in rugged Chino Canyon on the north edge of Palm Springs did not just happen. It was a long crusade. After many years of dreaming, Crocker enlisted the aid of desert pioneer and co-manager of the famed Palm Springs Desert Inn, O. Earl Coffman.

Such a project was more than an engineering challenge. It was a political chasm. A tramway-enabling bill passed the state legislature twice, only to be vetoed by the governor. With the outbreak of World War II, the plans were shelved.

With the war's end and a new governor, the plan was back on track, and the Mount San Jacinto Winter Park Authority was created. Coffman, who had labored long and hard to see the vision realized, was named the authority's first chairman.

The ride to the top requires about fourteen minutes. As your eyes stretch from one tower to the next, you inevitably marvel that the tower could cling to its precarious perch. You're bound to doubt that its construction was possible. Hold your questions until you reach the Mountain Station where a twenty-minute video film titled *Crocker's Dream* helps visitors understand the engineering problems. Thanks to the tram's 8,000-foot boost, I can boast. I have climbed, and stood atop Mount San Jacinto!

The House on the Rock (Wisconsin)

If this attraction doesn't blow your mind, it's possible you're brain dead. I haven't words to describe the creation of Alex Jordan, fifty miles west of Madison.* Jordan was a genius architect living alone in Madison. He envisioned a citadel attached to the stone—a place away—a high retreat. Well, he overdid it.

It grew like Topsy. There can't possibly have been a master plan, not at the start, not at the finish. Scratch that—there is no "finish." In time, it became a labyrinth of amazement. To describe it would take a book, an endless assortment of pictures. And after reading, you might insist it is fiction.

How does one describe the Stradivarius of carousels? A menagerie of 269 mythical creatures, seven deep, dance round and round to organ music, bathed in 20,000 dazzling lights! You needn't ask if it's the biggest in the world! "Would you believe it?" is heard endlessly from room to room.

I ask my guide, "Whence came the money? Jordan must have had unlimited funds. Where was his gold mine?" The

---

* Between Madison and the House on the Rock you pass through Baraboo. Tarry to check out the Circus World Museum. This is the starting point for the two-day circus train to Milwaukee.

guide insisted not so. OK, I don't believe it, and that adds to the mystery.

For whatever reason, Jordan sold his House on the Rock and as part of the sale consideration remained near to his creation with a consultant's role (at $500,000 annually). He carried back a contract for $20 million. He died within a year. Had no immediate family. Jordan was a demonstration of the message in my next chapter: The creator gets his satisfaction from the result of his work; those of us who view it get our kicks vicariously. Mr. Jordan spent a lifetime creating a delight that is open to the public. In my judgment, he is a philanthropist. Whether that was his purpose makes no difference!

Go see. Allow a full day. There's a husky admission charge. Don't argue—just pay it and be thankful you've discovered your legacy from a mad genius. This spectacle is an orgasm.

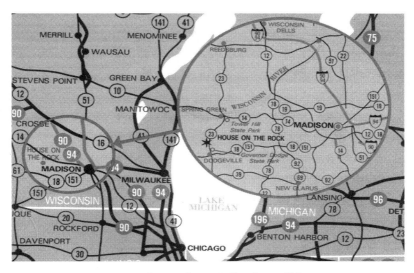

House on the Rock 200 Miles from Chicago

Travel Bonus

To make travel more special, Jeanne and I have stayed in classic hotels and resorts that shared the vicinity of our legacies. Examples: Grove Park Inn (Vanderbilt mansion), Hotel DuPont (Longwood Gardens), Del Coronado Hotel (Balboa Park), and Harrison Hot Springs (Minter Gardens) in British Columbia. The rates may seem expensive until you adjust your perspective. Most rich people feel compelled to build monuments. Since they have funds, they create with style. Tell yourself, *Someone spent a fortune and/or half a lifetime creating an exciting hostelry that I can own for a night (or a week) for a pittance.* What if the room did cost $xxx.xx? It's a sure bet there'll be that much left when I die.

That analysis can add to your pleasure when you cruise. When you stand on the bow of a luxury ship, letting the breeze blow through your hair, watching the ocean swells undulate below you, staring at the sunset turning the clouds yellow and pink and gray, congratulate yourself:

Hey buddy, did you ever imagine that for a paltry sum you could have the run of a $200-million floating palace? This is better than owning the ship because you have no worries about meeting the payroll. You're eating like a king, being waited on hand and foot. Your bed will be turned back with a chocolate on the pillow. You're richer than you ever dreamed! The few thousand bucks you spent for a ticket was money you can't take when you cash out. What an easy way to feel successful!

You're living rich with **Other People's Money!**

15

The Gospel of Philanthropy

Philanthropy: "1. The effort or inclination to increase the well-being of mankind, as by charitable aid or donations. 2. Love of mankind in general" (*American Heritage Dictionary*).

Andrew Carnegie was a poor boy from Scotland who became a huge success. He made tons of money, part of it from abusing his labor, but the bottom line was he knew he couldn't take it with him and got busy giving it away. True, he could have shared it more generously with his labor force, but because of his wealth, our country now has over 2,500 libraries, and I have a card that gives me free access.

This Scotsman, pondering his money at age 67, wrote, "I knew the task of distribution before me would tax me in my old age to the utmost. It's wrong to die with it."

This sentiment has been dubbed "The Gospel of Wealth." Carnegie wrote several magazine articles to expound on the merits of giving money away. As a person of modest substance, I assure my peers it does not require impressive wealth to affiliate with Carnegie's club. Today, our citizenry, more than any other people on earth, donate generously. We call it *philanthropy*. One does not need to be rich to give back that which we can't take with us. One only needs a kindly spirit and an open purse. It is a good feeling.

Jesus' Sermon on the Mount may have been the earliest seminar on estate planning: *It is more blessed to give than receive.*

Charitable giving has a tax advantage. I believe your tax consultant will tell you that a charitable remainder trust is a smart strategy for disposing of appreciated assets and depreciated real estate. Recapture (of depreciation) often requires cash outlay. With your accountant's cooperation, this may be avoided with the C.R.T. Instead of cash outflow, there can be cash conservation. A special advantage is that it, in contrast with a will, allows the donor to witness the results and the gratitude.

Charitable remainder trusts need the guidance of an expert. Most charitable organizations will furnish this. To illustrate the flexibility, a good friend had a property that seemed an ideal gift and of dubious interest to the heirs. Our friend was able to split the acreage of a fully depreciated citrus grove, allowing both our City College Foundation and Planned Parenthood to be beneficiaries. Each sold its parcel. Our friend avoided recapture tax and got a tax deduction to boot. He is now divested of management headaches and regularly receives checks in the mail.

Santa Barbara is fortunate in having a community college and an adult education program beyond compare. Its Omega classes are specially oriented to senior citizens. The program manager, Maryellen Kelley, seems to know that we seniors need a jumpstart to cope with health of the body and lethargy of the mind. It has helped me play catch-up for the college I missed and the years in Alaska lost to isolation. I can even the score by contributing to its foundation.

"The Mentor," Campus of Santa Barbara City College. Sculpture by
Aristides Demetrios. Gift of Santa Barbara philanthropists,
Eli and Leatrice Luria and Michael Towbes, with
Dr. Peter MacDougall, SBCC President (at right).

Gifts Tailored to Match the Attitude

Runaway population is spoiling the planet's quality of life. California brings the message to my doorstep. However, the problem is worldwide. It is too hot a subject for the political powers to confront, especially since it doesn't offer rewards at the polling place. The solution is controversial and perhaps will be solved only by the four horsemen of the Apocalypse. Planned Parenthood dispenses sanity and compassion that deals with family planning and education. Supporting its mission is a philanthropy that is in everyone's long-term interest.

It is my opinion that one can be poor with a fat portfolio and one can be rich with no portfolio. It depends on how wealth is viewed. To be short on assets while long on happiness is preferable to being rich and miserable. Peace of mind is a luxury difficult to put a price on. A person's attitude can change the criteria.

Over the past 100 years, many people with big money have moved to Santa Barbara for its weather and scenery. They have been motivated to shower this city with gardens, beach facilities, parks, and architectural beauty. Their gifts have been an astonishing legacy. The same happens in New York City, Chicago, Dallas, and Denver. It happens all over the land. Because of these philanthropists we have untold riches, vicariously. How lucky we are. This chapter is my opportunity to say, **I thank you!**

What better summary for my commentary than to style my beatitudes after the ultimate mover and shaker—Jesus—whose Sermon on the Mount (Matthew 5) is a guiding light.

Blessed are the peacemakers, for theirs is a lonely vigil indeed.

Blessed are the devout believers, for they have found peace of mind.

Blessed are the agnostics, for theirs is the ongoing search.

Blessed are the protesters, for they refuse to be brainwashed.

Blessed are the environmentalists, for they treasure God's wilderness.

Blessed are the skeptics, for crackpot theories should be examined.

Blessed are the bicyclists, walkers, and bus takers, for they conserve.

Blessed are the artists, for without them the world would be drab.

Blessed are the philosophers, for truth is a work in progress.

Blessed are the scientists and inventors, for they make our life easier.

Blessed are the rich, for their philanthropies enrich us all!

Mother presenting her unicorn tapestry to Janell (and Randall), 1987. Jeanne is skilled at needle-point, quilting, china painting, cooking, sewing, gardening.

Jeanne's knitted caps modeled by the family, gathered for wedding of
Kirsten to Phillip Suttner, Christmas week 2002.

16

Gospel of the Believing Agnostic: A Benediction

*agnosticism: n. 1. Philosophy. The doctrines of the agnostics,
holding that certainty, first or absolute truths, are
unattainable, and that only perceptual phenomena are
objects of exact knowledge. 2. Theology. A theory that does
not deny God but denies the possibility of knowing Him.*
(American Heritage Dictionary)

That label suits me. I am a *believer*. I believe this amazing
cosmos, planet, earth life, humankind could not possibly
have happened by accident. It is too fantastic! Too miracu-
lous! There just has to be a creating intelligence/power/force.
Its capability is beyond human comprehension and much too
almighty to be encapsulated by ecclesiastic dogma.

Aristotle offers me a perch. He believed humankind is in
a privileged position: The human soul has the divine gift of
intellect, which makes us kin to God and a partaker in the
divine nature. This godly capacity for reason puts us above
plants and animals. As body and soul, however, each person
is a microcosm of the whole universe.*

---

* See *A History of God: The 4000-year Quest of Judaism, Christianity, and Islam*, by
Karen Armstrong (New York: Alfred A. Knopf, 1993).

Throughout history, a divinity has been worshipped in a thousand ways, with as many struggling portrayals, and given myriad names, especially *God,* the prevailing label for simplistic discourse.

Inasmuch as humans have now, and throughout history, innumerable differing beliefs, each convinced it is God's chosen, the only conclusion must be that there are just a lot of Gods. That doesn't bother me, and whether one religion is truer than the other, I humbly concede I haven't the slightest idea. I think it is normal to want to know why we are here and where we are going. Religious leaders, usually in churches, mosques, and temples, try to provide the answer and to make it believable and personal. In doing so, they shrink God to one-size-fits-all. For the vast multitude, it answers the need. For myself and a few like-minded nonconformists, it doesn't.

When I define myself as a believing agnostic, I open lots of discussion. How do I worship? Yes, I attend service. At Santa Barbara's Arlington Theater, when the mighty Wurlitzer rises to the stage and the gold console dazzles my eyes and pipe organ classics fill the auditorium, I feel I'm in the divine presence. When I sit in a park under blue skies, listening to our Santa Barbara Prime Time Band, all seniors over fifty, I'm worshipping. If I can watch the Radio City Rockettes, I'm in heaven. If I go to the Palm Springs desert to count the golf courses, I make a hole-in-one at the Follies. This troupe of ex-singers and dancers, fifty- to ninety-year-old professionals, rekindle my spirit. It gives me reason to pray: *God, don't let them expire before the curtain call.* Yes, I'm content with my agnostic worship.

For soul food I can easily tap into Frank Kelly's spirit. Frank is a Santa Barbara writer who exudes an elixir of exuberance. He is one of the founders of the Nuclear Age Peace Foundation and actually believes humanity has a future. Frank offers the following antidote for my skepticism:

A Center for Humanity's Future In the coming centuries, in which we will face more complex problems than ever before, it will be essential to evoke the godlike qualities inherent in every person. To act with the unconditional love transmitted to us by our Creator, we will take joy forever from a full appreciation of what we really are—embodiments of the cosmos, each of us aware of the strength we can draw from the universe, each of us absolutely original and upon our understanding of the fact that what we think and what we do will have repercussions through the whole future.

To serve the global community now arising through the efforts of Glorious Beings all over the world, I advocate the creation of a Center for Humanity's Future. Such a Center could be a place of light and listening, a place of exploration and encouragement for people to become even greater than they are now, a launching pad for ideas from everywhere. It would enable all of us to become more aware of what marvelous capacities we have and stimulate us to become more creative than we have ever been.

If a traditional Protestant church service blesses me with a sermon that is fresh and has substance, my time is well spent. Because I was captive to my father's ministering, I have squirmed through a thousand sermons that wrung a half-hour harangue out of an irrelevant Bible passage. I have had a lifetime supply of dogmatic exhortations.

Call me a religion junkie. My church attendance is impressive. In the '20s, I watched Billy Sunday as he climbed onto the pulpit and exhorted us to "hit the sawdust trail." In the '30s, it was Aimee Semple McPherson charming me as only angels can. I have been overwhelmed by Riverside Church in Manhattan and popped my eyeballs in the Crystal Cathedral at Garden Grove. The Crenshaw Christian Center in Los Angeles is on my "places to experience" list. I sat in the cheering section with 5,000 yuppies in the charismatic Willow Creek Church near Chicago and with similarly dedicated enthusiasts this past Easter when Jon Ireland ministered to his Ocean Hills congregation on the lawn at our City College. I'm tolerant of all, and as proof, I chanced to be in Lynchburg, Virginia, on a Sunday, so I attended the Thomas Road Baptist Church with Jerry Falwell behind the pulpit. I'm willing for people to believe what they need to believe, Moslems included.

Heaven is the domain of organized religion. I hear it's a place so trouble-free we should want to be there, and never more so than when the body we inhabit has exhausted its spirit. The churches should speak out on this but don't. It is a subject I would expect to hear sermonized. Today's message from the Lord: "A good life deserves a good death. Heaven need not wait."

The laws of this "nation under God" don't allow us to exchange unendurable pain for heaven. Not even if a person hurts so bad, hell would be a good alternative. Our attorney general, a born-again zealot, is hounding the State of Oregon for its break with regimen. Why must it remain for secular advocates to intercede for the afflicted? Out of sympathy for terminal sufferers, I have asked Faye Girsh, dedicated past president of the Hemlock society, to define its mission:

The Hemlock Society fights for the right to choose a peaceful, gentle death, in the company of loved ones.

It is the ultimate civil liberty. To deny a person assistance to achieve this goal, to force someone to endure suffering, loss of dignity and personhood, because of another's beliefs, is cruel and tyrannical.

Church suits me best when the message opens my eyes. Nelson, a soul mate, and I were attending service at the National Cathedral, Memorial Day Sunday. The patriotic occasion gave theme to the bishop's recitation of the third verse of the "Star Spangled Banner." (Does anyone know there is more to the song than what we sing to open the ball game?) A club I attend regularly begins with our national anthem. I'm annoyed that the first verse gives emphasis to the rockets' red glare and bombs bursting. This national anthem originated with a war we didn't need and lost. To me, a war theme is wrong. But if sing it we must, the third verse has lines more appropriate to a nation that claims to be well behaved:
"Praise the Pow'r that hath made and preserved us a nation!"
Then conquer we must, when our cause it is just."

"Just?" There's a pledge worth living up to.

I am learning. I attend a popular Adult Education class on understanding how and why the Old Testament was written. It attracts a host of mature and educated adherents of nearly every faith. Fundamentalists, Catholics, mainline Protestants, Jews, and atheists sign in religiously in the hope of solving the puzzle. No person is there to defend his or her dogma. I ask the leader, Dr. Pete Diamond,[*] for his critique of my "Wilderness of Man" chapter:

---

[*] Instructor, Santa Barbara City College, Continuing Education Division, Humanities and Computing.

Hal takes the path of Job and complains. He protests the arrangement of things, all the while confessing gratitude and wonder with regret.

The need for comfort causes us to shrink from the thought of arbitrary transcendent cruelty. Why not abandon the journey. Embrace your bitter death in the wilderness. Its dysfunctions, hostilities, and arbitrary cruelties are insurmountable.

Entranced, we confess, "There is still beauty in the world!" We keep on, hunched along the pilgrim way.

To find an explanation of this focus group, I asked a couple to lunch. (The Montecito Country Club should convince them I'm in search of profound truth.)

"Kurt, you are a graduate lawyer and CPA. You went through the paces at the temple. Why are you attending Dr. Diamond's lectures when you could be cruising?"

"Hal, I try to be objective. It is easier when I have heard all versions of the subject. I'm looking for light at the end of the tunnel. What menu item do you recommend"?

Maybe I could learn more from Kurt's wife: "Marion, you have a PhD in French literature. Isn't this class far afield for a Jewish lady of letters?"

"Hal, when I hear Pete ask "am I making sense" I'm thinking, 'Does anyone?' Should we order?"

I explained to my friends that Dr. Diamond's depth of analysis was missing in my religious training. "Makes me wonder if I was educated in the dark ages. Some of the stuff I'm hearing is way over my head. Am I the only one?"

Kurt was candid: "Hal, the search for truth is unending. It's a work in progress."

Unfortunately, the human species does not agree on a

universal religion. Neither can it tolerate differences such as boundaries, sovereignty, and especially economic models that might be named Capitalism or Communism. That should be no reason to spill blood, but it is. I can't believe God (or Yahweh) wants it this way, and I do believe it is further evidence that God doesn't interfere.

For addressing 21st-century problems, our Bible doesn't scratch the surface. Of course, ancient narrators could not foresee modern problems such as corporate fraud, insider trading, abortion, narcotics, divorce, child abuse, women's rights, racial prejudice, terrorism, and crime in the streets. Revised scriptures are badly needed. It would make more sense if God had delayed issuance of the worshippers' operating manual until a population of 6 billion was dealing with these recent problems. A logistics-smart God would have waited until computers could standardize communications.

If medical technology functions as I expect, I will live well into my nineties. At that point, I may aim for one hundred. It has been a good life. I am happy with the hand fate has dealt. For my final curtain call, I want this life to end with a good death. In the Bible, I find no help for confronting the most critical contingency we seniors live with. It falls to the Hemlock Society. At their recent National Convention, the Bishop of Newark (Episcopal Church), in his keynote address, expressed my feelings precisely:

I want to live my days surrounded by those I love, able to see my wife's beautiful smile, and to experience the touch of her hand. I want to share in the joy and vitality of my children and grandchildren. But when those realities are taken away, then I want to leave this world, and those I love, with a positive vision. I want them to see in me one who lived and loved deeply and well, until no longer possible. I want them to remember me as a person who was vital to the end, as one who was in possession of all that makes me who I am, and as one who died well. My deepest desire is always to choose death with dignity over a life that has become either hopelessly painful and dysfunctional or empty and devoid of all meaning.

—John Shelby Spong

The Miracle We Call "Home Sweet Home"

The Benediction

As a habitual churchgoer in my youth, I recall the benediction as the best part of the service. It marked the long-awaited end. It meant the kids could now get loose to play, mothers could get Sunday dinner started, and work ethic fathers could take a nap—unless the minister was overzealous and sprung an altar call. Such was life in the Bible Belt.

The benediction was the minister's synopsis. Hopefully, it would be short. It could be grist for conversation afterward, but not likely. Good or bad, it was the preacher's parting shot. In recent times, I was reminded of it when a Unitarian friend told our Rotary Club that a program should always leave the audience with something to take home. Don's smart advice prompts me to conclude with the message from the cenotaph that speaks from our yard: It is Jeanne's art and my conviction, set in concrete. It is my benediction:

Our ancestors' shadows stay with us forever.
Their genes permeate our persona; however,
choices we make control mating who(m)ever.
careers opted. risks taken, locale and whatever.
If lucky, we're healthy — what counts most then
is honest values & ethics, esteem of family and friends.
—H.T.

About the Author

Harold Thornton comes by his autobiography the hard way—he earned it. During his 88 years he has experienced the most dramatic changes of any century in history. Born to two evangelist ministers, he was immersed in the harsh light of God's wrathful love. As a teenage minister during the Depression, he traveled the Bible Belt with the word of God, seeing a nation through the eyes of rural America. Sensing failure, he fled to the Alaska wilderness where he learned to fly, both literally and figuratively. In this pioneering society, he met and married the woman who would share his mistakes and successes for the next 60+ years.

— Jo Evans

As viewed by a seasoned Alaskan:

Work, wit, and an adventurous heart, were the essentials for Hal's success in Alaska. Passionate storytelling recounts the ups and downs of entrepreneurship, flavored with salty opinions and a frontier romance. This book has good advice even today. Stick with bootstrap endurance, have faith in yourself and live your life with generosity and verve. Thornton did it.

— Muriel Ganapole